Confessions
of a Modern
Dentist

Confessions
of a Modern
Dentist

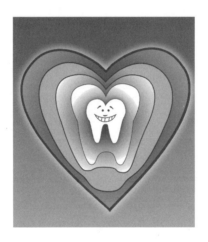

True Stories from Above
& Beyond the Chair

Dr. Sherwin Shinn, D.D.S.

**DRILL
PRESS**
Sammamish, WA

Published by DRILL PRESS
704-228th Avenue, N.E., #204
Sammamish, Washington 98074

Publisher's Cataloging-in-Publication Data
Shinn, Sherwin R.
    Confessions of a modern dentist: true stories from above and beyond the chair / Sherwin R. Shinn. -- Redmond, Wash. : Drill Press, 2001.
        p.   cm.
    ISBN 0-9672610-0-7

    1. Shinn, Sherwin R.   2.Dentists—United States—Biography.
    I. Title.
RK43 .S55 A3   2001   99-62707
617.6/0092   B—dc21   CIP

PROJECT COORDINATION BY BookPublishing.com

05 04 03 02 01 ⌐ 5 4 3 2 1

Printed in the United States of America

To my family dentist, Dr. Robert Keller, *who taught me the empowering value of positive reinforcement by raising each person's self-esteem with the acknowledgment of their greatness.*

To my mother, Hilda Recks-Shinn, *who showed me how to use the creative power of my imagination to keep Life joyful, meaningful, and fresh by putting humor into every situation.*

To my father, Thomas S. Shinn, *who introduced me to the glorious wonders of the great outdoors and demonstrated the importance of knowledge, perfection, and professionalism.*

Contents

Acknowledgments

THE PROCESS OF WRITING AND PUTTING TOGETHER this book was rewarding and multifaceted. It's something I've always wanted to do. With the help and guidance of many other caring people it happened. An inspiring speech by Jerrold Jenkins and the tireless patience and professionalism of Nikki Stahl, Theresa Nelson, and Eric Norton at Jenkins Group, Inc.* helped me initiate and wrap up the package.

The conscientious editing and gracious suggestions from Alice Thomas helped me say what I wanted to say.

The high-tech wizardry and innovative computer skills of my nephew T.J. Chambers and sister-in-law Judy Chambers got my words out of the Dark Ages of pencil and paper and onto the hard-drive domain of the digital age.

The generous support and creative ideas and input from Dane Spotts and his daughter Athena at LifeQuest Publishing Group** focused my mind and kept me moving forward.

To my lifelong friend Dick Schlicting, who was pure fun from day one and who continues to show me how to laugh at life and how to make it up as we go along. To all the rest of my friends and companions who contributed to making the memories in this book, whose names have been changed to protect the not-so-innocent.

To Jim Whittaker, who not only told me what adventures were possible, he went ahead and lived them.

To all my teachers, instructors and advisors over the years who have provided the opportunity for real learning and education by caring and believing in me: Mrs. Tveten, Mr. Gilbert, Dr. Tom Lewis, Dr. Dan Middaugh, Dr. Peter Domoto, and Linnell Isoshima. To the University of Washington Dental School, which provided the solid foundation for my career dreams to flourish. This school, which I am proud to call my alma mater, is led by Dean Paul B. Robertson, an enthusiastic advocate of the student and a champion of effective education. His leadership has produced the ongoing reputation as the #1 rated dental school in the nation.

My heartfelt thanks to all of the wonderful dental assistants, hygienists, students, and staff who have sat next to me over the years, quietly doing all the work and not getting any of the glory. You have lovingly cared for all the patients, supported my personal philosophy, laughed at all my really dumb jokes, never flinched in the face of adversity, and have continually handed me nothing but success.

To all of my patients who have opened wide with your trust and confidence and allowed me to "practice" on you. If I have been successful in helping others, it is only because of the accumulation of gentle guidance and patient wisdom that I have received from you.

Most of all, to my wife Jerri and our two handsome sons Josef and Michael. I have never met anyone who is more beautiful on the inside and the outside than Jerri. Her gentle, enduring strength raised our children, manages our family business, tolerates my idiosyncrasies, counsels my confusion, administers a practical wealth of medical knowledge as a sage and caring nurse, and has cultivated "love, honor and cherish" to lavish abundance in my life. She is an angelic force with a radiant peacefulness that beams from her face. Together we have always shared the common vision of honoring each person we meet until we're all together on the same plane of understanding and compassion. Her steadfast, loyal support has been my constant cornerstone.

And who can say enough about their kids? Joe and Mike have proved to me that Life goes on forever, always getting bigger, better, bolder, and brighter! They are young adults now, but they still give me hugs and take me along as a friend on their own adventures, challenging me to remain youthful and pushing me to stretch my limits. When I need their help they are always there. We're all proud of each other. What more could a father ask for?

Together, these people and more have made it possible for me to share with all of you *Confessions of a Modern Dentist.*

* Jenkins Group, Inc. 121 E. Front St., Traverse City, MI 49684
**LifeQuest Publishing Group, P.O. Box 1444, Issaquah, WA 98027

Foreword

BY JIM WHITTAKER

THERE ARE MANY PATHS HUMANS CAN TAKE AS THEY climb life's mountains and descend into its valleys. Chance encounters and the many forks in the trail open up a whole world of opportunities or disasters.

It seems to follow that when one is at risk doing something we learn the most. Churchill wrote, "When you play for more than you can afford to lose, you learn the game."

Sherwin R. Shinn was 14 years old when he came face to face with his own mortality. His life on the edge is a humorous, heartwarming tale of using his profession and gifts of modesty, sensitivity, intelligence, and curiosity to erase national boundaries and reach out to all who have been given the gift of life on this magical planet.

His book is a story of Love, happiness and the power of the incredible human spirit. Yes, it's a good read!

All the best,
Jim Whittaker

Statesman, peacemaker, environmentalist, adventurer,
author of *A Life On The Edge*, and the first American to reach
the summit of Mt. Everest

Introduction

AHHHH, YES, THE DENTIST! HAVE YOU EVER WONDERED what sort of personality would choose to spend their profession putting their faces and fingers into the mouths of perfect strangers, politely poking them with pointed needles, probing around with penetrating precision, and pulling out pieces of people's body parts with a pair of pliers? What a puzzling phenomenon!

I am a dentist and wonder about this same thing, too, especially while lying upside down, gazing up into the mask-covered face and peering eyes of my own dentist. How did we get this way? What's the secret truth behind our purpose? Are we overreacting to some suppressed childhood nightmare of the awful, gleaming fangs of a saber-toothed tiger, or are we unconsciously drawn as close as possible to the engaging power of the human being's smile? Did we endure all the hardship, expense, and exhaustive focus of our training to get rich, or is there something miraculous that we saw in this calling that allows us to receive fulfillment by enriching others? What were the remarkable events that led us down this path, and what unrevealed initiations occurred along the way? Who is the Tooth Fairy? What goes on behind the scenes?

The public has a right to know these things and I'm going to tell them because I know what happened to me. The answers are sometimes frightening, funny, hard to believe, inspiring, and possibly life-changing. They allow you to see inside my mind. Don't worry, it's the kind of stuff that happens to all of us. Maybe I just interpret things differently from others because I am fascinated by intrigue and the meaning of Life, but now I'm going to let you in on it, too.

These pages are filled with wild escapades, death-defying leaps of faith, unexpected accidents, embarrassing moments, crazy antics, uncommon knowledge, unusual people, and enlightening experiences. They are absolutely true and told just the way they happened. Through it all there is something lurking in between the lines. It is for you. It slowly builds as you read along from story to story. It is my intention to let it come out a little at a time because that is the way it happened for me, finally culminating in a grand realization.

It's about the thrills of riding bareback through the jungle on an Indian elephant and scuba diving in the prop wash of a powerful ferry. It's about climbing over the jumbled ice and past plunging crevasses in the highest mountains and doing surgery on tiny children in primitive conditions. It is witnessing firsthand the wisdom and power of certain indigenous people and counting shooting stars with your family sitting around the campfire at a secluded place on the shore of a placid lake. These things and a whole lot more are here, waiting for you to search them out and explore on your own.

Can we influence the events of our future by how we view the past and what we believe in the present moment? Is it by random chance, Fate, design, or choice that we become what we turn out to be? I've always wondered about stuff like that (until just lately) and I've always wondered why I became a dentist. Now I know. These are my confessions—the confessions of a modern dentist.

As you read them I want you to see where I am coming from. I hope you are amazed, that you laugh out loud with gleeful abandon, that you see your dentist regularly for the real person he or she is, and that the message lurking between the lines comes out for you.

Enjoy,
Dr. Sherwin R. Shinn

It's always what we want to be and feel, and not what we do, that drives our passion to go forward with Life. Stay in touch with those feelings and follow your dream.

*"Life is a
work of art
designed by
the one who
lives it."*

CHAPTER 1

Man The Lifeboats

FOR THE LAST WEEK I HAD BEEN HAVING THE MOST unusual and vivid dreams. Maybe it was from all the exotic food I was eating, or the hot and humid conditions of the South Pacific. I knew one of my wildest dreams was about to begin when I heard the words ring out, "Man the life boats! Abandon ship! This is not a drill!" Not wanting to accept that this was really happening, we reluctantly donned our life jackets and calmly climbed over the rail into the open lifeboat.

My wife, Jerri, and I were on an expedition-class ship somewhere in the Solomon Islands heading for Papua New Guinea to do health care assessment in the remote and primitive regions of this remarkable part of the world. For ten years now we have experienced the most incredible adventures, empowering wisdom, and unbelievable fulfillment from traveling to the isolated areas of Nepal, Tibet, Bolivia, Costa Rica, and the Cook Islands to deliver medical and dental treatment, health care supplies, and disease prevention education. It meant making all the necessary and responsible arrangements to take time off from our busy dental practice and family obligations. We had dreamed about doing humanitarian health care together from when we first met in college 34 years ago. I had become a dentist and Jerri a nurse. Now we were living our dreams and it was wonderful! It was so rich with unexpected rewards that we had just recently formed our own non-profit organization called "The International Smile Power Foundation" to allow us to give more care and travel more frequently.

We were continually surprised by the things that happened on these forays into the unknown, but this was totally unpredictable, implausible, and mind-boggling. Two hours ago we were happily cruising through tranquil and transparent aquamarine waters. Now we were marooned on a small and secluded tropical atoll waiting to be rescued.

It was the end of April 2000. We had been standing on deck talking to shipmates in the mid-afternoon when a sudden grinding, groaning lurch tossed me forward. I struggled to maintain my balance and reflexively grabbed the elderly gentleman next to me who was also falling over. Together we held each other up. In less than ten seconds it was over, but it was obvious we had struck the reef! At first I thought it was no big deal, a benign brushing of the shallow bottom. But soon the captain announced that there was a leak and called us to our muster stations. As we sat there waiting for further instructions, it became undeniable that our ship was steadily listing more and more to the starboard, especially when glasses started sliding across our table and bottles began crashing to the floor from the bar. When the call came to "man the lifeboats" I still believed this was only a temporary inconvenience. I was wrong!

As our crowded lifeboat lowered jerkily to the sea, Jerri and I held hands and confidently smiled at each other. The sun was out, the water was warm, and we could see land. We would probably just float around out here until they fixed the leak, then we would continue on as if nothing had happened. As we waited for the other lifeboats to deploy, I glanced at the horizon and saw an ominous-looking squall skirting across the waves in our direction. Soon it was upon us. The sky darkened and gusting winds blew in sideways sheets of torrential rain. The tremendous deluge threatened to swamp our heavy-laden boat. A huge rubberized tarp was pulled over our heads to keep the water out, but a murmur of concern soon ruffled through the crowd when we realized it was trapping the noxious fumes coming from the center-mounted inboard engine. Someone produced a pair of scissors and cut a hole for the exhaust pipe to vent through. The mood of the passengers remained composed, positive, and friendly.

All signs of land were now obliterated by the intensity of the cloudburst. The menacing ocean was the color of black coffee with the top four inches whipped into a white froth by the surging turbulence of the downpour. It looked like a gigantic, double-tall mocha frappe. Jerri and I looked at each other and shook our heads in disbelief.

We floated around aimlessly in the impenetrable cloud trying to stay in contact with the other lifeboats. Suddenly two natives in a small dugout canoe materialized and offered to lead us to a hidden beach through the maze of shoals and shallows. The green palms and white sand of the island finally came into view and a lively and joyful chatter broke through the self-imposed silence of the voyagers.

When the hull finally scraped to a stop on the bottom, we climbed out and waded ashore onto the most gorgeous island I had ever seen. Huge ancient trees leaned out over the shimmering lagoon as if protecting it and sent thick tentacle-like roots probing into the pristine jungle. The ground was littered with beautiful ornate shells of every conceivable shape, size,

CONFESSIONS OF A MODERN DENTIST

and color. It was the picture-perfect paradise. The crew directed us to follow a narrow path through the dripping forest that led to a solitary thatched hut that someone had built about 300 yards up the beach from the landing site. We stopped in a clearing next to the mysterious shelter and waited for everyone to gather together. We soon discovered we weren't alone. The isle was inhabited by a bunch of curious and sly-looking natives who stealthily appeared, one by one, out of the dense emerald-green foliage on silent bare feet. They seemed friendly enough, but stood close by staring at us without speaking.

The weather started improving and soon sun rays were peeking through the tropical canopy above. We could see our ill-fated ship languishing on its side about two thirds of a mile out. It was heeled over so far that the top of the propeller was showing. Inexplicably the engines suddenly started! The spinning prop shot a white wall of water spraying high into the air. The stricken vessel began moving toward us, picking up speed. I figured the captain was going to position it nearer to us for convenience in shuttling supplies, but he kept coming closer and closer, faster and faster. We all watched in dismay as the large ocean liner came ramming straight into the beach, plunging into the jungle only 100 feet from us, snapping off big trees and crashing through the underbrush. It was like witnessing an unbelievable scene from a high-budget disaster movie, except this was real. Surreal!

Just when I thought it couldn't possibly get any more astonishing, the captain threw the engines into reverse. With the propellers chewing through the sand he backed the ship out, and parallel parked it on the shore like it was a lonely stretch-limousine. There it sat, leaning over on its side, creating a totally incongruous scene. No mistake about it, we were shipwrecked!

The crew informed us that the distress signal from the ship

had been heard by a small cargo ferry in the vicinity. We were lucky. It would come to rescue us and should arrive sometime before morning. Darkness slowly enveloped us while we waited, giving us seclusion with our own private thoughts.

As I sat there reliving the crazy events of this day on the high seas, my mind drifted... As I thought about the chain of events that had led up to this present moment I slipped into a reverie of memories and recollections while our ship continued to silently take on more water. All of the remarkable occurrences, meaningful experiences, favorite moments, highlights and low points, influential lessons, and profound realizations that brought me to where I am today, flooded my thoughts and washed through my mind's eye one at a time. I was able to view them in detail, remembering things I had done that I hadn't thought about in years. In retrospect I realized it had been quite a journey. It started about fifty years ago when I was just a kid...

CHAPTER 2

Early Influences

I DON'T REMEMBER BEING BORN, BUT I'M SURE IT WAS quite a thrill. My earliest memories come from about the age of three when my parents and I lived in the High Point Housing Project in West Seattle. It was a large neighborhood set aside for government employees and their families. We lived in a long L-shaped row of duplexes. Our house was the one right in the corner of the "L". There was a grassy court-yard out front and woods out back to play in. My favorite play area was the open pit garbage dump behind the houses where all the local residents dumped their trash over the steep ravine into the forest. My first best friend Eddy and I used to love to go there and stomp on the light bulbs, throw bottles around, and search for exciting treasure in the piles of junk. He lived at the far end of the row of houses at the other end of the "L."

I enjoyed going to play at his place because his mother let us rough house more than mine. We used to jump off the top of his bunk bed, gallop around the house like wild horses, and play lots of hide and seek. I found the perfect hiding place behind his father's overstuffed easy chair which was shoved up tight into a corner. In order to get behind it, I had to climb up over the chair and squeeze myself down into the corner space. It was great! Eddy could never find me when I hid there. He would always give up and then I would mysteriously reappear when he wasn't looking. I relished the fact that I was so clever.

The one rule in his house was that no one was allowed to sit in that chair except Eddy's father. I had never met him, but from the stories I heard about him, he seemed like he might be gruff and mean. He was never home during the daytime anyway, so I wasn't worried about running into him. One afternoon we were playing hide and seek and I was comfortably crouched behind the infamous seat. I could see Eddy pacing back and forth looking for me, dumbfounded again. I knew he would have to give up sooner or later, so I just waited there feeling smug, and smiling.

Suddenly I heard the deep growl of an unknown man's voice. It startled me awake. I realized that I had fallen asleep back there for several hours and now Eddy's father was home for dinner. I heard them talking around the kitchen table in the adjoining room. His dad didn't sound too happy. His voice gave me the impression that he was really big, with thick, hairy features and dark sunken eyes. He could be the type who would grab you and squeeze really hard if he was upset by something you did. I was scared, petrified! I considered staying behind the chair forever, but I knew my mom would be calling soon to check on me. I was worried that at any second Eddy's dad would finish his dinner and want to rest in his favorite chair. It wouldn't sit well with him if he knew I was climbing over it, especially if he was sitting in it at the time.

My mind was whirling with doubt and anguish! I needed to do something fast before it was too late. Summoning all my courage, I hurriedly crawled out from my solitary confinement, put my head down and raced through the house, traversing the kitchen like a blue streak of lightening without ever looking up or uttering a sound. Eddy's family was calmly eating at the table when I sprinted past them, blasted through the front door slamming it behind me, and madly dashed all the way home! It was the kind of startling occurrence that could have caused someone to choke on their food. I didn't go back to visit Eddy for weeks.

But I never heard a word about it, and to this day I still wonder if Eddy and his parents ever knew who or what it was that suddenly burst through their kitchen that night? I hope not. I hope they're still wondering about it too.

Party Crasher

I WAS QUITE accident prone as a child, suffering more than my share of mishaps and broken bones. One day I was watching my mother shovel coal into the monstrous, cast iron furnace in the basement. I was bending over, looking through a crack in the staircase when I lost my balance and rolled all the way down to the concrete landing, breaking my right collar bone. Subsequently, I sported a plaster cast that went from my shoulder all the way down to my wrist. It immobilized my arm and kept it sticking straight out all the time. It didn't seem to slow me down much, however, and Eddy and I continued to have our usual rough and tumble adventures.

Halfway between my house and his house lived a girl about our same age. Her place was the only one in the entire neighborhood that was surrounded by a fence, a white picket fence at that. She was never allowed to play outside of her enclosed yard. She made it known to us that she was too good for our kind and lived in a social strata that was obviously way higher than the rest of us. Most of the time we just ignored her. She seemed just too prissy for us.

One day, as we wandered past, she proudly announced to us, "Tomorrow I'm having a birthday party and you're not invited!"

We said, "Big deal," and continued on our way. We didn't believe her anyway. But, sure enough, the next day her yard was filled with balloons and a bunch of unknown kids all dressed up in fancy-schmancy party clothes. Eddy and I went over to take a closer look and the birthday girl started laughing at us, calling us names and showing off for her friends. We were right outside her fence and Eddy reciprocated. He picked up a small pebble and threw it straight down into her yard as an act of defiance and disgust. It wasn't directed at anyone, and landed closer to us than any of them. The little girl, acting as if she had been mortally wounded, started screaming and threatened to run inside and get her mother. We said, "Go ahead." I felt confident that what Eddy had done was totally innocent and couldn't possibly warrant any punishment or retribution.

The girl made good on her threat and soon returned with her mother and several other parents in tow. Now she was crying her eyes out. Her mother asked her what happened and the little girl pointed directly at me and said, "He spit on me!"

I was completely flabbergasted! I had done no such thing! Nobody had! I was just an innocent bystander to an innocent action, but now a false accusation of a truly more serious nature was being leveled against me. Before I could protest, one of the other kids at the party claimed that he witnessed the foul deed. He was a big, chubby kid and he offered to defend the birthday girl's honor. He opened the gate, ran out into the grassy courtyard and started chasing me around a small birch sapling that was only about five inches in diameter. Around and around we went. In my mind I was scared at first, but somewhere during the third revolution I realized how ridiculous this was. I stopped abruptly, turned around, and gently aimed my cast toward his head as he ran into it. He dropped to the ground like a sack of potatoes hitting a warehouse floor. I had heard of someone being "knocked out" before but this was the first time I had actually seen it happen.

Now all the birthday party mothers who had gathered on the porch started screaming and all ran outside the fence to help. Meanwhile, I ran home and told my mother what had happened. Pretty soon the phone rang and she defended me to our hostile and irate neighbor lady. I felt really good about all the support I received that day from my mom, and was intrigued with the power and satisfaction that came with that knockout wallop.

The stunned and burly would-be hero came to quickly with no obvious lasting ill effects, and everybody went inside. I don't remember ever seeing the little girl out in her yard again after that day. I always wondered why she and her family were so different and unfriendly. I never figured it out. Shortly thereafter we moved to the shores of Lake Sammamish on the east side of Seattle where I spent the rest of my childhood. The old Highpoint neighborhood, the garbage dump, and my friend Eddy became just a fond memory.

BOXING LESSONS

IN COLLEGE MY father was a champion boxer. He was undefeated in the fly-weight division and even considered going professional. After breaking his nose for the third time, he decided to give it up for more painless pursuits. When I found out his exciting history, I started pestering him to give me boxing lessons. The gratification of that one punch knockout in the old neighborhood still lingered in my mind. I was only four years old, but I already had a thirst for that "king of the hill" adrenaline rush.

My father was eager to teach me some self-defense skills and to have a workout center of his own, so he set up a first-class gym in our basement, complete with body bag, speed bag, regulation gym mats, several sets of leather boxing gloves, and professional quality jump ropes to help me develop quickness of feet and coordination. I learned the proper stance and how to transfer all my weight into my jabs, how to defend myself, and how to deliver a dazzling volley of counter punches and uppercuts. I practiced all the time. By the time I was five and a half years old and ready for the first grade, I was a ferocious little fighter.

After I started school I had no qualms about slugging someone for the simplest infraction. Stepping in front of me in the lunch line or leaning on my desk would prompt a battle. I always got in the first blow and always had the skills to be the eventual winner. The more mayhem and havoc the better it was for me. I remember that my parents talked to me once about not fighting at school. I guess the teacher complained about it. But I continued to practice and regularly punch the body bag in the basement and throw my weight around at school. It was my identity at the time, my *raison d'être*.

Evidently the teachers had complained to my parents more often than I knew. One day I came home from school and headed for the basement in my usual pattern. What I found there completely shocked and staggered me. The room had been completely transformed into a totally new and foreign environment. Gone was the body bag and gym mats. The boxing gloves and jump ropes were nowhere to be found. I looked everywhere for them. In all the boxes and corners and shelves that we had there was not one hint that a gym had ever existed. The room was now a sedate living room with book-cases and couches, rugs, and lamps. Unbelievable! The effect was total and complete. The feelings of confusion and uncertainty were very humbling.

Without one word from my parents, I realized that what I had been doing must have been very dishonorable to cause them to make such an overwhelming response and reaction. The utter shock of that stark alteration was like enduring a primitive initiation rite instituted to separate me from my foolish, fighting ways so I could attain a certain degree of maturity. It worked. It was quite a lesson. After that day, I never engaged in any physical combat or violence directed toward others. I remembered the feeling of shame that it had brought on before and I wouldn't choose to bear it again. It was much worse than being tagged by a solid right hook.

GIRL TROUBLE

I WAS ALWAYS pretty shy around members of the opposite sex, especially the girls who I thought were really cute. When I was young my timing was bad, my pickup lines were stupid, and my moves were awkward. By the time I entered college, the memories of how I had blundered through the previous years were still with me, and they influenced how I got dates.

My first romance was in the first grade with a girl named Sherry. It only lasted a day or two but it was intense. We had the same teacher and rode the same bus together. I remember sitting in the back seat of the bus with her, kissing her all the way home. I was in heaven and I think the feeling was mutual. I didn't even know where she lived because I got off the bus before she did. The next day her neighbor, a kid named Mike, came over to talk to me while we were at school. He was in the first grade too. He roughly grabbed the front of my shirt and said to stay away from Sherry because she was his girlfriend! He was a big guy and threatened to beat me up if I didn't. I believed him. Puppy love was quickly replaced by genuine fear.

Later that year, Sherry lost her lunch money on the bus on the way to school. It was a $20 bill. She was afraid to tell her parents the truth so she lied and accused me of stealing it. I was appalled when her parents called mine, demanding a refund. My dad, suspecting the truth, called the bus driver who found the cash while sweeping out the litter. I felt vindicated, but my self-assurance with girls had withered somewhat.

In the fourth grade my confidence rebounded. I had a big crush on a girl named Joan. I wanted so badly to be able to tell her how I felt, but I was scared. Finally, one day I summoned up the courage and promised myself that as soon as I saw her that day I would go right up to her and tell her my feelings for her. As the school bus I was riding pulled into the school yard that morning, I saw her standing there on the playground. "Dang it!" I said to myself, "I didn't think I would see her this soon!" But I kept my promise and nervously walked over to her. Stammering, I told her I really liked her and hoped that she could be my girlfriend.

She smiled graciously and said to me, "I used to really like you too, but now I'm in love with Elvis." Then she walked away. It was a bittersweet moment for me. I felt enthused that she had ever liked me at all, but I was really upset that I had spoken up too late.

I wondered who the heck is this kid named Elvis anyway? I'd never heard of him. He must be a new kid in school that I didn't know about yet. For about two weeks I brooded about this and tried to discover whose class Elvis was in, what he looked like, and what he had that I didn't have. One day I heard a new song on a friend's radio. (I wasn't allowed to listen to anything other than classical music at home, so I wasn't exactly in tune with the current scene). The radio announcer said the song was by "Elvis." I realized then, that the Elvis I was searching for was a grownup, and a popular rock and roll singer to boot! There was no way I was going to be able to compete with that. From that day forward I never liked Elvis or anything he did. Sorry about that, you Elvis fans, but I was nine years old and he stole my girl, and that was that! My confidence declined.

My next resurgence of romantic zeal was in the seventh grade. A month before school started a new family moved into our neighborhood. My mother was the first person to greet them. They had a daughter my age, so they asked my mom if I would be willing to show her around the area and introduce her to the other kids in our school. I was most enthusiastic because she was absolutely beautiful. Her name was Donna. We became somewhat acquainted, but not close friends.

When school started that fall it was a big deal! It was our first year of junior high. It was scary being around all those big kids. There was a lot of pressure to be cool, to fit in to the right group, and to do the right thing. Everyone was nervous. My first class was homeroom, a two-hour session that was very important to do well in. I walked in and there stood Donna. Since I was the only person in the room that she knew, she naturally sat next to me. I felt so proud to have this beautiful girl sitting by me, and I felt so important that I was the one who got to show her around. It was like a big feather in my cap that signified that I was indeed very cool. As the weeks went by we became better friends and I grew to like her more and more. I didn't know how she felt about me, but I decided I wanted to ask her to "go steady." I struggled with how to do it, and with what I could say that would be really neat and appealing. After agonizing over it for days, I finally came up with the perfect way to ask. We both had braces on our teeth so I decided to use that to my advantage. I waited for the perfect moment during class, right before recess break. I got her attention, leaned over, and said softly to her, "Wouldn't it be great if someday our braces got locked together?" She just stared at me for a brief moment but didn't say a thing. Then the bell rang.

I didn't see her during recess. When the second half of the class started afterward, her chair was empty. I wondered where she was. Then I saw her sitting clear across the room in the front row. She was as far away from me as she could get. Evidently I had come on too strong, or quite possibly I was just totally inept. In any case, I had blown it again. She had asked the teacher to move her away from me. I don't know exactly what she told the teacher, but she never talked to me again after that day. She went on to become a cheerleader and prom queen, and I went on to become a nincompoop.

I gave up on girls after that. The prettier they were, the farther away I stayed. I busied myself with homework and music lessons. By the time I was in eighth grade I was a very good pianist. The school's drama teacher enlisted me to play for all the auditions and rehearsals for the upcoming play and talent show. The final production was a big hit with the school and the parents. They openly praised the skills of the drama teacher and he felt really honored. To show his appreciation, he invited the four students who helped him the most to go out to dinner with him and then to a professional play at a downtown theater. I was one of those four. The other three were all ninth grade girls. They were all at the top of their class. They were smart, gorgeous and a lot older than I. They were good friends with each other, but because of my shyness, I hardly knew them. I felt very puny around them.

I dreaded having to ride in the car with them to the restaurant, but they were nice enough and included me in the conversation while our teacher drove. This was my first, real dress-up social event, so my parents gave me plenty of helpful hints on proper etiquette and table manners. We went over them several times before I left the house that evening.

When we got to the restaurant we were shown to a corner booth. It had a large U-shaped seat around the table. The three girls slid in and sat together at the curved part of the U, and the teacher and I sat across from each other at either end of the U. I was glad that I had been prepped by my parents on table manners. I knew exactly what to do. I unfolded my cloth napkin and tucked the end of it into my belt. I kept my elbows off the table and my left hand in my lap. The conversation continued from the one started in the car and I was beginning to feel a little more accepted now. After a while, the three girls mumbled something to each other and then announced that they were all going to the restroom. They started sliding out of the booth in my direction so I held onto my napkin and stood up to move out of their way.

Unfortunately, in my nervousness I had mistakenly tucked the corner of the tablecloth into my belt along with the napkin. I pulled two complete place settings of dishes and silverware onto the floor, along with spilling the water, before I realized what was happening. I can still hear the echoes of the shattering plates and the tinging sounds of silverware bouncing around on the linoleum. That was followed by the deafening roar of silence that filled the entire restaurant as I endured the weight of dozens of pity-filled eyes looming down on me. My newly found confidence collapsed. Unbelievable humiliation came over me. It was happening again. I was a dufus!

My teacher and the waiter quickly started cleaning up the mess while the three girls escaped to the ladies' room, trying to put as much distance between them and this embarrassing scene as possible. When they returned later, the table was back in order and all the broken pieces were gone except for me. I hung my blushing head as they slid in past me. I don't think I looked up again for the rest of the dinner. Fortunately, the play and the ride back home in the car were in the dark, so I felt like I was hidden. Even so, it seemed like the awful image of those dishes crashing to the floor was still clearly visible, lingering in the air about me. I didn't get over it for quite some time. The three girls were very kind and polite to me for the rest of the year, but I was at a loss for words around them. It was one more piece of evidence that seemed to prove that we would all be better off if I stayed away from girls.

I had two really great girlfriends later on in high school, but they were the ones who approached me and asked me out. They evidently were unaware of my past history.

~~ ~~

HITTING THE WALL

THE SUMMER BETWEEN junior high and high school proved to be extremely important for me in many ways. I was 14 years old and starting to search for real meaning in life. Who was I? What were my talents? Where did I fit in? What would I do for an occupation? Would I ever be able to talk to girls again? I knew I was lucky to be growing up with a beautiful lake as my backyard. Many of the other kids my age who lived on the lake were popular at school, and just riding the school bus with them made me feel proud.

I remember how excited and surprised I was when I received an invitation to a summer party at a girl's house along the lake. She was very well connected to the in-crowd at school and I knew they would all be in attendance. It was going to be a water-skiing and beach party. I was sort of known by my peers as the studious, shy type with a talent in music, but that was the extent of their knowledge. No one realized that I had a passion for water-skiing. Since I lived on the lake, I was able to indulge in my zest for water-skiing every day if I wanted to. It was the only athletic activity that I really excelled in and I was better than most kids my age but nobody knew it! Being an athlete was surely a way to get noticed in high school by the girls, especially those who were in the in-crowd.

I couldn't wait for the party because I kept visualizing all the praise, honor, and respect I would be receiving from the group when they saw me ski. I would finally break the mindset that I was just a nerdy, bump-on-the-log type of guy. Finally, the day arrived and it was perfect weather—hot and sunny, insuring a maximum turnout. Sure enough, they were all there at the beach, waiting for something to happen. I could hardly believe I was part of it, surrounded by the prettiest and most popular girls of the school in their swimming suits.

All the athletic and Romeo-type guys were there too, but I barely noticed them. I could tell with a little casual observation that most of them were unfamiliar and somewhat uncomfortable being around the water, boats, swimming, and such. This gave me a boost of extra confidence. When the hostess asked who wanted to go water-skiing, I jumped at the chance and volunteered to go first. Since this was uncharacteristically brave of me, I noticed a slight murmur of surprise, curiosity, and anticipation rippling through the crowd gathered on the dock. I put on the beautiful, laminated water ski that was custom-made for the girl's mother, grabbed the rope and yelled, "Hit it!"

The boat roared forward and I was up. It was one of those old classic, mahogany Chris Craft inboards that rumbled like a finely tuned hot rod. I had never skied behind it before and it was going quite a bit faster than I was used to, but the extra thrill of the speed made the whole scene just perfect for me. I was skiing great, kicking up huge walls of spray and flying across the wake going airborne on each pass. By their wide-eyed looks and dropped-jaw expressions, I could tell the people in the boat were "wowed" by my performance. I was showing off like never before. I hoped that the observers from the shore were caught up in the same sense of wonderment. I decided to do something special for all who had gathered at the end of the dock. At the end of my turn, I planned to come in fast, head straight for the dock, and at the last second turn and carve up an immense wall of water that would astound and soak down all the onlookers!

I signaled the driver to return and at the last possible moment I swung way outside and made a hard double cut across the wakes toward the throng on the float. As soon as I let go of the rope I realized I was going much faster than I had ever gone before—too fast to carry out my last minute ditch with out hitting the dock! My mind started racing, "What do I do to still get out of this looking good?" I quickly surveyed the scene because I had never skied at this beach before. The boat dolly for launching the boat was still sitting out in the water at the end of the marine railway. It had four 4x4 posts sticking up above the surface. I could ski in parallel to the dock, slalom expertly between the posts, and then fall (on purpose) to stop. That would be really impressive. I went for it. As soon as I successfully negotiated the posts a new dilemma arose. I was still going too fast! I could see the rusty heads of the railroad spikes protruding up from the ties through the water beneath me. It was rapidly getting shallower and I realized that if I fell now I would be filleted into ragged strips on the sharp metal on the bottom. I decided I needed to change plans again, so I quickly reevaluated the situation. So far, the total elapsed time from letting go of the rope was only a few seconds, but my mind was scrambling so rapidly that whole lifetimes were going by in a flash. It seemed easy to formulate, disband, and then reformulate probable scenarios in a split second while traveling at 40 MPH on an out of control ski. I decided to ski onto the beach and, at just the right moment, deftly jump out of the ski and gracefully run up on the sand like I had done a hundred times before at home. The only problem was that here, a tennis court was built up on a rock bulkhead just at the shoreline. I would have to turn gently and carefully to keep from falling on the tracks, but far enough to miss the corner of the rock wall. I was approaching dry land very rapidly! At the last instant I knew I hadn't put enough arc on my turn and I put my hands up to cover my face for protection. BANG!! The terrible force of the blow crumpled me like a rag doll. I clipped the corner of the rocks in the bulkhead. I almost cleared it, but not quite. Amazingly I felt no pain, just complete numbness. I found myself lying flat on my back on the sand with the waves lapping up against my left side. Someone yelled out, "Are you okay?"

I didn't answer back, but silently I thought that I was just fine. I began to get up from a prone position. I drew my legs up underneath me to stand, and all of a sudden my left leg fell over sideways into the lake. It was a sickening feeling of dread seeing my leg turn 180 degrees from the thigh. Like a separate piece of meat it hung from my body, seemingly lifeless, totally out of my control, bouncing in the waves. I grabbed it with both hands, turned it back around and continued to hold it in place, daring not to let it move even one inch more. I called out weakly, "I think I broke my leg."

Someone called the aid car and someone else went to get my parents. Meanwhile, as I lay there, my sense of feeling started to return to my body. With horror, I noticed with my tongue that my teeth were completely rearranged and some were obviously broken off. Blood was coming from somewhere and all the skin on both hands had been torn off. I had the sudden realization that I had gotten myself into quite a predicament. This nightmare was no dream! I was scared and feeling helpless. I needed some outside assistance. I prayed earnestly to God to help me. I had heard about the power of faith in church but had never really put it into practice. At that moment I put my complete faith and trust into God's hands. I totally entrusted Him with the complete healing of my leg and the rest of my body and thanked Him for being there for me. I immediately felt relieved and confident. In my heart I knew, then, that everything would be all right, and I relaxed, waiting for the future to unfold. It was a great feeling to have, that total confidence.

I heard my mother's voice as she was being escorted down to the beach. Several people were trying to explain what had happened. Her only comment was, "I don't care just as long as his face is all right." When she finally got close enough to stand over me and get a good look, I watched her heart sink as her face sagged. She uttered a barely audible, "Ohhhh."

I knew from her expression that my face was not so familiar any more. The sirens were screaming in the distance, coming down the lake road. Before I knew it, the paramedics were loading me into the back of the ambulance and then off we went. I remember the excitement of being whisked along with the siren blaring, but wishing it was just a joy ride instead of a real life emergency.

My father met us at the emergency room where the doctors checked me over. Along with breaking my nose and six teeth, I had also broken the largest bone in my body. My left femur was shattered into seven pieces. It was so bad that the doctors didn't know how to fix it. The pieces were too numerous and small to pin together. From my bed I could hear them conferring with my dad out in the hall. The doctors' consensus seemed to be to amputate. When I heard that, I felt ashamed that what I had done was causing my parents so much grief and anguish. The decision was left up to my dad. He decided to get an outside third opinion and had an orthopedic specialist called in from a hospital in downtown Seattle. It took quite a while for him to arrive. Meanwhile, the spasmodic muscle tension in my leg was slowly collapsing it like an elongated accordion since there was no bone to provide any resistance. It was getting shorter and shorter. They gave me some pain medication and a sedative while we waited. After that I drifted in and out of coherency.

I opened my eyes at one point and saw two men working on my leg. They had a solid stainless steel brace and bit. (One of those old fashioned carpenter's drills). It glinted in the bright lights and they were boring a hole through my knee with it from right to left. The sight of this happening to me was surprising, but there was no pain, so I watched intently. After a while, one of the doctors noticed I was awake, so he calmly asked me to close my eyes and rest.

The next time I woke up I looked exactly like one of those cartoon pictures of someone lying in a bed, completely covered with bandages, with ropes, pulleys and trapezes hanging down from above, supporting various body appendages. Instead of cutting off my leg, the specialist decided to try an experimental procedure. Thirty pounds of traction were hanging from a steel rod that protruded from the drill hole on either side of my knee. It was to stretch my leg back out to its original length. Meanwhile, my entire left leg was tightly wrapped with gauze tape, binding a wooden plank to my side that acted as a splint. The hope was that the constrictive wrap would consolidate all the broken pieces into one lump while they healed and coalesced together into a hard callous along the straight line defined by the board. The doctor told my father that it might not work. Even if it did, I would always have a permanent limp and probably need a crutch or a cane for walking assistance. I was secure in my belief that I would prove the doctors wrong. I had the healing force of the entire Universe on my side.

For six weeks I lay in this immobilized state. The pain killers weren't totally effective and they caused nausea. Keeping more than small bites of food down was impossible so I lost a lot of weight. There was plenty of time to think and to observe the day-to-day hospital routines as other patients came and went. I thought about how my accident must have thrown a gigantic damper on the party and wondered what happened after I left. My performance certainly couldn't have dispelled the notion that I was a nerd.

Many of the kids came to visit me and I was surprised at the ones who showed a genuine empathy for me. They were people I hadn't known very well and I was enthused that so many actually cared about me. As I thought about it more, I realized that there was really no such thing as an "in-crowd" or an "out-crowd." We were all just people who needed to get to know each other more. The fear of rejection was a powerful force that dissuaded you from reaching out beyond your safe zone of established contacts. This fear was artificial and worthless. Everyone contains the same divine life force inside that drives them forward. We all come from the same common ground. We all belong to the same clique. I resolved to conquer my cowardice and to start feeling comfortable around all types of people. It was a skill that needed practice and it was going to take a while before I got really good at it.

I also thought about what had caused this accident. When I analyzed it, I came to the conclusion that showing off was the source. I promised myself never to show off again. Having a talent was something to relish for your own entertainment and enjoyment. It was not for inducing others to like or admire you. The payoff came with the thrill I experienced while doing my best and with sharing that excitement and sense of achievement with others. Not being afraid to share was the important part. Freely sharing success acts to uplift others and encourages them to go ahead with their own accomplishments.

As I felt myself beginning to heal, I was so grateful to all the doctors, nurses, staff, and volunteers who cared for me. I knew that I wanted to do the same for others. While lying in that hospital, I decided I would become some type of doctor. I thought about all the different doctors I knew. I didn't think I would be good at handling death and dying issues, so I searched for alternative choices. I remembered how my family dentist treated me over the years. I looked up to him immensely because he always made me feel like I was a great person and that he was glad to know me. He had a knack for raising my self-esteem and greatly empowering me every time I went in for an appointment. When I left his office I always felt like a million bucks. I felt like such a good and worthy person even though half my face was completely numb. That's what I wanted to do for other people! Have the opportunity to make them feel great about themselves and their abilities. That in fact is our true nature: we are all great! From that day forward I was on track to becoming a dentist. It would be my avenue for helping others find out the truth about themselves.

After six weeks of being wrapped up like a mummy, the bandages finally came off. They were replaced by a huge body cast that extended from my neck all the way down to my ankle. A space was left in the middle so I could use the bedpan. But there was a problem. Every time I moved a little, an excruciating sharp pain came from my private area. I put up with it for a few days because I was too embarrassed to have a nurse check it. Finally, one evening an orderly who I trusted came in and I asked him to take a look. He said, "Oh, I see what the problem is. Hold still." He gave one quick yank and a blood curdling scream gushed from my shocked mouth that was so loud and shrill it must have come from my ancestral primal center. I'm sure no one in that hospital had ever heard one like it before. I know that even today it is still echoing through those halls like a ricochet. Turns out that when the plaster on the cast was still wet, all the hairs on my backside got embedded in it and trapped. In one swell whoop I was free! It was instant relief.

After setting the record for the longest patient stay in that hospital, I was finally released to go home. It was the day of the frightful Columbus Day storm in 1962. Trees and electrical lines were down everywhere. The wind and rain were pounding. Yet another challenge for my poor parents—dodging fallen branches and fording flooded sections of road to get me safely home to a dark and cold house without power. My life was turning into quite an adventure and I was dragging them unwittingly in to it. They persevered through love.

It was good to be home again, even though I was restricted to a prone position in my body cast prison for six more weeks. I faced dire consequences of missing my entire first year of high school because of my immobility. But a solution emerged. The phone company rigged up an elaborate system that connected my bedroom with the school via intercom. It was transmitted over the phone lines. A large speaker box was carried from classroom to classroom by my fellow students and plugged into a wall outlet. I could hear the conversation in each class through another speaker next to my bed at home. There was even a button I could push so I could respond back to the class when asked a question. Other students along my bus route picked up and delivered my homework every day. The system worked flawlessly. It was the height of technology for its day and was the first time on the West Coast that this type of telephone hookup had been tried. It was quite an accomplishment. It required the cooperative efforts of the school, the phone company, and the community at large. The story made the top ten events of 1962 for our local community of Redmond, Washington.

Friends who delivered my homework were jealous of me. They explained that all of the girls from the other junior high schools in my classes were in love with my voice. They had never met me and could only fantasize about the personage that went along with that deep, rich, and resonant voice that came from the speaker every day. Six months after the accident I was finally able to walk well enough to return to school on my own. That first day was one of great anticipation for my teachers, my classmates, and me. The first class was French. I'll never forget the look on the faces of all the girls sitting in the back of that room when I first appeared in the doorway. I don't know what they expected, but I could literally see the emotion drain out of their faces as they paled in disappointment. There I stood, still terribly skinny and frail, covered with acne and limping noticeably. Clearly, more than one person's hopes were dashed that day.

I recovered steadily over the next year. Because of my notoriety I was well-known in the school. I was still pretty shy but getting braver. It took a while for all the things I learned while lying in that hospital to take hold of me. But it happened. I continued to excel in music and academics. High school was fun, but I considered it just a stepping stone to dental school. The impact of hitting that rock wall had a much greater effect on my life than I realized at the time. I learned firsthand about real friends, real pain, and real faith. It helped me realize my life's purpose. I learned that life is not about showing off, but about performance for the sake of others. By the time I graduated from high school I was no longer limping. I was climbing mountains! There was no doubt about what I would become in the future.

RANDOM NUMBERS

ENTERING COLLEGE REMAINS one of the supreme high-lights of my life. I was bolstered by my academic accomplishments in high school, gleeful to be on my own, and enthralled to be starting the first tangible steps toward achieving my dream of being a dentist. I was filled with zeal and everything was pure fun. There were so many new people to meet, unfamiliar sights to see and explore, and new adventures were around every corner. I took full advantage of every opportunity to broaden my horizons except, of course, going out on dates. I was still suffering from all the indignities that I foisted upon myself in my youth. Though still keenly interested in meeting women, I couldn't force myself to do it face to face. Not knowing exactly why, I was self-conscious about my appearance. I felt there was something visible about me that belied my feelings of incompetence around women. If I was going to be rejected I didn't want it to be because I looked weird. Being inept was resolvable, but being unattractive was a permanent condition that would be just too extreme for my fragile ego. I decided the best way to get around this was not to show my face.

In those days (the 60's and early 70's) college men and women lived in separate residence halls. There was no such thing as living on the same floor, much less in the same building, and strict curfew rules were imposed on the women. At 11:00 PM the doors were locked on all the women's dorms. If you were still out somewhere, you couldn't get back in without setting off an alarm. In addition, the house mother did a bed check, and if you didn't answer, distress and misfortune started happening in your life without hesitation. Your parents were informed and it could lead to expulsion and a whole raft of troublesome and disconcerting interrogation.

The telephone system on campus was unique. The first

three digits connected you to the university exchange. The next number distinguished the particular residence hall, while the last three were the room number of the person being called. Once I comprehended this system, I embraced it as a way to ask for dates and still save face. I would dial the first part of the phone number, making sure it was for one of the women's dorms. Then I closed my eyes and randomly let my fingers do the walking.

Whoever answered was engaged in a conversation that would inevitably lead to a request for a date. I was very confident about the quality and richness of my voice, having been told many times that I should be a disc jockey. Knowing that the sound of my voice was intriguing, I figured that with sincere friendliness, attentive listening, and a little bit of schmoozing I could convince the female on the other end of the line that at least one live encounter with me was worthwhile. Surprisingly, I was never turned down. My self-confidence grew based on the fact that once a commitment to meet me was made, it was good for at least one date. Finally, I didn't have to worry about my looks interfering with my social life so much anymore.

I met many genuinely friendly gals this way. They were interesting to talk to and fun to be with, but so far none of them ever really wound my clock or rang my bells. There was no zinging or zanging of my heart strings. No feelings of deep abiding love. No feelings of love at all.

One night, just for the sake of conversation, I did my usual dialing routine with my eyes closed. The phone rang several times before a quiet and subdued voice answered. When she found out that I was a stranger making random calls she chastised me for waking her up from a deep sleep. She was trying to get some rest for a big test the next day and didn't particularly appreciate the intrusion. Taken aback by her reaction and my mistake, I told her I would call again another time. I apologized weakly and hung up. There was something sweet and endearing about her voice and her sincerity. I sensed something special about her, plus I really wanted to apologize properly. There was only one problem...I had no idea which number I had dialed. For the next two or three days I spent my spare time madly calling one wrong number after another, asking the confused party on the other end if they had talked to any strangers recently. Many of them had, but their strangers were not the same stranger as I. It was a strange interview scenario.

The failure rate was climbing and I was starting to feel pretty desperate. I just had to find that number! Finally, I hit the winning combination—5624—and she answered. She was astonished that I had called back and impressed with my sincere regret at disturbing her previously. Her name was Jerri, and we stayed on the phone talking for over two hours. The time flowed by like butter melting on a hot ear of corn. It was a delicious and glorious conversation. By the time we finished, we knew everything important about each other: our beliefs, our likes and dislikes, our goals, and hopes for the future. The amazing thing was that they all seemed to match up with each other right down the line.

The only thing left was to see if our physical attributes appealed to each other. We set up a meeting time and "Voila!" She had beautiful long hair, a beautiful face, curvaceous body, and the sweetest, most genuine smile I had ever seen. Before long we fell head over heels in love and we have been together ever since. I'm sure it was a match made in heaven.

I'd never been particularly lucky at games of chance, picking horses, or playing the numbers. I certainly had never been lucky with members of the opposite sex before. I sported a long litany of goof-ups, near misses, wimp-outs and letdowns. All these experiences had groomed and prepared me. They molded me so that I would play this game in a certain way.

They finally all came together and I was the winner of the biggest jackpot payoff in random number history: # 5624— Jerri, I love you!

IN THE BEGINNING...

ON SEPTEMBER 1, 1968, it happened! We had a beautiful outdoor wedding on the shores of Lake Crescent on the Olympic Peninsula. We decided we would drive to San Francisco for our honeymoon, so as soon as the reception was over we set off down the road. Our friends and relatives gave us a really special basket of goodies so we would have snacks to eat along the way. It was filled with cheese and crackers, fruit and nuts, cookies and candy, and an expensive bottle of champagne.

It was a hot, bumpy drive in our old car, but we didn't have reservations anywhere so we just kept going until we were falling asleep at the wheel. When the sound of our tires hitting the gravel on the side of the freeway woke us up several times, we decided it was time to find a place to stay. We saw a nice looking motel and checked in.

I decided that a toast with our champagne would be a good way to start out the evening. As we stood facing each other I popped the cork and the warm, agitated bottle erupted like it was a fire hose. The spray blasted Jerri right in the face! I immediately turned the bottle to the side as fast as I could and the rest of it emptied out all over the bed. It happened so fast we were both stunned. I quickly reassured Jerri that everything would be okay and that she could take a relaxing shower while I got all the wet blankets off the bed and cleaned things up.

She went into the bathroom and started running the water

to warm it up. Suddenly I heard a strange noise and she started shrieking. I ran into the bathroom and saw that the shower pipe had broken off inside the wall. A gusher of water was spraying straight out of the plaster board, all over Jerri, ruining her beautiful hairdo and soaking her new white jacket and blouse. I turned the water off and this time it took awhile longer for both of us to calm down. I told her I would fix the pipe and get the bathtub working. Meanwhile she went out to hang up her wet clothes. About 30 seconds went by and then she started to scream at the top of her lungs. I had never heard her or any woman scream like that before. I raced out into the bedroom to see what was the matter, and there, standing in our closet, was an old man in his underwear! I slammed the closet door and leaned against it. My heart was pounding and my mind raced as I tried to figure out what to do next. Then I noticed a small hook lock on the outside of the door.

The motel had two wings and was shaped like an "L". We were in the room right in the corner where the two halves met each other. Because of the high class nature of this place, we were sharing the closet with the people next door. I wondered why the man had such a shocked look on his face. It was just a pure coincidence that the poor man was in there hanging up his clothes when Jerri opened the door. He must have been completely mortified. I'm glad no one had a heart attack.

Later that night as I was adjusting the curtains above our bed, I discovered that our window was stuck open and that someone had punched their fist through the screen from the sidewalk outside. It would have been easy for anyone to reach in from the parking lot and choke us while we slept. I kept this fact a secret for several years.

The next day we awoke with renewed enthusiasm and reached San Francisco in the late afternoon. We went to the first big hotel we saw and asked for a room. The man at the desk said there were two huge conventions in town and that all the rooms in the city had been booked months in advance. Nothing was available. We decided we could find one if we looked on our own. After three frustrating hours we had made a complete circuit of the city and no rooms were to be found.

Out of sheer desperation we called Jerri's eccentric uncle who lived in a nearby men's boarding house. He said he had a room for us. We were excited when we arrived at his building. It was a 100 year old, beautiful hand-crafted wooden architecture. As he led us up the long flights of stairs to the top floor, I marveled at the smell of the old wood and creaking of the varnished steps under our feet. I knew we were going to have a special penthouse room all to ourselves. He opened the door and we looked in.

It was an oversized janitor's closet containing a large floor sink, jugs of cleanser, stacks of buckets and toilet paper, and dozens of mops. There was a thin, single wide mattress lying on the floor next to a broken window. That night the continuous flashing of the neon sign next door, the constant dripping of the sink, and the noise of the trucks coming and going to the delivery entrance below kept us restless and wide awake. Every so often I would roll over, half on the mattress and half off, and open my eyes to see a forest of tangled stringy mops gently swaying above me, suspended from the ceiling. At one point during the night we turned toward each other and decided as soon as it got light we were heading north, back to our abode, to get on with our lives. When dawn finally arrived we high-tailed it out of there, escaping toward home and our new life together.

When we were married we looked into each other's eyes and we knew we would be together forever. Our honeymoon was a test, a crazy trial by fire, and it melded us together into one solid unit. September 1, 1968, was just the beginning.

SPLIT PEA SOUP

IMMEDIATELY AFTER GETTING married and returning from our honeymoon we moved into a duplex. It was located in a large housing project which had originally been government housing but was now reserved for low income families. In order to be accepted, you had to go through a qualification process which included a review of your income and ability to pay for rent and food. We were both full-time students so I was only able to work on weekends, bringing home $120 a month. We qualified for a rent payment of $40 a month. Later, this was lowered to $26 a month after an updated review.

Since most of our income went for books, tuition, and other school expenses, there was little left over for food. Because of this, we also qualified for a government food commodity program. Surplus food left over in warehouses was distributed monthly to those of us in the program. We never knew what we would be getting. One month it might be a ten pound brick of cheese, the next it would be a 25 pound sack of corn meal and the next, a large block of cooking lard or butter. One month we got a huge bag of split peas.

We would supplement these with meat from dried up old dairy cows that were way past their prime. They were occasionally available from a local farmer who sold them to be butchered before sending them to the glue factory. We shared half a side of cow (I hesitate to call it beef) with our brother-in-law. All the meat was cut into "steaks" for easy packaging. It was the toughest, most tasteless food I ever had. There was a very fine line between it and real leather. It was so tough that it was almost impossible to chew, even after pounding it into oblivion with one of those iron club meat tenderizing hammers. Dinnertime lasted longer than it should have because our jaws got so tired from chewing that we had to rest a lot in between bites. The only consolation was that we could truthfully tell all our friends that we ate steak every night!

It was a meager existence but we were proud to be making it on our own and happy to be together. After all, we were living the American dream, albeit starting out close to the bottom of the dream ladder, but we knew we had the right steps in place to climb to the top. We decided we would have a small dinner party to celebrate our independence and to showcase our wedding gifts. It was going to be the first time we had had company over for dinner as newlyweds. We wanted it to be special, so we knew that serving the leather-like steaks was out of the question. The only other option was to utilize the 40 pound burlap bag of split peas that was still sitting unopened under the sink. We had never made split pea soup before, but it sounded good and it would be a welcome relief to our munching muscles.

The recipe called for cooking the peas in a pressure cooker, which we didn't have, so we took a quick jaunt to the nearest St. Vincent de Paul secondhand store. There was a large pile of donated cookware. Rusted pots and pans with broken handles or burn holes in them were plentiful along with a few nicer items. Way down at the bottom of the heap we discovered a heavy cast iron pressure cooker with its lid still intact. The only thing missing was the pressure relief valve that fit on the top. One of the store clerks said he had a drawer full of them in the back. He picked one out for us and we were on our way back home.

Our kitchen was small but functional. The only cabinets were a set of open shelves that were hanging above the stove. We decided that this would be the best place to display our beautiful wedding gifts. We carefully unpacked and dusted the fanciest presents and arranged them neatly on the shelves.

There were fancy crystal goblets and dinnerware, along with ornate vases, cut glass dishes, an exquisite wine decanter, and a china teapot from England. It took longer than we thought it would to get all the stuff properly situated, but when we finished the whole cabinet sparkled with elegance. After this, we put the ingredients together for the soup, filled our pressure cooker with them, and put it on the stove to cook for the recommended three hours. We spent the next two hours cleaning the house and tidying up so that our dinner guests would be duly impressed.

Finally, with an hour or so to go before our company arrived, we sat back to relax a little bit. Jerri was pretty nervous about how the dinner would turn out. It was the first time as a new wife that she had cooked for anyone other than me. The rich smell of the split-pea-laden, superheated steam whistling from the stove was encouraging, so we folded napkins, set the table, and tossed the salad. Suddenly, there was a loud "pop" followed by a deafening, whooshing roar coming from the kitchen. The pressure relief valve had broken and blown itself clear off the top of the cooker. There was an intense, dark green geyser of boiling goo erupting through the hole in the top. It was spraying up, all over the walls and ceiling! It was too hot and scary to approach so we just stood there at a safe distance, watching in disbelief and waiting for it to settle down to a small spurt. I was afraid the pot itself was going to explode and scatter dangerous shrapnel all over the place!

We were flabbergasted! Icky, sticky, khaki-colored paste was dripping down from above. The beautiful glassware in the cabinet was plastered with green froth, not to mention the floor, walls, and ceiling of the kitchen and dining area. The only room left unscathed was the living room. Jerri was crushed and exasperated. I, on the other hand, found more humor in the situation than she did, which didn't help to alleviate Jerri's feeling of panic and hopelessness. After a brief moment of despair, we resolved that we could still salvage the evening. We flew into a maelstrom of activity. Jerri found some surplus noodles and hastily threw together a sauce while they were boiling. At the same time, we were both wiping, washing, and cleaning up the mess. It was a frantic race of quiet desperation to get everything back in order before people started showing up.

Finally, unbelievably, we got things looking pretty spick and span. No one would ever suspect the tragedy that had taken place only a short time before. As I was sampling the sauce, I glanced out the window to see the first couple walking up to our door. Something was wrong with the sauce. It tasted terrible! It was revolting! Jerri agreed with me, but there was no more time or ingredients leftover to enhance the flavor. To make matters worse, the old noodles had turned out like glue and tasted like paste. Jerri was silently fuming with embarrassment and I didn't know what to say. We answered the door with forced smiles on our faces and invited them in. Shortly thereafter we all sat down to eat. From my perspective, when Jerri served the food, it looked like two bowls of slop. Of course, the rest of the people had no idea what had transpired up to this point, or what they were about to get themselves into. The bowl of noodles was passed around the table first and everyone helped themselves with the wooden serving spoon. Then came the bowl of awful sauce. It went first to my friend Dick, who wholeheartedly scooped out a large portion of it and then to my horror started to dig in for more. I knew he would hate it, but would be too polite to say anything and would suffer through trying to eat everything on his plate. I decided I should warn him. I leaned over and whispered in his ear, "Don't take too much of that stuff."

Unfortunately, Jerri either heard me or read my lips. I

unintentionally had hurt her feelings. It was the last straw. Finally, the toll of the day's anxiety and frustration were too much and they boiled over. She grabbed the wooden spoon, wrapped a big wad of noodles around it and angrily slung the slimy mass at my head. At the last second I saw it coming and ducked just in time. The noodles flew over my head and landed in the living room. As they flew through the air they spread out like a shotgun blast and covered the carpet and our new couch, which was a wedding present from Jerri's favorite aunt.

On one hand I felt happy and smug that I had dodged the projectile, but on the other I was taken aback at Jerri's reaction. I had never before (or since, for that matter) seen her lose her temper. Our guests were stunned, shocked, and silenced! They weren't privy to the prior chaos and there was no good way to explain it to them now. We just sat around the table without speaking, politely choking down the meal. Our friends all had strained looks on their faces but I didn't know if it was because of the food, or the food fight, or both. I'm sure some of them got the wrong impression about our relationship, but who could tell? I finally excused myself and scooped up the noodles from the other room so that we could sit in there without further embarrassment after dinner. We had ice cream for dessert and that was a hit, but the rest of the evening's conversation seemed subdued.

We laugh about it now, but it was definitely a rough start to our social life together as a couple. We hung on to the pressure cooker for quite a while after that, but we got rid of the remainder of the split peas the next day.

COATS

EVER SINCE CHILDHOOD I have thoroughly disliked coats. I've made it a life-long, one man crusade not to wear a coat. I never wear one, no matter what kind of weather it is. I go bare-chested when I can and wear a short sleeved shirt the rest of the time. I believe, along with many epidemiologists, that going out in the cold and wet without a coat on has nothing to do with catching a cold and I want to demonstrate that to others. Besides, coats are a nuisance. They're bulky, cumbersome, and get snagged on stuff. You always have to find a proper place to put them when you get to your destination, or you have to carry them while you're inside a heated area, leaving you with only one hand free. What's more, you always have to remember not to forget your coat when you leave. I think they're fine as a fashion statement, but other than that they're useless baggage.

The only coat I do like is one I found discarded in a roadside drainage ditch. It is tattered and torn, the pockets are nothing but holes, and some of the stuffing is hanging out. It is perfect for protecting my other clothes in emergencies because I never have to worry about ruining it. It looks so bad, though, that my family won't let me wear it in public. I've had it for years but don't wear it much, either, except when working on the car or doing messy yard work

Anyway, I really enjoy the aliveness I feel with my bare skin exposed to Mother Nature. It's like an intimate relationship that I can depend on, it's invigorating, and I never get sick from it. Besides, my body is so used to experiencing rapid climatic changes from wet to dry and hot to cold and back again that I'm sure it has stimulated my immune system to become more resilient and resistant to erratic conditions.

Many people are surprised and concerned when they see me out in inclement weather without a coat on. They either don't believe in my philosophy, or think that I can't afford a coat, or don't have a nice enough one to wear. Consequently, those people closest to me are always giving me coats for presents. I have a closet full of wonderful coats. I keep them around for a while, so the giver feels appreciated. Then I donate them to charity.

One year, early in our marriage when we were still struggling financially, my wonderful mother-in-law gave me a beautiful winter parka. It was a top-of-the line survival jacket, insulated for cold, lots of pockets, a ton of zippers and snaps, a hood, and pretty enough to wear anywhere. It was expensive and I knew that she went way beyond her budget to get it for me because she was worried about my exposure to the elements. I felt very honored by her caring and didn't want to hurt her feelings by telling her that I would never wear it.

Jerri and I were invited to a party one night and since her parents were staying with us for the holidays I decided to show my appreciation to them by wearing the new coat. In those days we were living in a large, low income housing project where all the duplexes had exactly the same floor plan. The party was at one of these other houses. When we got there, the party was going on full bore, but the place was mostly dark on the inside because it was only dimly lit with festive candles. I didn't know where to put my new coat so I tossed it under the stairwell which was where the closet was in these houses. Hours later when the party was over I went to retrieve my coat. I turned the lights on and saw that our host had converted his stairwell closet into a photo developing darkroom. There was my coat, soaking in a vat of acrid chemicals. I was mortified! There was a huge dark stain on half of it, and part of the lining was starting to melt away. I gingerly picked up the wet dripping rag and sheepishly drove home, wondering what I was going to say to my mother-in-law.

Fortunately she was asleep when we got there, but over the next year or so whenever we got together, she would inquire about where that coat was and how I liked it. I had to think fast to come up with some reasonable replies, and occasionally, when the timing was right, I would let her catch a glimpse of it hanging in the closet with only the good part showing. Finally it became a forgotten issue and we gave it away to someone more deserving.

This experience only strengthened my convictions about coats. What a hassle! Now thirty years have gone by and people are still giving me coats. I just got a real nice one for Christmas. I'll keep it for a while in remembrance of the giver, but I know I'll never need it. Some other person who really does like coats will end up getting it soon enough.

MY FRIEND DICK

I HAVE A LIFELONG best friend named Dick. There is some debate as to when we met, but it was either in the first or second grade. Dick really knows how to laugh! I was drawn to him because his laugh is so infectious. It acts to validate your worth as a fellow human being, breaks the ice in a tense situation, and uplifts you from feelings of doom and gloom. Whenever we get together we revert back into our childlike state, and a synergistic vortex forms that compels the universe to create unusual and unbelievable circumstances that can only be described as supernatural oddities and the best adventures that life as to offer. It happens so regularly that now we expect the craziness. We just don't know when or what it will be. Our exploits center around our favorite pastimes: hiking, boating, playing music together, and shopping.

Every year we go on our annual Christmas shopping spree. Our mission is to have fun, uplift the spirits of our fellow shoppers and sales staff, and find some meaningful presents for our wives. We usually overdress in holiday attire and laugh our way through the mall until closing. Our joy is genuine and contagious and it spreads to those around us.

We try to be sedate and businesslike, but we're just so exuberant and thrilled that kid stuff starts to happen. We'll spend hours posing as pretend mannequins, secretly spraying each other with tester perfumes, trying on outlandish outfits, and teasing the security people at the fitting rooms. We'll carry on conversations in fake foreign languages, try to buy merchandise with phony million dollar bills, and entertain people on the instruments in the music stores.

One year we were shopping in a large mall and Dick had purchased a pillow which he was carrying with him in a large shopping bag. Later, when we were in a competitor's department store, we decided to compare prices on their pillows to see if he had gotten a good deal. We asked one of the clerks to show us the bedding section which was tucked in a back corner of the store out of sight of the main area. She accompanied us back there and then left us alone to return to her checkout counter because we were just goofing around. We were too embarrassed to tell her why we were really there. We checked over the merchandise and when we were satisfied that we had gotten a good deal, we left. As we were walking away, joking with each other, I turned to wave goodbye to the gal who had helped us and saw that she had a look of dread on her face and was madly dialing the phone. It seemed evident that she had not noticed our shopping bags when we came in. But now there was the unmistakable outline of a pillow in one of them. I figured she might be calling security because she thought we had stolen the pillow from her store.

Sure enough, at the bottom of the escalator we were met by a large, gruff-looking security guard who came right up to us but didn't say anything. We knew that the policy was to not accuse anyone of shoplifting until they tried to leave the store. So we just ignored the cop and headed for the cosmetic section with him tailing us about 25 feet behind. I saw a beautiful display of tiny perfume bottles. I thought getting one would be a good gift idea for Jerri. There were hundreds of them setting on a fragile-looking tier of four round glass shelves. I saw one that interested me in the middle of the third shelf and picked it up to examine it more closely. Meanwhile, Dick was looking at something else and the security cop was eyeing us from the end of the aisle. I don't know if I was nervous because of the surveillance, or if it was because the bottles were packed so closely together, but when I reached in to return the one I was holding I fumbled it, and it knocked over the one next to it! Suddenly, a chain reaction occurred and they all started falling over like dominoes. The resulting vibration caused the whole display to shake and I feared that the glass shelves were going to shatter. Finally, after an eternity, it was over and the loud clattering ended, replaced by a penetrating hush that overwhelmed our end of the store. Every eye was looking at me in shocked disbelief, and poor Dick was incredulous. The policeman held his ground. My hands were shaking as I attempted to upright all of the fallen bottles without starting the whole thing happening all over again.

Relieved when I had successfully finished this task, we retreated to the kitchenware department. We were looking at toasters and sets of steak knives. The knives were displayed on a small table covered with a tablecloth that drooped down to the floor. We didn't realize that underneath the table cloth, hidden from view, boxes and boxes of knife sets were precariously stacked. The entire inventory was there. Dick accidentally kicked it and the pile fell over, spilling knives out all over the floor and into the aisles. One of the clerks tried to help us, and I remember how ludicrous it seemed with the three of us on our hands and knees under the table cloth trying to rebuild the leaning tower of cutlery that was already too tenuous to begin with.

When we finally re-emerged, the security guard had disappeared. He had evidently been called away on more urgent matters. Relieved, we decided to go get a bite to eat so we left the store via the pet department. Dick donned a small pair of reindeer antlers made up as holiday fashion wear for your dog. He did a perfect imitation of a bull moose shaking his head to discourage flies from landing, pawed the ground, snorted, and we left for the restaurant.

We were chuckling about something when we sat down at our table. I don't remember what it was but it progressed into a case of the uncontrollable giggles. It was just like the ones they show you on those blooper out-take TV programs where news reporters lose it and can't quit laughing. We struggled to contain ourselves, but every time the waitress came over to take our order, we would burst out all over again, unable to answer her coherently. It was really humiliating, two middle-aged, slightly graying men unceremoniously chuckling like two giddy idiots. We dared not look at each other because it only made it worse. We couldn't even talk to communicate that maybe we should leave. I haven't laughed like that for years and boy, did it ever feel good. I realize now that the stares we got were ones of envy.

Finally the tears subsided. We had a nice meal and the shopping spree was over. We wished each other Merry Christmas and returned to our homes. I wonder what will happen next year?

Dental School Life

A CHEAP THRILL

WHEN I WAS IN DENTAL SCHOOL, JERRI AND I DIDN'T
have much money or time to spend on entertainment and
socializing. We still had lots of fun, but we had to look for
things to do that were inexpensive and easy. The friends we
hung out with were all in their mid-twenties, married, and
shared similar economic circumstances. Three of us couples
got together one warm weekend and decided to drive up to
the state fair about 30 miles away. When we got there we
noticed that the admission price was $4.00 per person. We
were disappointed because we were hoping that the price was
going to be per carload instead of per person. While we sat
there discussing what to do, we decided that if two of us hid
in the trunk we would have eight more dollars to spend at the
fair. Since the car belonged to my friend Dick, and it would-
n't be proper to put any of the wives in the trunk, we decided
that the only two logical candidates were Kurt and me.

There were no other cars around at the moment so we hurriedly opened the trunk and climbed in. It was a much tighter squeeze than I had anticipated, but it was doable. The mischievous excitement overshadowed the crowded discomfort. We got situated the best we could. Then I reached up, grabbed the trunk lid, and slammed it down! Suddenly, it was pitch dark and we were squashed together like sardines, barely able to breathe or move. A few seconds of silence went by, then I discovered I was still holding the car keys in my left hand. It was a horrible realization. It got worse when I noticed that the car engine was still running. (It was one of those old cars from the 50's that allowed you to remove the key from the ignition without shutting it off.) A great feeling of dread came over me there in the dark.

I decided I should share the bad news with my cohort Kurt who, unbeknownst to me, was secretly discovering that he was severely claustrophobic. When he found out we were hopelessly locked in, he totally freaked out! By now we could smell the exhaust fumes coming into the trunk and he started screaming and wailing, "We're going to die! We're going to die!" At the same time he was violently trying to claw his way out of there with both his hands and his feet scratching and kicking at the metal walls all at the same time. Due to my extremely close proximity with him, the panicked yelling and thrashing around started to get to me. His reaction was causing me both physical and emotional distress. Along with the abuse from the frantic pummeling, waves of fear started coursing through me. I did my best to ignore them and think of a rational escape plan.

By now Dick had ascertained the situation and started pounding on the exterior of the trunk. I was able to convince Kurt to stop screaming for a moment so we could communicate with the outside world. We decided that since it was such an old car, maybe we could bend the back seat forward far enough to create a space big enough for a hand to reach through. The overly concerned wives all got out, and Dick began yanking and tearing at the back seat. We could hear fabric ripping and metal creaking several times. Kurt was desperate to get out and started groping at the area where the sound was coming from, but the first two attempts were unsuccessful. We couldn't reach through the tiny space. Kurt started sobbing and murmuring incoherent stuff. Finally, Dick heaved on the seat with all his might and the metal groaned. Suddenly, a little shaft of light appeared and we could hear Dick's voice much clearer. Straining, we were able to just touch fingertips and transfer the keys. Dick shut off the motor and came back around to let us out. Meanwhile, a much relieved Kurt made me promise not to reveal his phobic tantrum to anyone.

When the lid finally flew open, the sudden burst of bright light took me by surprise. So did the long line of cars that had formed behind us, waiting for us to move so they could get in to the fair. We sheepishly climbed out, much to the amusement of the onlookers, and got back into the car. We considered ourselves to be grown men at the time, but in retrospect I guess we weren't. We paid our eight bucks and had a great time at the fair.

Shots

GOING FROM THRILLING excitement to absolute dejection was a typical range of emotions on any given day in the life of dental school. As students we felt very passionate about learning all the skills and knowledge required for our profession and we were hungry to acquire the same level of proficiency as

our instructors. We were used to getting top grades and positive feedback when attaining our undergraduate degrees
because in order to be accepted into dental school we had to
be among the best students in the nation. But now that we
were there, the circumstances were totally different. We were
held to the exacting standards of our instructor's level of expertise. Nobody got A's or B's anymore. Getting a D on a project
was a common experience and a source of emotional dejection.

Before dental school, even getting a C for a grade was an
indication of failure. Now it was a sign of accomplishment
and cause for celebration and jubilee. More than ever before,
we had a sincere interest in applying ourselves, but we just
couldn't seem to make the grade we were shooting for. We had
finally made it to the place where we could learn what we had
always really wanted to know, but our zeal for achievement on
every project was often tempered with rejection and a request
to do it over because it just wasn't good enough. With bruised
egos, we would feel downcast and unworthy for a while, but
driven by our youthful passion, our confidence arose again,
and, relatively undaunted, we continued on toward our goal
of becoming doctors. This constant struggle against assuming
a permanent negative self-image was more difficult for some
than for others.

Eighteen-hour days were common in order to complete the
requirements of attending classes, finishing the laboratory projects, and doing the reading and study assignments. This went
on day after day. Sometimes there just wasn't enough time to
get it all done so you had to prioritize. Certain assignments
were absolute requirements. The rest we completed according
to our own personal interest in that particular subject and to
what we thought might be the subject of the next inevitable
pop quiz. We wanted to be as prepared as possible to avoid
looking like a fool in front of our fellow classmates, not to mention our instructors who could at any time randomly pick you

from the crowd and ask you to recite the anatomical structures of a certain nerve's pathway, or give the pharmacological properties and physiological ramifications of a specific drug or medication. We were all scrambling to be on top of it all and avoid sleep deprivation, but it became obvious after a while that each student developed different areas of confidence and expertise. It was equally possible that there were other areas in which some students were still untested, unskilled, and unprepared.

One day during the latter part of our second year we had a surprise announcement of yet another pop quiz. Not knowing what it was to be on, we were asked to pick a partner for the test. We lined up into forty pairs of expectant dental students and the instructor walked down the line. On each one of us he softly touched his finger to three places on our face and said to our partner, "Get this numb, this numb, and this numb."

Well... we all got numb from worry, anxiety, and shock! We gazed wild-eyed at our partners, silently praying and hoping that he had read the proper chapters on anatomy, anesthesia, and needle-handling techniques. Most of us had never given an injection before, much less even handled or properly loaded a syringe. That long, shiny, stainless steel implement was part of the array of instruments that we had purchased and heretofore had gazed and marveled at, but had never used. The techniques were all there in the textbooks, but we figured we would have a little more simulated practice before giving actual shots, cold turkey, to our nervous friends.

It turned out that my partner was pretty needle phobic, so I volunteered to start out as the numb-ee and he was the numb-er. We quickly reviewed our collective knowledge of the procedure and then set about this heinous task. We were moderately successful at achieving the desired results. Surprisingly, with a maximum level of anxiety but a minimal amount of pain, our faces started to tingle and turned into rubber-like, lifeless caricatures of their former selves. Our lips and tongues became immobilized. We could no longer talk properly or even feel ourselves breathe. This lasted for hours, well into our next class where we were expected to eloquently articulate our knowledge on a moment's notice when questioned.

My partner and I, however, fared far better than many of our colleagues. Some of them apparently failed to adequately absorb the essential teachings of the appropriate, assigned chapters. We observed that some of our classmates had slunk away into hidden corners and dark recesses in the clinic to administer the dreaded Novocaine away from other watchful eyes. Some emerged from this tortured experience with pure white, ghostly faces filled with a look of deathly trauma and horror. In many cases they had failed to deaden their counterpart's features even after repeated forays into the relatively unknown. A few had gone too far, rendering lifeless areas of the head and neck that weren't part of the assignment. Others nicked vessels and unknown to the numb-ee they walked around sporting a small trickle of blood running down their anesthetized chins. This of course, when noticed by an instructor, was immediate grounds for failure for the numb-er. For some, the completion of this test was just too much. Several loud thumping crashes were heard as they fainted and dropped to the floor. At least one person was unceremoniously taken away on a stretcher that day.

Finally after an hour or so, those of us left standing had to line up again. The instructor walked back down the row and checked each of us to determine if the appropriate level of anesthesia had been attained. We were very smart. We all acknowledged that total numbness had indeed occurred, whether or not it was actually true. None of us wanted to risk finding out what a "no" answer would mean at this juncture. Satisfied, the instructor finally let us go. After that day we all redoubled our efforts to study and learn everything as thoroughly as possible. We knew that the trial was over. The next time would be the real thing, on a real live patient. We were determined to do it painlessly, professionally, and perfectly!

ANXIOUS MOMENTS

I'LL NEVER FORGET my first patient in dental school. He was a nice man but very nervous. He made me nervous, and I was already nervous because I needed to get him numb and do some fillings on him. I had never done this on a real person before. I tried the best I could to disguise my anxiety and hold it all inside, but he wasn't helping matters any. He asked incessant questions and wouldn't quit talking long enough for me to get a dental mirror in his mouth edgewise. I spent two, 3 1/2 hour appointments just examining and cleaning his teeth and trying to reassure him. At first he would startle and jump, then quickly look around at every unusual sound or movement I made. As time passed, however, he started to calm down a little.

By the third appointment I knew I wouldn't be able to delay doing the fillings any longer. I explained to him in advance what the procedure would be. He seemed surprisingly relaxed about the whole thing, so I reclined him backwards in the chair to rest while I got things ready.

The dental school was built in the 1940's and the clinic was situated on the top floor of the building. To maximize the amount of light coming in, the ceiling was 30 to 40 feet high with tall windows all around the sides and skylights above. It was an impressive cathedral-like place where 150 to 200 wanna-be dentists could be working all at the same time under the same roof.

While I was setting up my instruments, I noticed that my patient was lying there with his eyes closed and his mouth wide open. I realized he was probably just as tense on the inside as I was, and I prayed that nothing would happen to disturb his composure. Finally I was ready. I turned to the sink and thoroughly washed and dried my hands again, for the third time. When I turned back around, there it was... a big black spider had come down from the tall ceiling and was dangling from its tiny, 35-foot long, single strand of silk thread! It was hanging two inches above his face, centered absolutely perfectly over his open mouth. I gasped silently, and started praying again that my patient wouldn't open his eyes and that the spider wouldn't drop any further and go into his mouth. I quickly reached out, grabbed the spider, and threw it into my waste can without my patient being any the wiser.

The extra adrenaline burst propelled me through the rest of the procedure. I don't really remember any of the details except that it must have gone okay because we both appeared to be happy and relieved when it was all over.

What's So Funny About Laughing Gas?

AFTER WE BECAME familiar with the basic routine of working with patients in the dental school clinic, it was time to be introduced to more sophisticated procedures. One of these was learning the proper use of nitrous oxide, or "laughing gas" as it is more commonly known. On that fateful afternoon we were divided into groups of five students and one instructor. The aim of the instruction was to demonstrate the safe and suitable operation of the equipment utilized to administer the gas and to have a chance to experience the feeling induced by the drug so we could accurately prepare our patients for what they would experience. This "live" experience was beneficial in learning the proper concentration of the gas to use, so it could be tailored to the comfort of each individual patient's need.

Nitrous oxide is a wonderful tool to have for calming and alleviating the fears and apprehension of nervous patients. It is relatively safe, easy to use, and dissipates quickly with few side effects. At proper concentrations it makes you feel like everything is just peachy, *no problemos,* "I don't care man, it's cool"!

You are still aware of everything going on around you, the experience just loses some of its intensity and you just kinda float through it. The original experiments and studies with this gas have shown that at very high concentrations, (higher than used in dentistry), it can induce exaggeration of your sensations and emotions. Most commonly this would be feelings of extreme mirth and gaiety causing the patient to laugh and giggle almost uncontrollably at the most mundane issues and comments. However at these high levels, it can also exaggerate other emotions, such as anger, grief, passion or paranoia. These extremes are never encountered in the normal application of this medication, but this day would be different.

The instructor started the session with a demonstration of how the equipment worked: how to turn it on and off, adjust the concentration, monitor the flow rate, and how to change the tanks safely. Then it was each student's turn to act as a patient. We had all heard crazy rumors about nitrous oxide so we were both eager and a little apprehensive to try it ourselves. Each of us had about a ten minute exposure to the gas. The instructor operated the equipment and set the concentration at a standard level. We all watched intently for the reaction of the first volunteer but nothing ever happened. He reported some mild tingling in his toes but that was it. Nothing profound. The same was the case for the second person. As time went by, the rest of us became more and more disinterested in the process and just started talking among ourselves while each student had his turn. Even the instructor became absorbed in the socializing going on and soon we were basically ignoring the guy in the chair.

Finally, it was my turn. After watching the unresponse of the others before me, I was relieved that this would be an easy way to satisfy yet another dental school requirement. I laid down in the chair, put the mask over my nose, and began to breathe. After a minute or so a slight feeling of lightness came over me. It was barely perceptible but it was there. I thought to myself, "No big deal!" At that moment, one of my so called buddies in the group quickly reached down, turned one of the knobs on the apparatus, and gave me a quick wink. The others in the group were engaged in talking and didn't notice.

Suddenly, a great whooshing sensation overtook me. It felt like a giant, invisible hand was lifting me straight up into the air. I was definitely floating! I couldn't feel the chair underneath me any longer and I couldn't force myself to speak. I felt totally immobilized and slightly panicked. I tried screaming out through my eyes to get some attention, but, as I looked up, the rest of the guys were still busy conversing, totally unaware of my plight.

As I focused on the group standing over me, I became aware that when one person was talking I could predict who would respond next, and what he would say, and then who would reply to that person and what he would say. At first, I thought it was just an odd assumption, but as I paid closer attention I realized that I was precisely correct to the word. I was two people ahead in the actual conversation. I knew what they were going to say and who would speak next. As soon as one person finished, my mind automatically jumped ahead to accurately predict the next speaker and his response. It was eerie and unnerving. The surrealism started to sink in and I was worried that I would be trapped in this zone forever. But the fantastic nature of this ability to forecast the future was fascinating to me. I wrestled with how and why this was possible.

Just as I was almost getting used to it, the instructor glanced over at the dials, got a look of wonder on his face, and turned up the oxygen level. I could feel my prescient ability starting to fade and I mentally grasped to hold on to it. On the other hand, I was relieved to be returning to familiar reality. Going, going, gone, I was back. I acted as if nothing out of the ordinary had happened and I didn't tell anyone about it for years.

I thought about it a lot, though, trying to analyze it. The experience was real, and it raised profound questions in my mind about Life. Was it totally predictable? Was it all pre-planned and plastic and were we just unwittingly going along for a pre-programmed ride? Could we change anything by our own choice? Was there such a thing as free will? I was uncomfortable believing that there wasn't.

To counteract this possibility of predestined fate, I promised myself to always be unpredictable. To be fresh, to be original. To say and do things that are unexpected and out of the ordinary in order to stimulate those around me to react in new and unpredetermined ways. Refuse to just maintain, but be creative, rediscover the uniqueness in others and the environment. Always be searching for the hidden treasures that exist all around us. They are there. I've seen them. They are waiting for us to go out of our way and discover them.

ALIENS

SEVERAL YEARS LATER I had a vivid dream that reinforced my resolve to always keep this promise. I dreamed that there was a separate race of beings or aliens who were from another dimension or planet. Their technology was advanced well beyond ours. They had a television-like device that could tune into any one of us humans as if we were each a separate program. When they did, they could experience everything we were experiencing as if they were right inside our brains. They could watch our lives unfolding as it happened, "live".

The aliens used this device as a source of entertainment, much like we use our TV to watch sitcoms. The difference was that they had billions of possible "channels" to choose from— us. I resolved that if by chance one of these aliens was flipping through the channels and happened onto me that I would be doing something noteworthy, exciting, or intriguing at the time. Something that was captivating and entertaining to watch. I didn't want to be boring and mundane and risk getting canceled. It meant that I pretty much have to be creative and "in action" all the time.

You never know when your chance for stardom will occur, so I always try to be in a leading role. I want to be known as a serious comedy, setting examples in a lighthearted way.

MORE LAUGHING GAS

THREE YEARS AFTER my first nitrous oxide experience I signed up to participate in a study that the oral surgery department was running. They were trying to determine if using acupuncture was as effective as nitrous oxide for controlling pain. I volunteered because at the time I was interested in applying to oral surgery school and I thought that the extra exposure would help my chances of being accepted.

The experiment went as follows: I was the patient. One doctor used an electronic stimulator (pulp tester) on several of my front teeth. He would slowly turn up the current and when I felt something I was to raise my hand. A second scientist was administering the laughing gas. After each round with the electronic pulp tester he would turn the laughing gas up to a higher concentration and the routine would be repeated. A third researcher, the head professor, sat in the back of the room behind me and recorded my responses. To eliminate any bias, I was to keep my eyes closed. No talking was allowed. All information was passed back and forth between them using predetermined hand signals.

Toward the end of the experiment, when the gas concentration was at its highest, I saw the man in the back of the room raise his hands over his head. Evidently, this was a signal to the others that this part of the procedure was almost over. I unintentionally broke protocol and asked the professor why he had raised his hands?

He responded curiously, "How do you know that I raised my hands? I am sitting behind you, out of your line of sight. Besides, your eyes are supposed to be closed."

I told him I didn't know how, but I could see him. He decided to test me by holding up several fingers, asking me how many I saw. Each time he did this, it was crystal clear to me and I responded correctly every time. He finally asked the assistant next to me to make sure I wasn't cheating somehow and peeking out of the corner of my eye. He checked, and to our amazement discovered that my eyes were still closed tightly. I didn't believe him at first, but when I deliberately opened and closed them I realized it made no difference, I could see equally well either way. Not only that, I could see the whole room, in front of me and behind me, in 360 degrees. Every corner was viewable all at the same time, eyes open or shut!

When the scientists grasped the unusual nature of this data, they quickly jumped up, looking really agitated, and turned the oxygen on full blast, terminating the experiment. Because of my weird and unconventional reaction I was not allowed to participate in the rest of the study.

I don't know how to explain what or how it happened, but I've heard of out of body experiences. Maybe that was one. For me, Laughing Gas was no laughing matter! Maybe they should change the name of it to Unnatural or Supernatural Gas.

A HIDDEN GOLD MINE

ONE OF THE skills we learned in dental school was how to make gold crowns. We used the "lost wax technique." It is the same technique that is used to make gold jewelry. Using a centrifuge, molten gold is spun into a form and solidifies into that shape when it cools. It could be the shape of a tooth or a ring or a brooch. Whenever the centrifuge is spun, a little gold is always splattered out to the side. Most of the time it was very insignificant. Sometimes during a miscast a lot of gold would be spilled. It was burnt and black from the heat and oxidation and difficult to recognize, but it was gold.

During the course of the school year hundreds of students would attempt to cast their crowns and bridges. Every day after class I would go down to the lab and pick up the splattered remains. I would put the little globules and paper thin, foil-like pieces in a jar and save them. Sometimes I found huge solidified sheets of precious metal that had been unknowingly left behind. After several years of regular prospecting, I had enough gold to make jewelry for all the members of my family for Christmas presents. They all thought I was extremely generous. I thought I was just being prudent.

Twenty-five years later I took my two sons by the school to show them my old stomping grounds. Just for fun we cruised through the lab area and I checked, just like the old days. Sure enough, it was still there, the vein had not run out. Gold! I picked up a few tiny nuggets, laughed, and showed my boys the scorched little nodules. They were amazed. So was I.

CHAPTER 4

On Our Own

BIRTH AND REBIRTH

IMMEDIATELY AFTER GRADUATING FROM DENTAL SCHOOL, Jerri and I decided to take a little vacation. We had earned it. Jerri had worked extremely hard as a nurse at the university hospital, making money to pay the expenses of living and the high costs of dental school. I was spending all of my time attending classes, studying, and working part time as a dental lab technician and musician. Trying to achieve our "American Dream" was a grueling task, but it was coming true. Now it was time to congratulate ourselves for completing another major step toward our goals. We pooled together all of our $700 in savings and went to Hawaii for ten glorious days. We camped on the beach, hiked through the jungle, swam in the waves, basked in the sun, made Puka shell necklaces, and gorged ourselves on freshly picked pineapples and mangoes. We spent every last penny and we were proud of it. We knew that as soon as I started to work we would have lots more money but fewer chances to take time off, so we lived it up. It was like our second honeymoon, except it was much more successful than the first.

After we returned home I started extensive preparation for the Washington State Board Dental Exam. I needed to pass it in order to receive a license to practice dentistry in the state. It was the next giant hurdle and involved much apprehension. I spent most of my time screening patients to find the appropriate preexisting indications for the proper assessment of my clinical judgment and technical skills. The rest of my time was devoted to studying for the x-ray analysis and written phase of the test. I was in the library studying one evening when Jerri walked in after work with smiles all over her face. She sidled up next to me at the table and whispered in my ear, "I'm pregnant."

My blood pressure skyrocketed, causing my heart to swell up like a balloon, and my adrenal glands shot off about two pints of secretion before I could even take my next breath. Wow, what excitement and pride! I actually had it in me to be a father! Of course, so far I had only accomplished the easy part. We had purposely waited to start our family until we had a secure future guaranteed. Now was the time, and it had happened just like we had planned it years before when we dreamed of our lives together as husband and wife.

We hurried off to our favorite restaurant to celebrate, and downed enough pizza and ice water to swamp a life boat. We reviewed all the plans we had made and marveled at the way in which they had all managed to work themselves out. It was hard work but, ahh yes, it was the American Dream coming true. In my youth the essence of life was to find a beautiful girl, fall in love and get married, have some kids, buy a nice house and have a worthy career. To do so was the definition of success. So far so good. I was on my way. Confirmation that we were going to have children was one more giant step toward our goal.

Jerri's pregnancy was uneventful except for the unusual cravings that set in about the fifth month. Tomato soup and peppermint ice cream covered with hot fudge were relatively easy requests to fulfill. Trying to find banana milk shakes at three o'clock in the morning was more of a challenge. The futility of the quest was often quelled after I had pulled my clothes on over my pajamas and was headed out into the night. Just as the door clicked closed behind me, the intensity of the craving would lessen and Jerri would change her mind and call me back, much to my relief. I would lie there in bed grinning, thinking how lucky I was, and feeling happy that I wasn't driving around searching for an all night deli that made gourmet ice cream treats.

As the due date got closer and closer, I started getting the pre-delivery jitters. I thought about all the things that could go wrong and prayed that everything would go just right. I also noticed, much to my amazement, that my stomach was taking on a life of its own in sympathy with Jerri's. It was getting bigger for no logical reason. I had heard of this phenomena, but I didn't appreciate how eerie it was until it happened to me. I liked it. It confirmed that we were a team in this endeavor, and that something miraculous was happening that was beyond our immediate control.

The due date came and went without so much as a twitch or a spasm. All the previous nervous anticipation now turned into uncomfortable uncertainty. In order to ease the tension and divert our attention for awhile, we decided to go to a movie. There was an all night Clint Eastwood marathon playing at a drive-in theater nearby. We called another couple and made it a double date. They drove so we could have the more comfortable and spacious back seat. A construction project in front of the theater necessitated taking a detour down a long, bumpy, dirt access road. It was filled with dips and humps and huge pot holes that suddenly appeared out of the dark without warning. Even though we drove slowly, the old car bucked around wildly on its worn out springs over the bombed out road. We were tossed airborne from the seat several times as we bounced and jumped and jostled along. Jerri let out several little whelps of surprised exclamation on the roughest portions, but by the time we reached our speaker pole things were back to normal. We hung in there until dawn. The cowboys were still fighting it out up on the big silver screen but it was time for us to go. We endured another rugged and jarring ride over the ruts but we made it home all in one piece. Two hours later Jerri's water broke!

It was still controversial to allow fathers into the delivery room in those days but because I was a doctor I was invited in. After 19 hours of labor a baby was born. A boy! A son! We named him Josef. The nurse cut the cord and immediately handed him to me. His tiny but perfect body was still wet with the dew of creation. In that instant something totally unanticipated and mysterious happened that changed my life forever. A gigantic moving wave of intense emotion hit me. Feelings were evoked that I never knew existed before. It was an indescribable mixture of intense reverence, fear, and ecstasy. I shuddered with a new realization about Life. Inside that little body was a Soul. A surging spark of true Divinity. Somehow, I had had something to do with its appearance. I knew then that Life was not just a game setup to see if you could capture the American Dream, and that children were much more than just markers to demonstrate your status on the way to success. It was distinctly obvious that Life was an awesome responsibility. That each and every individual is supremely important.

Success is not about becoming a carbon copy of everyone

else, but about each person becoming fulfilled inwardly. Every individual's dream is worthwhile and attainable. I knew then that with confidence, commitment and action, anyone can accomplish any dream. It is the nature of the universe and the spirit of creation to make our dreams come true. Hold your dream in your imagination until you can see every part of it very clearly. Then confidently step into it and live it in the present moment. Take it on as if it already exists and it will. Your success will be a catalyst for others to succeed with their dreams. Soon, bigger and bolder dreams will be dreamed and realized and we will all be uplifted by them.

As we gazed down at our infant son, both Jerri and I had joyful tears in our eyes. We had both experienced a miracle! As I carried Josef to his bed in the nursery next door, I thanked him for coming into our lives. I vowed that I would teach him what he had just taught me. Eighteen months later another miracle occurred. Our second son Michael was born. The same tremendous ecstatic and thrilling wave of passion hit me again! Even though I was ready for it this time, it came out of nowhere and completely bowled me over. I knew it was from God. Michael's infant form served to reconfirm the precious nature of life and its potential. The wry little smile on his blissful face reminded me that he already knew more than I did.

The births of our two sons were the most amazing, fulfilling, and fascinating events of my life. Volumes of books could be written about being with them through all the many stages of maturation and development that we willingly experienced together. Jerri was the perfect angelic mother and I was the big bruiser dad. Our sons became my best friends, my buddies, my teachers, my helpers, my source of inspiration, and are the apples of my eye. A bond has formed between their births and my rebirth that will last forever.

LONG HAIR LIBERALISM

THROUGHOUT MY YOUTH I always had the same kind of haircut: a crew-cut. The only time there was any variation in this theme was when I temporarily ran out of butch wax. Then I had a flat-top. I can still remember the sweet smell of the butch wax and the precision strokes of my hand that were required to properly apply it so that the front of my hair would stick up perfectly straight like a short wall of organic spikes. It was so stiff that it was almost painful to touch it on the upright ends. It never got longer than 1 1/4 inches, even in college.

At about the same time I got my acceptance into dental school, my prejudices about life started to soften. There were people around who had long hair and beards. We called them "fringies." (It was Seattle's transition term from "beatniks" to "hippies.") We lived in separate worlds. My conservative upbringing convinced me that those people had no redeeming values. I had been taught not to judge a book by its cover, but that advice didn't seem to apply in the case with fringies. I just stayed away from them, minding my own business and keeping my head in the sand along with many others of my era.

My attitude changed after I met Sam. It was a chance meeting at a friend's party. He was a friend of a friend and had long hair. Somehow I wound up talking to him. During our conversation I felt a genuine unconditional warmth coming from him. He was articulate, intelligent, gentle and confident, and exuded genuine wisdom, spirituality, and love. It was the opposite of what I thought fringies were capable of. It was clear that he grasped a set of universal, fundamental principles about how life worked. As he explained them I could feel them ringing true somewhere deep inside of me. He was matured way beyond myself and I was duly impressed. He represented the kind of person I aspired to be, despite the long hair.

Somehow a one hour conversation with him completely broadened my understanding of other people and their potential. It was a life-changing event. I learned to give everybody a chance. To be open to everyone, regardless of their physical appearance, was the ultimate way to learn about yourself. It was an important lesson that freed me up.

I decided that maybe I should expand my comfort zone and try something other than a crew-cut. I would let it grow out to regular-length hair. It was early 1970 and my fellow classmates who were also going into dental school in the fall noticed my hair getting longer. The change worried them. Everyone in dental school had short hair. It was the most conservative of all professional groups. My hair had barely started to touch my ears when they started questioning me. "When are you going to cut your hair?" They would come up behind me in the halls and whisper it over my shoulder.

I hadn't planned on growing it any longer, but their insecurity about it reminded me of my previously prejudiced nature and what I had learned from Sam. I decided I would become a champion for "don't judge a book by its cover." I vowed I wouldn't cut my hair until people quit asking me about it. I wanted to show that even though I had long hair I could still be a righteous and honorable person. I would grow the longest hair ever had by a dental student, man or woman, if that's what it took. At the same time I would demonstrate consideration, care, and concern for my fellow man and be a dedicated, hard working student. We were going to be taking the Hippocratic Oath, swearing to provide dental health care to the best of our abilities to all those who needed it, regardless of their circumstances or station in life. That didn't leave any room for prejudice in my book.

When I graduated 4 1/2 years later my hair was almost to my waist. I hoped I had made my point. I made it through just like everyone else. I had my doctorate degree now and was ready to begin the next phase of my life. It was to use dentistry as a vehicle for uplifting people's self-esteem and for empowering them to become what they always dreamed about but thought they could never attain. "Everything and anything is attainable with imagination, solid intention, and perseverance." That would be my battle cry for the rest of my life, person by person, patient by patient. Along with this I would deliver the best dentistry possible in the kindest and most gentle way. It was a good goal. I was ready to take the next step.

I looked in the mirror and realized my long hair was part of my past. It had to go. I shaved off my muttonchops, trimmed up my mustache, and then I grabbed my ponytail right up close to my head, thanked it for serving me, wished it luck, and cut it off with scissors and dropped it into the waste basket. I walked up to a local barber shop to get the loose ends trimmed and sat down in the waiting area. I had never been there before but it soon became obvious that it was one of those places where the local people came every day to sit around and socialize. It had its collection of regulars who were old friends of the veteran barber who had been a fixture in this location for over 30 years. They were all members of the so called "establishment." Since I was much younger and a newcomer, they were curious about me and immediately included me in their conversation. My presence gave them something novel and fresh to talk about in lieu of repeating the same old stories that had been told a dozen times before. By the time it was my turn in the barber chair we were all well acquainted and "friends." The barber asked me what kind of cut I wanted and I said, "A regular."

He and a very talkative lady in the group asked me numerous questions while he snipped and pruned away on my head. They wanted to know why they had never seen me around before? I explained that this was my first hair cut in almost five years and that only minutes before I was the proud owner of a two-foot-long ponytail. The woman gasped and immediately the easy friendship turned into instant revulsion. She almost threw up at the thought of allowing herself to be this close to a "hippie." She stood up and stormed out. The barber was more professional but quit talking and silently finished me up with a neat looking "regular" that was a little on the short side.

I paid the bill and walked back home. On the way, I was feeling just like the "regular guy" that I always had been, but the rest of the world had changed. All the long-haired young street people who had previously thought they had some special rapport with me because of my long hair now avoided my gaze and ignored my presence, knowing that I couldn't possibly relate. On the other hand, the conservatively dressed "shorthairs" who had scorned me only 30 minutes before were now smiling and waving at me, delighted to encounter another one of "their" kind.

None of them looked carefully enough to recognize me. The whole socialized world had flipped over backwards because my appearance had changed. It was a huge lesson for me about prejudice and how hard it dies. But I knew that if I could conquer it, then anybody could. I was just a regular guy but I had an inordinate amount of hope for all of mankind.

I vowed to do what I could do to make prejudice disappear in my lifetime. That was 30 years ago, but I still have the same goal, and the very same mustache that I grew in the 70's. Yes, things have changed since then. My hair is slowly disappearing but so is prejudice. We still have a long way to go, but so do I.

ON OUR OWN

LIFE AFTER DENTAL school was great! Freedom! It was hard to get used to. No more staying up all night studying for exams or being on call for the hospital. No more grilling and drilling on teeth just to prove how much you knew about them and the bodies they were attached to. There were so many other things to learn about Life, and we set out to learn them all. Jerri and I moved out to the Kitsap Peninsula and set up housekeeping in the quaint old fishing and farming village of Poulsbo. Finally, we were doing our own thing. We found a huge, three story, 80 year old farm house that had been vacant for a while. It was in bad shape. The doors were missing, most of the windows were broken out, and several walls were kicked in. The only heat source was a gigantic wood-burning furnace located down in the cobweb-filled basement. It was delicately perched on a ridge crest on ten overgrown acres of rolling farm land. The entire length of the Cascade Mountain range filled the view to the east, and the oversized covered porch on the west side overlooked the lofty peaks of the Olympics, the shining waters of Puget Sound, and the everyday activities of the town at the foot of our hill. I thought it was perfect. Jerri was a little less enthusiastic, but it was shelter, had lots of potential, and cheap. So we moved in.

We paid part of our rent by doing labor to fix the old place up. We threw ourselves into planting a garden, growing and canning vegetables and fruit, learning about landscaping and carpentry, raising dogs, cats and kids, and cutting lots of firewood. It was fun! No more tests, or so I thought. All we wanted to do was settle in, become part of the community, and eventually start our own dental practice in town.

One of our first tasks was to cut back the mammoth mound of blackberries that had overtaken the back side of the house and had overgrown all the fruit trees in the large, neglected orchard. I wanted to bring those poor choked-out fruit trees back to life. I worked long and hard cutting and raking back the vines, and they were doing their best to resist me. They repeatedly lashed out at me with long barbed tentacles, clawing at my clothes and skin, trying to reel me into their clutches. Many times their volleys were on target and their sharp teeth painfully bit into me. I was always able to slowly wriggle free, but not without sustaining numerous lingering lesions that stung sharply and filled with tiny pools of blood that threatened to intimidate me into retreat from this war zone.

I was slowly winning the battle but I needed one of those long pole cutters to reach the tall stuff and finish the fight. We lived only several blocks from downtown so I decided to walk to the local hardware store to buy what I needed. Still sporting my dirty old work clothes, I walked into town thinking that since I was still a stranger in this picturesque rural hamlet that it was important to make sure I made a good first impression. I figured the best way to do so was to show them that I was an earthy type of guy who could work the land with his bare hands just like the rest of them. Having grimy fingers, soiled pants, muddy boots, and fresh sweat on my brow was just was just the perfect thing to win them over.

I pranced into the hardware store, smugly gathered up the tools I needed, and took them up to the counter to pay. The crusty old shop-keeper eyed me suspiciously, especially when I wrote out a check. He looked back and forth at it and me several times. Finally, he pointed to my name printed at the top and asked, "What does D.D.S. mean?"

I proudly announced, "Doctor of Dental Surgery."

He responded, "Does that mean you're a dentist?"

I answered, "Yes."

He looked at me sternly and advised me with a sound of authority in his voice, "Dentists around here always wear a white shirt and tie when they come to town!" He held out his index finger as if he were going to shake it at me and emphasized the point so I would never make the same mistake again.

To save face I tried to explain my circumstances but it fell on deaf ears. He reluctantly took my check and I walked back home feeling confused, a tangle of thoughts coursing through my mind. I wasn't about to change clothes every time I wanted to go four blocks and do some shopping. I was here to learn how to live off of the land. For the time being, I was living here, but practicing dentistry somewhere else, across the sound in West Seattle. I wanted to fit in here, but I wasn't prepared to change my ways and conform on the advice of just one man.

I found out later that a large portion of the town's real estate had been owned for years by a group of dentists who lived on the mainland. They were wealthy, big shot, tycoon types who were represented by conservative agents wearing conservative suits. (Ironically, one of these dentists was a man I had previously worked for as a laboratory technician.) No wonder dentists were regarded with such prejudice out here! I was still a liberal in a conservative community. No matter, I would work it out later. I would win the hearts of the local people when they got to know me better. It was yet another test and I would find a way to pass it.

I grabbed my new pole cutter and lunged at the towering blackberry vines. I pretended I was a great champion called upon to joust for the honor of the king. I charged into battle with an unrestrained surge of adrenaline. With every deft snip of the blades another dragon's head would fall and before long I had defeated the entire beast. It lay there at my feet. I had won. The kingdom was mine. Putting a successful dental practice out here would be a piece of cake.

A Rude Awakening

PART OF BEING on our own was having pets. We had three cats named Holly, Wheezer, and Blackie, and two dogs named Silver and Gypsy. The dogs were brother and sister from a litter of Wolf/Malamute pups. They were huge animals, both weighing well over 100 pounds. They were very loyal and protective of our family, especially loving to our small boys, and great companions for me. They loved to run and sniff their way through the woods so I occasionally took them with me in the morning, dropped them off at my parents' place, and went hiking in the mountains with them after work.

My daily morning commute included a half-hour ferry ride into Seattle. I depended on the ferry ride to get another 30 minutes of sleep. I would silently tiptoe out of the house in the early dawn, being very careful not to make any disturbances that would wake the children and interrupt Jerri's much-deserved rest. In the winter we all slept together on the floor, huddled around the opening of the metal grate from the wood burning furnace in the basement, trying to soak up the last bit of heat from the dying embers. To keep from waking the family, I avoided turning the lights on and blindly groped around in the dark for my clothes. Sometimes out of desperation I would choose incorrectly and wind up at the clinic with socks that didn't match or a different kind of shoe on each foot, much to the glee and consternation of my co-workers.

My ultimate goal for the morning, however, was to remain just barely awake so that when I got to the ferry boat I could go right back to sleep again. I kept one eye closed the whole time and squinted out of the other while driving to the dock. I knew the road by memory and drove in a state that was scarcely conscious. I had perfected a narcoleptic trance that got me to my car and the car to the dock without me being aware of any of my surroundings. I disdained anything that would jar me out of this luxurious world of soft floating images and unfocused thoughts.

The car that I drove to work was a 1961 Rambler Classic that we had purchased from Jerri's grandparents when we were first married. It was our first car and we affectionately called it Black Beauty. Over the years it had taken us from northern Canada to central Mexico and everywhere in between, never letting us down. It was somewhat banged up and battered, but it still got the job done. Several of the dials and switches were broken. The mirrors were missing. The heater and vent controls were hopelessly corroded into a immovable position. A loose wire somewhere caused the horn to honk twice by itself for every 360 degree turn of the steering wheel in either direction. You could watch the road pass by through a hole in the rusted out floor of the back seat. The front end shimmied so badly that it was impossible to control the steering at speeds over 50 MPH. The emergency brake never did work and a busted out rear wing window, covered with a cellophane bread wrapper that melodiously flapped in the wind, was the only audio entertainment on board. These were the minor problems. To its credit, it did have push-button drive, fold-down seats, a rebuilt engine, and immeasurable sentimental value. So ultimately, it was very very cool.

One drizzly fall morning as I slunk toward Black Beauty in my usual slumberous state, I decided to take the dogs with me for a rousing romp in the woods after work. I sleepily let them hop in the backseat as I climbed in behind the wheel and closed the door. A few short seconds of calm silence passed as I searched by feel for the ignition key with my fingers. Even though the light was still rather dim, I didn't want to open my eyes fully and risk waking up and losing my cushy, dreamlike condition.

Suddenly, just before starting the engine, all holy terror broke loose in the car! I was thrust into a nightmare of pain, horror, and bewilderment! It was as if I had been unceremoniously dropped into a giant blender, filled with large, heavy, sharp objects, all spinning, out of control, at high speed. Before I realized exactly what was going on, it was all over, and I was left bleeding, emotionally and physically wounded, scratched and scraped, gasping in pain and fright, and totally and rudely, wide awake! It all happened in the matter of just a few seconds.

The dogs had discovered a stray cat who had slipped in past the cellophane covered window to spend a dry and peaceful night sleeping on the ledge behind the back seat. Instantly the chase was on! What got my initial attention was the set of four cat claws that tracked deeply across my groggy face closely followed by two sets of wild dog paws using my chest for leverage as they bounded from seat to seat, their carnivore instincts raging in full blossom.

On the second revolution around the interior, the three animals had picked up enough speed and centrifugal force to run on the walls and windshield, their straining bodies hanging parallel to the ground and defying the force of gravity. It was an amazing wake-up call to watch them madly racing around my head like that. I was merely an inconvenient obstacle being used as a scratching post and door mat, and being brusquely buffeted by bouncing, behemoth bodies on every bypass.

On the third lap, the maelstrom abruptly died when the

lucky cat found its way out through the hole in the plastic. I sat there stunned and overstimulated, feeling like I had just been run over by a two ton buzz saw. Meanwhile, the dogs sat behind me, proudly panting and salivating heavily.

After determining that I wasn't mortally wounded and was able to go to work, I discovered that I had never been more wide awake or alert. On the way to the ferry that morning I saw things I had never seen before. Every minute detail was clearly visible. The fascinating texture of the pavement, the fragrant smell of the salt air, the sticky feel of the grip on the steering wheel, the unmistakable taste of kitty litter on my lips, and the sound of the fog horns in the distance and the plastic window flapping in the breeze were all new to me. My commute, my relationship with my community, and my awareness of the environment all took on an entirely different meaning that day. I realized that I was out of my element. That as charming and mellow as it was here, we didn't seem to be the right piece for this puzzle.

I knew then that I never would establish a private practice in Poulsbo. My job in Seattle was my first employment as a licensed dentist. I thought it would just be temporary while I got something established on the peninsula. It was clear to me now that my current job had captured my heart. Coincidentally, it was also in the very same community that I had been born into 27 years earlier, but had since been converted into a low-income housing project. I was working with disadvantaged children and teaching clinical skills to dental students who were rotating through the clinic. It was the perfect expression of my acquired liberalism. I grew to love my job and my opportunity to give something meaningful back to my old and dearly beloved neighborhood and alma mater. It was a chance to have a positive impact on the self-esteem of young people in hopes that it would make the difference to help them become confident and independent enough to break loose from the system of poverty and put-downs that they were caught up in. I felt so proud that I was actually given the chance to contribute in a personal way to the very community that had spawned me.

I knew I had to stay there for a while to accomplish this goal. I realized that my real passion was for being there, helping out however I could.

The relative quiet and beauty of the Kitsap Peninsula finally became overshadowed by the draw of the inner city. The virtues of the farm and country living were wonderful. Our boys came away from there with a permanent amount of soil embedded under the fingernails of their souls and a portion of salt water in their veins. It was a great beginning for them, but after two years of solitude and relative seclusion we decided it was time to teach them about people. We bought our first little house in West Seattle. We were close to the clinic, closer to people, and lived on a dead end street still close to the woods. We had learned a lot, and we were still on our own.

CHAPTER 5

More Spiders

THE TWO YEARS WE SPENT LIVING ON THE FARM ON the Kitsap Peninsula were filled with fun and adventure and many opportunities for learning. There were so many things that we hadn't done before, and so many unanswered questions about how to do them. How to be good parents and properly raise our boys, was at the top of the list, but there were many other minor issues as well, like: How do you fix a leaky faucet? When is the best time to dig up potatoes? Who gets to take out the garbage? and, What are we going to do with ten overgrown acres of ripe, plump, gorgeous, and delicious blackberries? I know, "Let's make wine for Christmas presents."

The recipe called for 30 gallons of berries. No problem, we had plenty. It was late summer. Spiders were everywhere! Great big ones and little tiny ones. There were shinning, quivering webs in all the spaces between the dense and thorn-covered berry vines. I had always been quite shy about spiders, and was initially very timid around so many of them. But as I spent day after day out there picking berries, I became more and more comfortable with them. There was plenty of time to observe their behaviors and become very familiar with their habits, movements, and lifestyle. They are actually very predictable and intelligent creatures. I grew to enjoy their presence as fellow companions, and was no longer bothered by their close proximity, even when they were crawling right on me. I knew they meant me no harm.

Our "Celestial Cellars" wine turned out famously and made fine gifts that year, but the best gift of all was conquering my fear of spiders. By getting to know them, I was able to make them my friends instead of my enemies. What is it about spiders that makes them so fearsome anyway?

Spiders! Spiders are so scary. Don't you just love to look at them? Eight long spiny legs, and bulging body parts all covered with prickly hairs. If you look real close you can see all six of their eyes. Then POOF, suddenly they're gone!

Have you ever walked face first into a large web? You know that spider is on you somewhere. Maybe it's on your back or underneath your clothes. Maybe it's in your hair getting ready to make a nest!

When a nest hatches it is a seething mass of hundreds of tiny red dots. All of them are spiders. If you're crazy enough to touch it, they all suddenly drop down on tiny silk threads. Now they're everywhere!

. . . As I sat there after the shipwreck, reminiscing and waiting to be rescued from our tropical island refuge, I remembered many other interesting encounters with spiders that had occurred during my life. My musing about them made me realize that for some reason spider confrontations occupied a substantial portion of my memory banks. Just like spiders they were hiding in the dark and recessed corners of my mind and came leaping out unexpectedly when I went searching for them. They were a significant part of my history from early childhood through all my adulthood travels around the world. They seemed to keep popping up wherever I went. I wondered why. Was there some kind of fascination that we held for each other? An ongoing history of stories started to unravel from the tangled web of memories in my mind.

~ ~

FEVERISH

WHEN I WAS a boy I got a lot of fevers. I hated them because they always caused such horrible hallucinations. The most common and abhorrent ones involved faces. I would be lying on my bed in a febrile state and terrible, frightful, horrid faces would appear out of thin air. If I let my eyes linger too long in any one place I would see them. They would start out as tiny spots and quickly grow into dreadful, ghastly, grotesque visages. They would suddenly rush in at me, quickly expanding into a gigantic size that would come shooting straight at my own face. Everywhere I looked it would happen, whether my eyes were open or closed.

Their tongues would be lolling around, dripping a vile extract. Their insane eyes would be abnormally big and bugged out. The other facial features would be in a fluid motion of constantly changing contortion. Their teeth were gnarly and menacing. I detested it! Even though I knew it wasn't real, I couldn't turn it off. I hated it! I usually gave in to panic and had to call one of my parents in for moral support to help me through it. Every time I felt the telltale symptoms of an oncoming fever I prepared for the worst.

Sometimes the delusions would assume a different form, testing my grip on reality. The last time this happened it started out as usual. There was no mistaking the generalized aching joints, simultaneous shivering and sweating, and the familiar burning sensation behind my eyes that I always got.

I crawled into bed that night and waited for the looming, frightful faces to appear. To my relief they didn't materialize. With my head on the pillow I turned toward the wall and closed my eyes to get some rest. After a minute or so I had a strange premonition that something was wrong. I opened my eyes and there, staring at me from two inches from my face was a very large spider. It startled me and I instinctively swatted at it. It disappeared. I shuddered and closed my eyes again. Before long I felt something crawling up my arm. I looked, another large spider! I knew then, that I was in for a new and different kind of nightmare experience.

As I lay there, I would feel one crawl across my face, down my leg, or over my stomach. Each time the sensation was so real that I thrashed out at them automatically. I was glad for the fact that when my eyes were closed I couldn't see them, only darkness. But in my foreboding thoughts I kept imagining them, so I looked every so often to check. Every time I did spiders were there. At first only one or two. But each successive time there were always more and more. Eventually, there was a whole army of them, marching across my body, my bed and pillow, and creeping up the wall from beneath the side of the bed. The wall in front of my face danced with the apparitions of small dark forms of tiny monsters appearing from nowhere. It seemed so real and it just kept building in intensity.

Unable to handle it anymore, I called out for help, waking up my mother. She was used to dealing with these fever-induced phobias. She came to my room and switched on the light. A moment of stunned silence was followed by her muffled screams and yelps. The spiders were real! They were everywhere! Some kind of massive arachnid migration was taking place. I was seriously stunned. This was no figment of my imagination. We flew into action, flogging at them with pillows until they were all gone. We made sure, checking inside, around, and under the bed. When everything was finally put back together again I drifted off to sleep. I felt vindicated that I hadn't experienced yet another phantom illusion. I also felt repulsed and shaken by the reality of the whole scene and what I had just gone through.

When I awoke the next morning to the welcomed light, I decided the whole experience of the dark night was just a crazy dream. I changed my mind when I saw all the brown, yellow and orange squish marks peppering my wall. Curiously, I've never endured anymore feverish fantasies since that night.

TROPICAL PARADISE

WHEN JERRI AND I went to Hawaii after dental school to celebrate successful graduation with some well deserved R & R after nine years of intense schooling, another couple of friends joined us. We wanted to get away from the beach scene for a night so we rented a place in the mountains of Kauai. It was a rustic log cabin, built up on stilts in the middle of the jungle. We arrived just at sundown and walked in. There was no electricity, and as we stood in the dim light surveying the place from the corner of my eye I saw something moving across the floor. It was a huge spider as big as my hand. It looked like a small salad plate with legs. It crawled under a kitchen chair that was just to my left and stopped. I knew that no one else had seen it yet so I decided I'd better warn them. Jerri was afraid of spiders and I didn't want her to be shocked. I said in my calmest voice, "Hey guys, the biggest spider I have ever seen in my life is sitting right under that chair. Don't be scared."

They all looked at it and in unison sighed, "Oh my gosh!"

I could feel the tension meter start to rise. We quickly formulated a plan. I would pick up the chair and my friend Kurt would immediately whack it with a broom.

So we counted down, "Three, two, one." I grabbed the chair and Kurt went wham. It was a weak kind of wham, not the hefty "whack" I was hoping for. He lingered for a few seconds and then picked up the broom. Pishoooo! That spider shot out of there like a bolt of black lightning. It ran right under the bed where Jerri and I were planning to sleep. Now, I wasn't particularly afraid of spiders at the time, but this one didn't even have to bite you. It was so big it could smother you in the middle of the night! I knew we had to find it!

I started crawling around on my hands and knees looking for it. It was nowhere on the floor. It must have crept up somewhere on the bed or in the wall. Finally I saw its shining eyes peering out at me from a crack between the logs about 18 inches above the floor. Meanwhile it was getting dark, so I asked Kurt to hold a flashlight so I could see while I tried to coax it out of the crevice with a small stick. The tension meter was going up even higher. I was concentrating hard. I kept poking in at it and it would move out of the way a little. I didn't want to lose it. I wanted to make sure we got the darn thing out of there so we could sleep.

I started hearing an odd clattering commotion that sounded like a distant train, slowly picking up speed over some old, loose tracks. I ignored it, not wanting to break my focus. The noise kept getting louder and louder, faster and faster, and sounded so strange that I finally had to look around. It turns out that Kurt was way more afraid of spiders that anyone else. He was holding the flashlight in both hands and was shaking so badly that the batteries were vibrating like a chorus of castanets. It was so comical and unexpected that I started silently laughing hysterically to myself.

I went back to work with his serenade in the background and a giggle in my belly. With a lucky flick of the stick the spider suddenly flipped out on to the floor and started racing toward Kurt. He yelped and dropped the flashlight. I grabbed the broom and swatted! Got it! The spider withered up into the size of a golf ball. We swept it outside and slammed the door. It was a fitful sleep that night wondering if there were any more of them around.

The next day when we left, the early morning sun was shining in underneath the cabin and through the stilts. As we coasted by we could see a dozen gigantic webs glinting in the light. In the center of each one was a huge, threatening, black shape.

It promised to be another hot tropical day, but for some reason we were all shivering when we drove away.

FLESH WOUND

ONE EVENING AFTER returning home from a routine day at the office, I was taking off my socks when I noticed an odd sight on the inside of my left ankle. There was a circular raw area there about the size of a nickel. No accompanying pain, itching or swelling though, so I forgot about it. The next morning it had grown to the size of a quarter and it looked a lot meaner. The overlying flesh was gone and the remaining tissue was all macerated and weeping. Still there was no pain or discomfort. I was slightly alarmed, mostly with curiosity, but had no time to deal with it. I had to go to work.

I wondered about it off and on that day but didn't get a chance to check it until that evening. I was dismayed when I removed my sock. Whatever it was had rapidly grown to the size of a silver dollar and looked exceedingly ugly and grotesque. I thought I was being attached by some strange flesh-eating bacteria or fungus. Maybe even leprosy had set in. Even Jerri who had seen everything as an emergency room nurse was surprised and clueless as to what it was. I resolved I would get an emergency appointment with my doctor the next day before I lost my whole foot to the oozing, alien presence.

The next morning it was even worse, with a secondary, unsightly crust starting to form in the center of the secreting mass. I booked a doctor's appointment at lunch hour and showed up feeling relieved that something was finally going to be done to stop the onslaught of this "thing." Curiously, instead of putting me in a regular exam room, the receptionist sat me in the central business office in one of the desk chairs. The nurses were all sitting around nonchalantly chatting and eating lunch, waiting for the doctor. One of them casually asked me what I was there for. I pulled my sock down to display the mysterious affliction and said, "To check this."

They took one look and immediately squealed with disgust. They recoiled back away from me and slunk together into a huddle in the middle of the room. Now I figured that if these seasoned nurses were reacting with such revulsion I must have truly contracted something quite deadly and terrifying. One of them ran to get the doctor. Evidently, briefed by the nurse, he kept a respectable and safe distance when he looked at my foot. He didn't want to touch it, and offered no diagnosis. He suggested I go to see a dermatologist as soon as possible, and I was politely ushered out of the office. Nobody there knew what it was. But whatever it was, it sure ruined their lunch. I was amused by the memory of the queasy expressions on their faces, but concerned that I had some rare ailment that defied the annals of medicine. Still, there was no pain.

I couldn't get in to see the dermatologist for another day,

and by then the center was on its third layer of crusty scabs and the borders were still growing, albeit slower now than before.

The specialist gave it a quick look and smiled. "It's a spider bite," he said. "Possibly a Brown Recluse or a Hobo Spider." He explained they like to hide in warm, dark places.

I thought back to how I could have come into contact with one and then I remembered. I routinely go into the garage barefooted every morning and step into my barn boots so I can go out to feed the chickens, ducks, cats, and dog. I recalled feeling a weird, itchy sensation one morning, the week before, inside my left boot. That must have been the bite. The poor astonished spider was using my boot for a bunk house when I stepped in uninvited.

The doctor gave me some special ointment to put on the wound, and it disappeared in about two weeks. He cautioned me to be careful about where I stepped, and not to go bare-footed in the dark anymore. I figured that this was a once-in-a-lifetime fluke, and probably would never happen again in a million years. My morning routine is still unchanged. Besides, seeing all those smug nurses drop their lunches and cringe together into a hair-raising human ball somehow made the experience all worthwhile.

"DON'T GET OFF THE PLANE"

JERRI AND I were in the magical country of Nepal on one of many visits there to help with dental and health care in remote villages. We had spent about a month in the relative cold, high altitude climate of the Mt. Everest area. Before going home we wanted to explore the warmth and greenery of Nepal's

Chitwan National Park. It is located in the southeastern part of the country where the land is only about 300 feet above sea level. Because of its latitude relative to the equator, it is a tropical forest containing many fantastic bird species, elephants, rhinos, tigers, and crocodiles.

We were eagerly waiting for our plane ride into the jungle in a small domestic airline office at the Kathmandu airport. We started exchanging pleasantries with a woman who was also waiting for the same plane. She was a very large, imposing-looking American who was traveling alone. She was friendly, jocular and loud spoken, but not abrasive. When we eventually boarded the plane she sat immediately in front of us in order to continue our conversation. It was a small, 12 passenger plane with two seats to the right of the aisle and only single seats to the left. The cockpit was not separated from the passenger area so the pilot and co-pilot sat with the rest of us in the same space, but they had swivel chairs.

Jerri and I were seated in the second row and our adopted friend was in the row, just behind the pilots. I noticed that she was so big that she literally took up most of both seats. She was sweating profusely, evidently a little nervous about the flying. I wondered how comfortable she would be in the hot, humid, untamed jungle. We were about 30 minutes into the 45 minute flight when she suddenly let out a shrill scream, threw off her seatbelt, and bounded out into the aisle, hugging the opposite side of the fuselage. Because of the sudden weight shift, the plane lurched slightly to the left. The concerned pilot turned around to see what was the matter. The lady was too breathless to talk but kept pointing with her burly, flagging arm at the wall next to her seat. Just above the window was a big, velvet black spider slowly inching its way toward us and the rear of the plane. The spider was about two inches in diameter. Fairly impressive for close quarters on a small airplane!

The lady just stood there, sweating, panting, and pointing. She was afraid to move. The pilot explained to her that we were getting ready to land and that she needed to return to her seat as soon as possible. The spider stopped moving and was higher up now, so the lady relented, and slowly crept back toward her seats. As she was lowering her heavy frame into the upholstery, the spider suddenly shot straight out from the wall as if it had been sitting on a tightly coiled spring that had just released. It ricocheted off the lady's shoulder and fell down on to her seat where it quickly disappeared over the edge.

The poor woman had an absolute conniption fit. She started bouncing around the plane like a frantic pinball in a rubber room. She crashed heavily into the pilots, disrupting their concentration. They were fighting to keep the plane level during the approach to the grassy field where we were to land. The plane kept veering back and forth in response to the panicked woman's unpredictable movements. The sound of the engines roaring to compensate for each unplanned bank was just audible over the shrieks and squeals of the lady. Some of the passengers started yelling at the woman to sit down. She was still leaning ponderously on the pilots who now were clearly irritated, and were trying to push her off of them and back toward her seat.

Meanwhile she kept murmuring, "It was so big, it was so big!" over and over again.

The whole scene was totally unbelievable but true. Our lives were in danger!

Mercifully, the wigged-out woman finally took her seat. The spider was gone now anyway. (It probably fell down into one of the open zipper pockets in the lady's carry on luggage that was stowed under her seat.)

The tense concern and commotion turned into dead silence as the airplane roughly touched down and rattled its way across the rutted pasture that doubled as an airstrip.

When it finally came to a stop and the door opened, a man's voice called out from the back of the cabin. "Lady, if you think that was a big spider, you'd better not get off the plane!"

Several people laughed and we deplaned. I don't know what happened to her after that. We went our separate ways at the small terminal.

The man was right, though. During our stay in the jungle we saw spiders that were 12 to 14 inches from end to end. They were nesting in webs that were six to eight feet across. We checked for them under our cots in the tent every night before going to sleep. The local people told us that there was an even larger variety that spun webs large enough and strong enough to snare birds in flight. I wondered about what our stout friend from the airplane thought about these giants and whether she was glad she got off the plane.

Spiders, what a trip!

CHAPTER 6

Cutting My Teeth

LITTLE BILLY

MY FIRST EMPLOYMENT AS A YOUNG DENTIST FRESH out of school was in a community public health clinic in West Seattle. I didn't think it would turn into a long-term commitment, but I vowed I would spend two years there to gain speed and experience and then transfer into private practice. The clinic was located in the same neighborhood that I had been born into 27 years earlier. The nostalgia of being back there felt good to me. It was almost as if I had been called back for some reason.

The clinic was setup to treat children from low-income families. Many of the children we saw were from broken homes, dysfunctional families, and abusive environments. It didn't take long to realize that there were many more things to learn about people and teeth that were not included in the dental school curriculum. I had learned what to do, but now I was going to learn how to do it. Unique experiences and learning opportunities presented themselves almost every day.

One of my earliest experiences was when little six-year-old Billy came in for his first dental checkup. He had a mouth full of cavities and other dental problems that would require numerous appointments in order to treat them properly. I could tell he was nervous and that he seemed unusually wary of the whole experience. I wondered how he would do for the actual dental procedures and if I had the necessary management skills to complete the extensive treatment plan and still provide a positive experience for both him and me.

When he returned for his next appointment the answer came quickly. He totally freaked out! We had barely even started when he began crying and yelling and thrashing about. He was filled with irrational fear and frantic. He kicked and hit and spit and bit, shredded up his bib and his chart and tried breaking the dental equipment, scattering the instruments across the floor. He was like a caged animal, totally panic-stricken and out of control!

The management techniques I learned in school to deal with this kind of behavior consisted of physically restraining the patient, firmly but gently, so they couldn't hurt themselves. At the same time you held one hand over their mouth to stifle their yells and to limit the amount of oxygen that was available to them. This promised to get their attention so you could look directly into the patient's eyes and instruct them to calm down. You were not supposed to remove your hand from their mouth until they complied with your request. It all sounded good when I learned about it, but in practice it didn't work for little Billy or me. In his state of mind, he was way stronger than I was and it was a no-holds-barred survival match as far as he was concerned. I held on as long as I could, but it only seemed to increase his conviction to escape. His flailing frenzy and irrational hysteria only grew in intensity. It was difficult under these circumstances to convince him that I was only trying to help him and meant him no harm. I finally gave up. Afterward, I felt exhausted and traumatized and was sure that he felt the same way, too.

His deteriorated dental condition needed help and I knew that I was his only resource. Deep down inside I knew there must be a better way to win him over. I prayed for guidance and mentally searched for the solution. I decided to forget about doing dentistry on him for a while and just be his friend. I scheduled him to come back and took him to the small community park across the street from the duplex that we were using as the clinic.

He was tense and resistant at first, but as I pushed him on the swings and helped him down the slide he started to have fun. I hoisted him up on my shoulders and ran around, bouncing him up and down, back and forth across the park and down an adjoining alley. He was having the time of his life, laughing and yelling at the top of his lungs, and I was feeling enthused that this approach seemed to be working. We returned to the swings and as I was pushing him again, a police car pulled up to the curb and two of the biggest cops I ever saw got out and started walking in our general direction.

Little Billy seemed very excited to see them and started screeching, "Police! Police!"

I assumed there was a local domestic disturbance going on nearby and they were there to check it out. But, they came right over to us and started asking me questions. They wanted to know who I was, what I was doing, what kind of car I drove and where it was? I explained who I was and what I was doing and why, and that my wife had dropped me off at work so she could use our black sedan for the day.

They didn't buy my story. Without saying why or checking at the clinic, said they would have to take me down to the police station for more questioning. I was scared and couldn't

CONFESSIONS OF A MODERN DENTIST

believe this was happening! There was no convincing them any differently. Just as I was being assisted into the patrol car, the clinic's hygienist who knew I was at the park nonchalantly walked out with some x-rays for me to look at. She was totally surprised by the police action and quickly identified me as the dentist, and verified that I was trying to help little Billy get over his fears of needed dental work.

The police then explained that there was a child abuser loose in the area and that a neighbor had called them when she heard Billy's yelling. I just happened to match the villain's description and the type of car he was seen in was a dark colored sedan.

The police apologized and praised me for what I was doing. Then the biggest and tallest one leaned over, pulled little Billy right up close, into his face, and said to him, "You listen to this dentist and do what he says or you'll end up like this!" Then he suddenly spit out his two partial dentures, dangling them from the front edge of his lips!

The sight of those artificial teeth ejecting out of his mouth totally shocked me and poor little Billy's eyes got bigger than baseballs. He must have been thoroughly jolted and perplexed by the unnerving spectacle.

I don't know if little Billy ever realized what had actually happened, but after we both recovered from the disturbing display, we walked hand in hand back to the clinic. I knew I had made a new friend and little Billy was a model patient ever since that day.

I don't know if it was the cop, me, or the combination of both that made the difference, but I knew my prayer for guidance had been answered. I discovered that the underlying common ground that everyone responded to was Love. I learned that children are especially sensitive to Love's vibration. The primary method of communication for children is more non-verbal than verbal. The younger they are the more they rely on physical cues for information about their world. They respond to the quality of your touch, the vibration of the sounds and motions you make, and the intention registered in your gaze. Their ability to accurately communicate through feelings is developed long before their capacity for understanding spoken language.

It took me several years to perfect this management technique. It requires consciously creating an atmosphere that is filled with the good intentions of helping and loving others. You learn to fill the room with your countenance of joy, nurturing, honor and respect, producing a climate of genuine caring. It is communicated through your touch, your voice, your posture, and your look. When you look at someone you purposely look past their physical form and interact with the Divine essence of Life that dwells inside each body that unites us all into Oneness. This acknowledgment of their greatness is felt by the patient, and they respond with trust.

Thank you for teaching me this invaluable lesson, little Billy.

SCARY MARY

ONE DAY AT the clinic we got a call from a lady who was having some unusual pain in her mouth. We had never seen her before and when she came in to fill out the paper work we learned that her name was Mary. She had a look of fear and suspicion on her face when I met her. I felt somewhat uneasy and intimidated around her at first. She was one of the largest people I had ever seen. I estimated she weighed at least 400 pounds.

When she sat down in the old dental chair she spilled out

about one-third of her body on each side. I felt bad that it was probably fairly uncomfortable for her but there was nothing else we could do. As I slowly started to recline the chair backwards I could hear the electric motor straining and start to bog down. At a certain point I heard the metal framework creaking with fatigue. A sudden wave of panic flashed through me as I realized that I was sitting with my legs under the back of the chair. If the chair broke I would be instantly dismembered from the hips down. I quickly turned to the side to free myself, trying not to be too obvious so as not to embarrass her.

The chair held together okay and I finally got her into the proper prone position to do an examination. She told me that the pain was way in the back on the upper left side. When I looked at her I realized that her cheeks were so fleshy and overfed that they almost filled the inside of her mouth and totally obscured most of her teeth. I gently parted her lips with my mouth mirror, and started slowly working my way to the back, trying to retract her overly thick cheek so I could see what was going on and find the problem.

Suddenly, without warning, she flinched violently! Both her hands flew up over her head and she grabbed me tightly by the throat! Her forearms were as big as my thighs and I knew that with only a slight twitch she could snap my head off. She held me in a vice-like grip with her thumbs pressing firmly on my Adam's Apple. She was definitely in control of the situation.

With a muffled, wheezing kind of voice I squeaked, "Mary, what's the matter?" I tried to reassure her that I wasn't trying to hurt her and that she could let go of me now because I was really having trouble breathing. I told her that the best way to let me know if something was bothering her was to raise her left hand. That would be my signal to stop before anything became painful.

After what seemed a very long time, I could feel her grasp

start to loosen around my neck and she slowly put her hands down to her sides. Wiping the huge beads of sweat from my brow, I changed into a clean mask and took a few welcomed deep breaths of fresh air, then we talked for a while. We socialized about her life and then we re-established the ground rules for the dental visit. Once we trusted each other and knew what to expect, it was much easier to proceed with the exam and diagnosis.

It turned out that she had a sore and swollen gum inflamed from an embedded popcorn kernel. It was easily removed with a dental instrument and we were done. I saw Mary many times after that day and we became good friends. Every time I saw her I felt so glad that she was on my side now.

LIFE ON THE EDGE

THERE WAS ALWAYS something new to deal with when working in the community dental clinic. For a period of time, we were having trouble with someone breaking in at night and stealing supplies. It was obvious that whoever it was had a key because there were never any signs of forced entry. One day the clinic director informed me that he was having all the locks changed that afternoon. Only he and one other person had new keys. The rest would not be issued until later in the week. We were relieved that there was funding available for this because the theft of the supplies was limiting our ability to treat the low income neighborhood who couldn't afford health care elsewhere.

Late that afternoon an emergency call came in. A lady with a bad toothache needed to be seen. I volunteered to stay after hours and take care of her. She came in with her husband and was nine months pregnant, ready to deliver at any time. In her mature stage of pregnancy she looked as if she could be carrying twins or even triplets. She was uncomfortable at all ends of her body. It took about an hour to fix the affected tooth. Afterwards, she was very thankful and also very ready to leave. We went downstairs, and discovered that everyone else had already gone home and we were locked in with no key for the new deadbolt locks.

I tried calling the two people who did have keys to come over and let us out, but nobody was at home. For fear of embarrassment, I stopped short of calling the fire department for help and decided we could find a way out by ourselves.

We found a window on the ground floor that could be opened. It was one of those old style sash windows that slides up from the bottom. We decided that climbing out of that window was our only option. The husband exited first and I was surprised when he reached the ground outside. He had to jump down to it because it was about two feet lower than the floor on the inside. In our semi-desperate state we figured we could gently lower his wife down if I belayed her from inside and he caught her on the outside.

She climbed up on the window sill and threw one leg to the outside. So far so good. Then she ducked down to get her back and head under the window frame. Her husband gave her a slight tug and suddenly she was stuck tight, hunched over herself, straddling the sill! She started moaning in a tone that slowly grew in volume. No amount of gentle persuasion would move her. There she was, hopelessly trapped, doubled up in an unnatural position, doing the splits with her chin on her belly, all at my suggestion. It was all quickly turning into one colossal window pain.

In my mind I started to panic, trying to recall the proper procedures for delivering a baby, and trying to silence the voice in my head that was screaming, "Lawsuit, lawsuit!"

At the same time, I'm sure her husband was having frantic thoughts of his own. As I was trying to calm the woman, her husband suddenly uttered a loud shout and at the same time jerked on her arm. She popped to the outside with a shriek and flattened her husband to the ground as he tried to catch her. Fortunately, he cushioned her fall and after a few choice words and some dusting off, everyone seemed to be okay. I climbed out, closed the window, and we went our separate ways.

Later I heard that she gave birth to a healthy baby boy who weighed in at more than nine pounds. I never saw them again after that day and I wasn't too surprised to learn that the child wasn't named after me.

RATS

WHEN I WAS working with children from low income families, I was frustrated that there were no resources for orthodontic care. Many of these children were in dire need of braces, but their families could not afford to pay the fees necessary to treat them. I decided that I would try to help them myself. Having a pleasing smile that you're not ashamed of goes a long way in building one's self-esteem.

I took as much continuing education in orthodontics as I could find and enlisted several local, generous orthodontists to help me with the treatment plans. I would show up after hours at their offices with a box full of plaster models of patients' teeth. We would go over them one by one until I knew what to do. I tried to pick cases that would show a dramatic improvement with a little straightforward orthodontic intervention.

One of these orthodontists was a good friend from school and had just opened a brand new office. It was beautiful! He and his partner had remodeled a spacious single level home that sat on the edge of a high woodland knoll. One whole side had huge picture windows that looked out over an expansive, beautiful green valley. The patients had a stunning and gorgeous view from their treatment chairs and the equipment and furnishings were absolutely first class. He was extremely proud of this place. It was like a palace!

After we finished looking at the models, he wanted to show me around. We went out to the treatment area where six cushy dental chairs were lined up in a row to take full advantage of the spectacular view. It was dark and the lights were off, so while he walked back up front to turn them on, I climbed into one of the chairs to admire the myriad of lights twinkling in the distance across the countryside.

As I sat there watching, I heard a soft rustling sound off to my left. I looked down the row of chairs and saw a small room with a sink in it about 30 feet away. Evidently it was a laboratory of some kind. Underneath the sink was an enormous brown rat, a big one weighing maybe three or four pounds. He was obviously a resident left over from the old days when this was still a house.

Now I'm not bothered by rats at all. As a kid I had two pet rats. I was very comfortable carrying them around in my pockets and letting them sit on top of my head. Later during college, I worked on a research project for two years with hundreds of lab rats. These experiences created familiarity with their habits and taught me that they were very intelligent and intriguing creatures.

Being entertained, I calmly sat there watching the big rodent snooping around, twitching his whiskered nose, swishing his fleshy tail, and searching around for whatever. Momentarily, a few of the lights came on and my friend reappeared. He stood on my right, while I remained seated and proudly pointed out all the state of the art fixtures and equipment that he had installed. It was an exquisite showcase, truly the best money could buy, and I was quite duly impressed.

When he had finished his descriptions, I noticed that the big rat was still in the lab. I pointed and said, "Hey man, check that out."

When he saw the rat he got real quiet. Even in the dim light I could see the color start to drain out of him. Soon he was pale white and started to teeter back and forth. Just as he fainted, I caught him. He came to, right away, but still shaking and weak, he steadied himself against the chair. I was concerned and surprised that he would swoon like this and I wondered if all of this fancy equipment included any oxygen tanks just in case he needed to be revived.

The rat was no real concern to me, but obviously it had a much greater impact on my friend's emotional state. I clapped my hands and the rat jumped up on the drain under the sink and disappeared into the wall, squeezing through the space between it and the pipe. My good buddy was devastated, not only by the sight of this fearsome creature, but also by the fact that such a vile thing could be living in his beautiful, mansion-like dream office. I couldn't help it—I started to laugh at the irony.

After he regained his composure my friend vowed he would call the exterminator the next day and also have the hole plugged up immediately.

He swore me to secrecy. I was never to reveal to anyone that this event had ever happened in connection with his name or whereabouts. I kept my promise. No one will ever know.

GO WITH THE FLOW

DAY TO DAY life in the community clinic was always unpredictable. We relied a lot on volunteer helpers to keep things going as smoothly as possible. Many of the local community residents were able to receive job training as receptionists or dental assistants. Consequently, from one day to the next I never knew who would be there to assist me. It could be someone well known and highly skilled, or it could be someone entirely new on their first day with no training whatsoever. It required patience and flexibility to properly attend to the demands of the children's dentistry, the constant coming and going of personnel, and the frequent breakdowns and repair of old, donated equipment. It was a challenge that I really enjoyed, for I was learning so much about people, things, and dentistry. It helped me become self-sufficient and confident about what I was doing and what I was teaching others.

One day I was working on a particularly demanding restorative case on a relatively young patient. No assistants had shown up yet so I was going it alone. All of my attention was focused on the job at hand. Sometimes just a momentary lapse of concentration will be enough to allow a young child to become restless and difficult to manage at the end of a long procedure. It is important to stay actively engaged with the patient in order to keep their attention away from what is really happening to them. At the most critical phase of the operation the receptionist walked into the room and said, "This is your helper for today. She is new. Her name is Lucy. She wants to learn how to be a dental assistant."

I was too absorbed to even look up at her and greet her. I continued working and only acknowledged her verbally, saying hello, and telling her to take a seat in the assistant's chair.

Twenty minutes later I was finally finished. With gratitude I wiped the sweat off by brow and gave my five-year-old patient a little hug and a sticker and sent him on his way. Then I looked up to formally introduce myself to Lucy. I instantly recognized that she was a tall, very attractive young woman. She had the most beautiful ebony colored skin I had ever seen. I was admiring her pretty face when she smiled and what I saw there completely shocked me! My body spasmodically flinched and I was momentarily speechless. Contrasted against her dark skin her gleaming white teeth seemed extra emphasized, and right in the middle of her upper front central incisor, radiating out like a powerful beacon, glared a large, heart-shaped, brilliant green emerald inlaid into the surrounding enamel!

I tried not to overreact but I was distressed. I knew she had had it done for cosmetic reasons and to make a personal statement, but all I could think of was how incredibly beautiful her natural smile already was. Why cut a hole in a perfectly healthy tooth and ruin a precious living jewel in order to insert a gaudy gemstone? I was having a hard enough time as it was trying to convince my patients to take care of their teeth without having my dental assistant's smile constantly remind them that fillings were cool.

I didn't say a word to her. I just gazed and smiled openly, silently absorbing the initial shock of seeing the decorated tooth and pretending that it wasn't even there. At the same time I was hoping that I didn't display any reaction that would cause her any embarrassment or bad feelings. For the rest of the day, every time I looked up at her I had to force myself not to stare at that glowing tooth.

As time went by, Lucy proved herself to be a fast learner—reliable and genuinely interested in learning a marketable skill. I looked forward to working with her because she cared about people, had a great sense of humor, and had become a valuable asset as a dental assistant. The bright green front tooth ceased to be an issue. I didn't even notice it any more.

One morning after about nine months of work study training, Lucy showed up with another big surprise. She smiled and it was gone! The ornamental piece of rock had been removed and was replaced by a natural looking, tooth-colored filling. I had the same reaction as the first time I had met her and I gawked at her in quiet but pleasant disbelief. I don't know what it was that had changed her mind about removing it or where she had had it done. I didn't ask, I just maintained my policy of silence about this particular topic like nothing had ever happened. Inwardly, I was glad that she had restored her natural appearance, but already knew she was a beautiful person with or without that stone embedded in her smile.

Shortly afterwards she was offered a well-paying job in a private dental office and left our neighborhood clinic. The training had paid off and we were all happy for her. She had learned a lot and so had I: don't let first impressions lead you astray. Beyond all the glitz and glitter there is always a real person to get to know. I wonder where she is now?

Since then I have seen many patients with "options" added to their mouths and teeth. Sports logos of their favorite teams fused to their crowns. Teeth colored pink, yellow and blue, or blacked out just for effect. "Dog tag" information profiles, encoded on microfiche, bonded to molars for emergency identification. Teeth ground into unusual shapes for religious or tribal purposes. Pierced tongues and tattooed lips done to make a statement. Hollowed-out teeth used for smuggling contraband. I even have a dentist friend in Canada who has made quite a business for himself bonding small diamond chips to people's canines so that there is a real live sparkle in their smile.

BURIED TREASURE

THE EQUIPMENT WE used in the community clinic was all very antiquated and had been donated from various sources. Most of the old-fashioned dental chairs were from the late 40's and early 50's and they broke down fairly often. Many times we had to borrow parts from one to make the others work. Limited funds were available to pay for professional repair services, so I had to learn how to mend, and patch, and service the units as much as possible by myself. We had six dental chairs to work with and all of them needed to be functional during the week because of the large volume of patients and dental students who needed to use them. Sometimes I did emergency repairs during lunch, jerry-rigging odds and ends together by using my pocket knife, dental floss, and plastic tape.

One day a thin wisp of acrid smoke wafted from a chair every time we used the reclining motor. It was obvious by the smell that electrical wire insulation was melting somewhere under the cushion. Hoping to avoid a fire, a broken-down chair, and a patient receiving an unexpected hotseat, I looked into it during a break between patients. To find the motor, I had to remove the seat pad and the upholstery to get to the metal frame and the motor mount. I had never performed this operation before so I blundered through it, removing way more pieces than I really needed to. I was trained to do oral surgery and root canals, but if that chair would have been a patient I'm not sure it would have survived this onslaught.

Anyway, I finally grabbed hold of and pulled up on the right part and suddenly with a loud "rrrrip" the whole seat section lifted up. The motor was there all right, but so was something else much more electrifying and surprising—25 years worth of patient's pocket change!

Piles of lost coins from hapless clients had accumulated

over the decades between the seat and the frame. It was a bonanza of copper and silver currency. It was like stumbling upon a treasure trove of ancient Spanish doubloons hidden under an obscure rock outcropping in the remote desert Southwest.

Like an excited kid on a scavenger hunt, I scooped up the money and dumped it into my pockets, more than five dollars' worth. I was energized by the discovery and soon found what I was originally looking for. A bare section of wire was touching against the metal frame, shorting out, and causing it to overheat. I insulated the area by wrapping it with a couple of Band-Aids, reinstalled all the pieces I had dismantled, and went back to work. I felt a powerful surge of pride that I had actually successfully repaired an electrical problem.

I had sworn off everything to do with electricity at age twelve, after I had helped my dad repair the electric fence around the pasture where my sister kept her horse. In order to test whether the fence was working properly, my father would tightly grab the hot wire with his bare hand. His hair stood straight out while I watched in terrified disbelief as all the muscles in his arm violently jerked and twitched in unison with each pulse of power pounding from the powerful battery.

For instructional purposes he urged me to grab it myself, but no way! Just that morning I had witnessed our boxer dog, Ginger, chase a rabbit across the field under the fence. Ginger's back just barely grazed the lowest wire. She yipped and yelped loudly as the jolt instantly threw her into 720 degrees of head over heels somersaults. When she finally stopped the tailspin she was obviously disoriented and dumbfounded, like a stray bolt of lightening had struck her from out of the blue. The hair on her back where she touched the wire always remained kinked into a obvious cowlick after that shock. No way was I going to grab that wire! I was already shocked beyond belief by my dad and the dog. I didn't need any more, ever. That was the day I decided never to touch electrical wires again.

But now the dental chair was actually working properly again and it gave me a satisfying charge to have fixed it. Looming more importantly in my mind however, was the issue of all that money I had found under the seat. There were still five more ancient chairs to explore. I couldn't wait until the end of the day! When it finally arrived, I conducted an exhaustive but thrilling examination of every nook and cranny of the remaining dental chairs. By the time I was finished tearing them apart and putting them back together again, I was an expert in dental chair demolition and restoration. I knew how every part and piece fit together and I knew where to find hordes of cash abandoned and concealed throughout the ages.

I found lots of it, and filled my pockets with loose change. I felt like I had been the winner of an all-you-can-carry shopping spree at the U.S. Mint. As I walked into the bank that night I sounded like the jangling of two overstuffed gumball machines bouncing down the stairs.

I was $31.09 richer! I kept it a secret from the rest of the staff until the next day when all-you-can-eat soft drinks and pizza arrived just in time for lunch. We had a great celebration thanks to all of those wonderful dental patients over the years who remembered to visit their dentist but forgot to check their pockets.

GOING FOR THE GOLD!

I FELT PRETTY smug after finding all that loose change in the old dental chairs until I heard about the experience of one of my classmates from dental school. He bought an existing practice from a retiring dentist who had worked more than 40 years in the same office space. The older dentist was a specialist who had only done crown and bridge work during his career. He was a gifted craftsman who worked exclusively with gold and did all of his own lab work. In order to achieve perfection, he cast, trimmed, polished, fitted, and adjusted all of his patients' gold restorations himself, right there on the spot. When he was finally ready to retire, he sold his dental practice and everything in his well-used office "as is."

My friend, the new dentist who bought the old practice, wanted to totally remodel the office, upgrade the used dental equipment, and replace the outdated furnishings. In the process of stripping out the office interior, he pulled up the original carpet and on a hunch, sent it to a rendering company to test it for any stray precious metal fillings or filings. Two weeks later he received a check for over $3,000!

Over the years, all the sparkling gold dust and tiny fragments from endless grinding and polishing had accumulated in the nap of the rug and provided my friend with a big surprise: a built-in tenant improvement bonus. When the rest of us colleagues heard about this gold dust bonanza we applauded the wisdom and ingenuity of our friend. We wondered if we would have ever thought to check our carpets for such a prize?

CONSTRUCTION ZONE

AFTER SEVERAL YEARS of successful operation, our community dental clinic joined forces with several other grassroots health care clinics in the Seattle area and formed a consortium.

This arrangement made it possible for more federal funding to be made available. We applied for a grant and were overjoyed when we received it. The money was earmarked to be used for physical improvements to the existing building which was a forty-year-old duplex with dental chairs roughed in to each bedroom, a sterilization area tucked into one bathroom, and the waiting room squeezed into one of the small living spaces. The fixtures were leaky, the lighting was dim, and the walls and floors were thin and noisy. It would be a welcome enhancement in comfort and efficiency to have the space remodeled as a dedicated healthcare facility.

We couldn't afford to shut down operations during the construction phase, so a plan was devised to rebuild teeth and redo the building at the same time. We would continue to see patients in one end of the structure while the remodeling began in the other end. It would slowly advance toward us until we met, then we would swap ends.

The plan sounded good on paper, but there were a few unanticipated glitches, like when the power or water shut off unexpectantly halfway way through delicate dental procedures. The whole process took about four months and at first the noise and disruption were minimal. But as they advanced closer toward us it became more obvious and annoying. Every day the atmosphere was punctuated by the whining of power saws and drills, the pounding of nails, the crashing and shaking as heavy stacks of lumber were dropped to the floor, and the yelling of construction workers as they barked commands back and forth using colorful expletives!

Since the communication between the builders and the clinic staff was only partial and sporadic, we didn't really know what to expect on a day-to-day basis. It was a freewheeling adventure in the melding together of the two disciplines.

There was so much dust suspended in the air that every time we picked up an instrument tray after doing a filling, a perfect outline had already formed around it on the table. I had to use my body as a shield to protect my patients from the chunks of plaster shrapnel flying across the room as the workers demolished the wall from the other side with sledge hammers, evidently unaware that we were working next door. My voice quavered from constant yelling so my patients could hear me above the ever-increasing din. Our noses were assaulted by the unsavory odors of burning rubber, plastic, and wood as overheated saw blades and acetylene torches cut through the old structure, and solvents and glue and new paint evaporated in our midst. It finally got to the point where construction was going on all around us. We were hemmed in by hanging, flimsy walls of plastic sheets, discolored canvas drapes and spattered drop cloths. We were eventually relegated to one single operatory in the corner on the second floor where we tried to fix teeth.

One morning an electric saw started up that was so loud it sounded like it was ripping away inside my head! It was impossible to converse with anyone over its screeching howl. It made the sound of the dental drill seem like a pleasant lullaby. The whites of my ten-year-old patient's eyes grew vividly more apparent as we continued working on his six-year molar in speechless surrender. The shrieking saw screamed on and on for an infinity of 20 minutes, doing what seemed like irreparable damage to our hearing and our psyches! Mercifully, it finally stopped. The silence was a stark and welcome relief. Then I heard a loud crack and a groan. Without warning, a three by six-foot section of floor about two feet to my right broke loose and collapsed, falling away into the first floor with a tremendous crash!

I sat there on my little dental stool with my patient and assistant in stunned disbelief as a giant mushrooming cloud of sawdust billowed up and over us. As I gawked over the edge of the gigantic hole right next to me, I could see the satisfied faces of the labor force one floor below me as they congratulated each other on a job well done. We had relocated so many times that I guess they forgot which room we were working in that day. Oh well, sometimes the price of progress is frightening. Now our only access to the sink and instrument supply was cut off by a deep pit similar to the traps hunters dig in the jungle to catch tigers in. I'm just glad that no one was walking through on their way to the bathroom when the floor gave way!

This incident prompted a little better communication protocol about the work schedule for the remainder of the construction process and before too much longer the facelift was complete. We had a brand new spiffy clinic to work in, maximized for patient comfort and work efficiency. It was bright, clean, and quiet. There were no more holes in the walls or floors to watch out for. Now, we could really concentrate on fixing holes in teeth instead.

THE CANDY MAN

DURING THIS TIME period our sons, Joe and Mike, were in their formative years. Jerri and I wanted to expose them to as many activities as possible to give them a reasonable database of experiences to draw from so that in later years they could make an informed decision on what they really wanted to pursue further. This included music lessons, soccer, baseball, karate, horseback riding, scouting, and campfire groups, snow skiing, boating, and of course, swimming lessons. Knowing how to swim is important, but in the Pacific Northwest it is a basic survival skill.

We took them to swimming lessons at the local pool two nights a week and usually attended one of the family swim sessions on the weekends. It was an enjoyable routine and we were encouraged to see that the skills and confidence of the boys in the water were growing.

After the lessons were over for the night, all the parents would congregate in the lobby and wait for their children to come out of the dressing rooms. The youngsters would appear one by one with their damp towels, dripping suits, and wet, slicked-back hair. In their disheveled clothes they would line up at the vending machines to buy a snack.

There was a pop machine on one side of the lobby and a candy machine on the other. Being a good father and a dentist to boot, I had always discouraged the consumption of pop and especially candy. As a matter of fact, we had never admitted to our boys that there was even such a thing as candy. To our knowledge, they had never tasted candy and didn't even know what the term referred to.

I felt good about keeping this secret. I knew that cavities were totally preventable with proper oral hygiene practices and the limitation of dietary sweets. No child should get cavities, especially the children of a children's dentist. Maybe I was just trying to save face or make up for the fact that I had ignored my own parents' advice to stay away from candy.

Consequently, I had a whole mouthful of cavities as a kid. I spent so much time in the dentist's office getting my teeth fixed that by the time I was seven, I already knew how to operate all the equipment. I could see no reason why my kids should suffer the same humiliating fate. The total absence of candy from their experience, for as long as possible, was our goal.

Our policy was to greet our shivering kids as soon as they emerged from the showers, give them some fruit or a sandwich for a snack, and whisk them out to the car and away from the temptation inside. It was a sort of modern day Garden of

Eden scenario, with the Tree of Knowledge being the vending machine.

One night we weren't quite quick enough. We were absorbed in conversing with some of the other parents and our boys were already standing there, tugging at our shirt tails. They were about three and five years old at the time and had noticed the long line of their peers forming at the candy machine and asked while pointing at it, "What is that?"

I looked down at them and replied weakly, "Oh, nothing." I looked back up to say some hasty good-byes and started to leave when a very husky man with a deep voice stepped out of the crowd and blocked our path to the door. I had never noticed him before. He had overheard the question posed by our kids and wanted to confirm if it was true that they really didn't know what candy was. When I proudly assured him that it was true, he suddenly became extremely upset.

For whatever crazy reason, he started speaking in a loud booming voice, saying things like, "What's wrong with you people? This is totally un-American! Every child should be able to have some candy! This is child abuse!"

The rest of the people grew silent and pulled back away from us, no one daring to take sides. Then the man confronting us stamped his feet and with a red face yelled louder, "I am going to report you to Child Protective Services right now if you don't let your children have some candy!" The man was clearly either insane or a large shareholder in the candy cartel. He glared at me and then pushed his way through the crowd toward the pay phone on the wall.

I could tell he was serious and I knew that any feeble explanation on my part would prove fruitless and may even enrage him more. We stood there surrounded by a circle of shocked onlookers, none of whom were privy to the facts. All they had heard were the words "child abuse." I could sense some accusatory stares starting to form on their faces, so with all their eyes focused upon us, I reluctantly reached into my pocket and fumbled around for some quarters.

We were in the spotlight when we walked up to the vending machine and had to show the kids how to operate the levers and help them pick a selection since they had never done it before. I naturally helped them choose items I knew I would enjoy, while the crowd of onlookers whispered to each other behind our backs about our obvious lack of parenting skills. As soon as Joe and Mike opened their packages and began chewing on the sugary contents, the big do-gooder man was apparently satisfied and quickly left the building without saying another word. The rest of the crowd slowly filtered out behind him. We stood there alone for a while, completely taken aback and feeling like we were in the middle of a bad dream. I purposely lingered for a while, trying to sort it all out in my mind and to give everyone else a chance to go home and avoid another possible confrontation with the "candy man" in the parking lot.

To this day, I still wonder about that incident. Were we being bad parents, or was the candy man just having a really bad case of the sugar blues? I don't know. I do know however, that tasting that candy was like opening a Pandora's box full of forbidden fruit for our boys, especially Joe. From that day forward he carefully saved every candy wrapper he opened as a memento of the treasure that was found inside to savor. Thirteen years later, when he left for college, his collection overflowed from a huge cardboard box which we hauled to the recycling center after a brief and informal memorial service.

Fortunately, neither of the boys has ever gotten a cavity. When candy came on the scene we really stepped up the oral hygiene program and they had almost daily visits from their family dentist. Now that's an indication of being a good parent, isn't it?

The boys are both on their own now, and have both lost their "sweet tooth." They are into fitness and nutrition and neither of them have any more interest in candy, much to my delight. I do have to admit, however, that in their absence I have completely rekindled my childhood zest for chocolate. Now they call me "the candy man."

CHAPTER 7

Transitions

WHEN I WAS FIRST OFFERED THE JOB AS STAFF DENTIST in the community clinic, I was so happy to have a chance to give something back to the same neighborhood that I had been born into. Looking back at the experience now, it seems that there was some kind of divine intervention, karma, or fate working in my favor. When I first took the job I only expected to be there for two, maybe three years at the most. Then I would go into private practice after I had perfected my clinical skills. But it took me two to three years just to perfect my child patient management skills so that each appointment was a win/win situation.

My goal was to always provide a positive experience for the patient and staff while effectively solving the dental problems that presented themselves. After I reached that point, I was on easy street. I enjoyed the interaction I had with students as an instructor, the friendships I made with the local residents, and the opportunity to be a positive role model for children in my old neighborhood that now had more of its share of distrust, despair, and misunderstanding.

In the blink of an eye 12 fulfilling years had gone by. I was secure there and had become a dependable fixture, but I wanted to accomplish other things that could only be done as a private business owner. I took advantage of a change in clinic administrators and decided to go out on my own. I would start my own private practice!

I started working two days a week with a pediatric specialist in a peaceful little suburb named Issaquah, 16 miles east of Seattle. Two days a week wasn't enough to support my family, so in order to pay the bills I continued to work part-time for several other public health clinics during the transition into full-time business owner. I even did some house painting and landscaping on the side to help pay the overhead of my new venture.

THE PANIC BUTTON

IT WAS TOUGH giving up a dependable income and going out on my own with no promise of support or regular salary, but Jerri and I were confident that we would be successful with our new vision. One of my many part-time jobs was as a substitute dentist in the old Seattle/King County Jail. I'll never forget my first day there.

After an extensive background check of my public and private records, I was approved for service and qualified to have my photo ID badge picture taken. Then a jail administrator explained all the important do's and don'ts. Mostly, they were don'ts. They included: Never tell an inmate where you or your family works or lives. Never ask an inmate what they are in jail for. Never carry a pocket knife or other sharp objects into the cell block. Never give anything to the inmates. Never turn your back on them, or leave any instruments out in the open, or leave any drawers open or unattended. Never completely trust them.

I thought these seemed like reasonable precautions to take owing to the circumstances, but they certainly were foreign to my usual way of interacting with patients. I reassured the interviewer that I understood the rules and could comply. Then we went on a tour of the facilities.

We rode the police elevator up to the fifth floor and emerged to a small waiting area. We walked up to a teller-like cage and showed our badges to the guard inside. He, in turn, signaled to the shadow of another man who sat in an elevated, glassed-in turret surrounded with 360 degrees of darkened windows. It was situated in the center of the cell block where he could see in all directions. He stared intently at us for a moment and then a loud electric buzzzz startled me as the lock opened on the barred door in front of us. As soon as we walked through, it quickly closed behind us with a noisy metallic clang.

We were now in the day room, which was a large holding area that was secure from the outside world and from the rest of the jail. Five or six men were being "booked in" as new prisoners and were inside still awaiting their cell assignments. They eyed us suspiciously. We walked over to a guard who was standing next to a long wall of bars. He made sure the coast was clear and then motioned to the mysterious man sitting in the central control tower. Suddenly with a clunk, the wall started to slide open. It was a huge electronic gate, mounted on a track and operated by a chain drive motor.

When we stepped across the track we were in a large central hallway. As we proceeded, we passed many individual cells and other smaller hallways radiating out on both sides of us, each with barred entrances. We wound our way around a maze of passageways, going through two more locked barriers, and finally arrived in the dental treatment room which was the last chamber on a long and narrow dead-end corridor. It was a fairly large room with concrete walls, ceiling, and floor. A desk and some cabinets lined one wall, a lone dental chair sat right in the middle of the floor, and an old behemoth air compressor was parked up against the far wall.

My tour guide quickly showed me how to turn on the equipment and unlock the instruments. She explained that I would be working alone, without an assistant, and that only one inmate at a time would be sent in to see me. Then, just as she was leaving, she disclosed that the only guard in this area was stationed at the other end of the hall. She pointed to a black button on the wall above the compressor and said, "If things get out of control and you need help, push that. It's the panic button!" Then she left and I was there all alone with my thoughts.

I was scared, nervous, and frightened all at the same time. My thoughts ran rampant. I didn't even know how to find my way out of this locked-up labyrinth on my own, much less deal with a psychotic criminal or a prison riot. What if my first patient was in here for murdering a dentist that pulled the wrong tooth? The fact that a so-called panic button even existed was not reassuring to me in the least.

After a few distressful moments of wondering what I had gotten myself into, an attendant escorted my first patient in. He was a middle-aged, graying man who looked just like a regular guy. He didn't look like a killer. He complained of pain in his lower jaw. I could tell from his expression that he knew I was a total correctional institution greenhorn. I wondered if he was just faking his condition to take a vacation away from his cell. My heart was pounding when I examined him, but I found a large cavity in the area where he was hurting, which convinced me that his complaint was legitimate. I explained to him how I could fix it. He agreed and we started the process.

About halfway into the excavation process, the compressor sputtered a few times then suddenly let out a prolonged sigh like air escaping from a punctured tire. My air pressure dropped to zero and the drills quit working. This occurrence would have stressed me out greatly in my own private office, but in this circumstance it was much worse. A knot formed in my stomach and started slowly rising toward my throat. I forced myself to stay calm and called the switchboard on the desk phone. I explained my predicament to the operator and she said she would send someone up from maintenance to take a look. Meanwhile, I sat there with the anesthetized convict trying to make small talk without saying anything too revealing about my personal life, which I felt could be in jeopardy at any given moment if I made the wrong move.

All of the inmates wore faded orange coveralls and plastic sandals. I had noticed on the way in that there seemed to be a certain hierarchy in the jail population. Some prisoners were restricted to their cells while others roamed freely in the secured hallways. A few inmates, (the trustees) wore drab baseball caps along with the regular hoosegow garb. This seemed to signify that they had special privileges or were trusted to take some responsibility for helping out around the place.

My patient seemed to be taking things in stride pretty well and after about 20 minutes of shallow conversation with him, two guys showed up. They were both wearing discolored coveralls and one of them had on a baseball cap. He said they had come to take a look at the compressor. I feared they were both prisoners. They had no tools with them and didn't really seem to be mechanic types. I doubted that they had been sent by the maintenance department, but I just wasn't sure, and I was too timid to ask them.

Not wanting to turn my back on anyone, I stayed with my

patient while they leaned over the huge compressor tank to hopefully find the problem. They immediately started laughing and whispering and cajoling each other, and I immediately started getting more nervous. They were goofing around so much that I finally threw caution to the wind and went over to see what was going on. They were fiddling with one of the air line hoses. I could see that it was split where it fit over the end of the metal outlet, causing all the air to leak out. It was definitely the source of the problem. The leak could be easily fixed by cutting off the broken piece of tubing and reattaching the solid part onto the coupling. It was a five-minute job.

They asked me if I had something sharp to cut it with and I instinctively reached for my pocketknife. To my horror, I found that it was still in my pocket! I had broken one of the basic rules and brought it with me into the jail. I feared I would be busted if I admitted that I had it, so I looked around for something else.

I still didn't know who these guys were and I wanted to trust them, but I was getting more and more paranoid of possible foul play. Maybe they were all members of the same vicious gang with an elaborate plan to escape and I was their fall guy. All three of them watched intently as I rummaged through the cabinet drawers. I tried to appear confident but I was shaking on the inside. The only things I found that would work were some surgical scalpels. I unwrapped one, and just in case these dudes weren't from maintenance, I removed the blade from the handle and gave it to them, along with a pair of old slip-joint pliers to hold it with. My mind was racing. I theorized that giving them a whole scalpel was crazy. It could be used as a serious weapon. But holding the blade with the pliers would be too unwieldy to be very effective. I just prayed that they would volunteer to return it to me without me having to ask for it when they were finished. I sat down next to my patient and pretended to ignore what was going on behind me.

Inappropriate snickering started again. I looked over my shoulder and saw the two men triumphantly jostling each other. Their hands were out of sight, down behind the compressor. I couldn't see what had become of the homemade knife. I realized that in the last 15 minutes I had broken all of the cardinal rules. I had brought an illegal weapon into the jail and provided inadequate supervision by turning my back on my patient while the cabinets were unlocked. (Maybe he had reached over and grabbed a weapon for himself while I wasn't looking!) I had actually given potentially dangerous contraband to prisoners and out of complete naiveté I trusted them with it.

The situation had gotten completely out of control. Full-fledged paranoia set in and I knew at that point that something drastic needed to be done. I'd had enough and there was only one way out. The panic button! Unfortunately, the two "custodians" were between it and me. I could try a surprise end run around them, trying to slap the button before they wrestled me to the floor, or I could just nonchalantly stroll over, as if to check on them, and shrewdly reach around behind them and hit the button before they stabbed me. I chose the latter scheme.

With my heart racing, I sauntered over and glanced down between them. What I saw made my heart leap into my throat! They were trying to cut the hose with the ramshackle, razor sharp and flimsy knife. I could foresee that the inevitable accident was about to happen. Their arms were in such a position that one little slip of the hose or the wobbly blade would cause a nasty slice across the wrist of one of them. Guess who would have to sew it up? Me.

I didn't want that to happen. I forgot about the panic button, called a halt to the operation, and grabbed the pliers. I finished cutting the end off the hose myself and watched as they reinstalled it properly. The crisis was over. It seemed that they never had any malicious intent. They were just on a joy ride from confinement. With smiles all around, they thanked me for my help and left, never to be seen or heard from again.

The air pressure was back to normal now, so I easily finished restoring my patient's tooth. Surprisingly, he also thanked me before he left. He had gotten a lot of entertainment value out of his dental visit, I guess. My nerves settled down after that first day and I began to appreciate the uniqueness of this alternate reality. As the weeks went by, I gained a newfound respect for the patients I saw from the inmate population. To a person, each and every one of them thanked me sincerely after their appointment. I could tell they really needed somebody who genuinely cared about them. I've never received so much universal gratitude or politeness from any other group, before or since.

Some of the men I met had incredible IQs. I wished I could be half as gifted as they. I could see that they were so intelligent they would be totally frustrated trying to have a meaningful conversation with the rest of us common thinkers. It was their inappropriate reaction to this frustration that got them into trouble in the outside world. It was too bad they didn't direct their disappointing discussions into more positive directions. They could accomplish so much if they weren't incarcerated and could find someone to believe in them and help apply their insights and ideas.

For many others, being in jail was the least threatening and most comfortable and secure existence they knew. They did what was necessary to keep themselves in there.

My biggest realization came at the end of every day when I successfully negotiated the intricacies of all the checkpoints and locked gates and walked out into the sunlight on the street below, a free man. That freedom to come and go as I pleased took on a new, thought provoking dimension. It was an indescribably sweet feeling that I cherished. A privilege that I am so thankful for! It made me determined to always use my freedom for something positive. I never would have achieved that realization and this internal drive to do good if I had gone one step further and hit that panic button.

 ⌁   ⌁

FEAR OF THE UNKNOWN

WHEN I WAS four years old our family moved from the busy and crowded government housing project in West Seattle to the quiet and secluded woods on the shore of Lake Sammamish. Whenever one of us kids got sick or needed a checkup, we went to see the same pediatrician that we had always seen. We would all pile into my dad's 1941 Plymouth and head for the doctor's office on "pill hill" in Seattle (where all the large hospitals and medical clinics were concentrated). These trips were always memorable and filled with anticipation. To us kids, it seemed like a major expedition to go that far. Anything could happen.

It was so exciting to see all the things that were happening in the big city as we drove by. There were so many different people and tall, intriguing buildings all around to see and wonder about. In addition our doctor was always so nice to us. He gave us suckers and had a really cool fish tank in his office. We probably made that trip three or four times a year for 14 years.

Each time, without exception, we would get to a certain street and my father would slow down, point to it, and say, "Never go down that street! Never go down that street!"

He didn't tell us why, but I always remembered his words. As I got a little older I was told that it was where all the "bad" people were. Crooks, pickpockets, prostitutes, drug dealers, and mean and crazy people hung out there. The regular repetition of that warning stuck with me and I knew as long as I lived I would never go down that street!

Thirty years later, when I was making my transition into private practice and working part-time at the jail, I still needed more employment to make ends meet. I was lucky enough to be offered a job two days a week at one of Children's Hospital's satellite clinics. It was a prodigious opportunity and I jumped at the chance. I had never been to this facility before, so on my first day I left early with a map of the city and the address. I didn't want to be late. As I zeroed in on the location, I realized I was getting close to the area that my father had cautioned me about so many years before. Sure enough, the clinic was on that very street! The warning, "Never go down that street," rang through my memory banks as I slowly and reluctantly turned on to it. As I drove along, I laughed to myself at the absurdity, silliness, and superstition of my reluctance. But I still kept an eye open for anyone threatening to jump on my car at the stoplights or trying to assault me in the parking lot.

I felt better once I got inside the clinic and started to introduce myself. When I walked in I noticed that all the doctors were standing in one corner of the room talking, while all the dental assistants were grouped together in another area. Any smart dentist knows that the assistants are the ones who really keep the clinic running. They do all the hard work, constantly cleaning up, reorganizing, restocking vital supplies, keeping the schedule running smoothly, helping to calm the patients, and meeting the various demands of the doctor. The assistants would be my support team and link to the community. It was important to get to know them, to find out their likes and dislikes so we could effectively work together. I walked over to their group first and introduced myself. They seemed to acknowledge that I recognized them as the vital force in running this place. They received me warmly and before long we were laughing and telling stories. What a fun bunch of ladies they were.

As time went by, I became totally comfortable being in that neighborhood and driving down that street. One of the local soul food restaurants even named the "Doc Sandwich" in my honor because I was there so much and ordered it so often. I found out that most of the assistants were local residents who had grown up in this neighborhood. They were all friendly, kind, and professional people, just like anywhere else. We became great friends, but I was still too embarrassed to tell them the story of my preconceived, prejudiced fear about their home turf that I had fostered and hung on to out of ignorance since I was a child.

Then one day the subject came up about where I used to work. I told them I had spent 12 years working in the housing projects in West Seattle and still worked there one day a week.

When they heard that, they gasped collectively and said, "It's so dangerous there! There is so much crime in that area. Aren't you afraid that something bad will happen to you there? Be careful, you might get mugged or have your car stolen!"

I laughed inwardly and shrugged my shoulders. I told them I felt right at home there and had actually been born in that neighborhood.

When I walked away to finish my charts for the day, I overheard one of them say to the rest of the group, "Dr. Shinn is crazy! I would never go down into that part of town, would you?"

CHAPTER 8

Private Practice

GETTING STARTED

IN ORDER TO MAKE MY PRIVATE PRACTICE DREAMS come true, I was working six and a half days a week. Some days I would do children's dentistry in the morning, general dentistry in the afternoon, and oral surgery at night in three separate clinics. These were very busy days, but the one and a half days a week in my own office were a different story. I was starting from scratch in a town that already had plenty of dentists. I hung out my shingle, placed a small ad in the Yellow Pages, and waited for the phone to ring.

At first, I had no employees. I sat alone in the office reading the same magazines over and over until I started to doze off. Then I would walk around town for a while visiting the other shopkeepers and introducing myself. I tried to eat lunch in a different cafe or restaurant everyday to maximize my exposure to the public. In the afternoon I would read the magazines again and think of advertising schemes that might work for me. I knew that the best advertisement is word of mouth from satisfied customers. When I did have a patient or two, I gave them the best service possible. The rest of the time I just tried to stay awake.

The hinge on the front door needed lubrication and was very squeaky, but I liked it that way. It alerted me that the door was opening when I was in the back with a patient. I would instantly put on my receptionist's hat and greet the new person. At first, it happened so infrequently that the screech of the hinge or the sudden ringing of the phone would startle me out of an unintentional nap. I snapped awake with the excited anticipation of getting a new patient, but nine times out of ten it would be a salesperson, insurance agent, pest control, or the fire department on their rounds doing a safety check.

I offered all kinds of inducements to people to come in to see me: free movie tickets, cassette tapes, discounts, and dinners for two. I found that what people responded to best was honest communication and good service.

The community was growing and I slowly started getting busier and busier. I finally hired my first employee. She was my bookkeeper, billing and insurance clerk, and dental assistant. She was a great dental assistant but sadly, three months later, when I attempted to do my taxes for the first time, the columns just didn't add up right. She was honest and reliable but unknown to both of us she had dyslexia. The numbers in the procedure codes, the addresses, the patient and doctor IDs, the charges and the insurance codes were transposed and reversed. It was a monumental mess, but it turned out for the best. It took me six months to straighten things out but rectifying the matter forced me to learn all the business office systems inside out and backwards. I became an expert in an area that I previously knew nothing about. I also got to endure the anguish of dismissing my first employee and finding the appropriate community agency to help her with her disability.

They were both important steps in becoming a successful business owner.

The growth in the community suddenly mushroomed and so did our practice. I was finally able to eliminate all of my outside part-time jobs, we hired more personnel, Jerri became the office manager, and we were on our way to a whole new set of adventures.

GHOSTS

IN THE EARLY days of starting a private practice there are sometimes long periods between patients with not much to do. I like to amuse myself during these lulls so I'm always looking for something that's funny or a practical joke to play. One such day, the two dental assistants were busy cleaning and sorting instruments in the sterilization area. They were happily chatting while standing next to each other. Our office was set up with a pass-through hole in the wall so that x-ray films and instruments from the adjoining room could be efficiently handed into the darkroom or sterilization areas. This eliminated having to walk around so much. The rooms were small and not conducive to a lot of foot traffic.

I noticed that the pass-through hole just happened to be positioned at eye-level right behind and between the two heads of the conversing assistants. I decided I would sneak into the back room and do something to scare them. I knew that one of the assistants was afraid of dogs, but the other one was fairly new so I didn't know too much about her. I thought this would be a good time to find out more.

I held my fist in the shape of a claw, and slowly pushed it through the hole so that it would come out right between their faces. At the same time I was making a low growling sound that grew and grew in volume. All of a sudden they noticed the claw and the growling and they just lost it! They started screaming and jumping up and down. Each one was fueling the other's hysteria and the screaming got uncontrollable. They were beside themselves with panic, yelling and beating the air with waving arms. I was completely astounded, to say the least. I hadn't figured that this would cause such an intense reaction. I was concerned because I remembered scaring my sisters when I was younger and afterwards they didn't think it was very funny.

I quickly ran into the other room to calm them down and to tell them it was only me playing a joke. As I hurried around the corner of the wall toward them, I glanced into the waiting room. A patient was there! He was brand new to our fledgling practice and was sitting down filling out the health questionnaire. He was a very distinguished looking, middle-aged gentleman dressed in a suit. There was an air of sophistication and intelligence about him. Before I could get to the screaming girls, I observed that with a look of dread on his face he abruptly leaped from his chair and started crawling rapidly across the carpet on his hands and knees toward the front door. This all happened so quickly that I didn't fully process it until I had successfully quelled the turmoil in the sterilization room.

First impressions are important and I figured I had blown this one. I was afraid to see what had happened, so we all stayed quietly in the back room for a minute, leaving the receptionist up front to handle the fallout. When I finally peeked around the corner again, I was amazed to see that the man was sitting back in the same chair again but with a nervous look about him this time. I was sure that he had left the premises and for good reason. I was surprised and elated that he was still there.

Smiling, I walked out confidently, as if nothing at all out of the ordinary had just happened, and greeted him. He was very gracious and refined, so I was curious about his unceremonious crawling across the floor conduct that I had witnessed just moments before. I knew he was unaware that I had observed it, so the embarrassment factor was not an issue for him, just for me.

When we got back to the dental chair and he got all settled in, I read his new patient information form, and listed under "occupation" was written "paranormal investigator." He was a real live ghost buster! His extreme and peculiar reaction in the waiting room suddenly made sense and I started to laugh crazily on the inside. The poor man had probably thought he had stumbled into a hellish arena filled with ghosts, ghouls, and other supernatural entities. In a way he was right.

He turned out to be a wonderful person and gifted scholar. He told many hair-raising stories about hauntings and exorcisms and I always looked forward to his visits. I have to congratulate him for the courage it took just to stick around on that first day. Getting up the nerve to go to a new dentist is tough enough, even under normal circumstances. But these were abnormal, or should we say "paranormal." I never did mention or explain to him about the screaming. But after he got to know me better, I'm sure he figured out that there was a good reason for it.

THE FAMILY

SHORTLY AFTER BEGINNING my private practice, I received a call from a mother who was looking for a dentist for herself, husband, and four children. She explained that they were on welfare and that no other dentists would take them. I said, "Sure, come on in."

When they showed up a few days later I was mortified. All four children were completely out of control, running around the waiting room throwing toys, screaming at each other, and terrorizing the other patients. Their parents ignored them, except for an occasional, outrageous threat of bodily harm. They continually argued amongst themselves, sometimes sharply swatting each other, and cursed and picked at each other in loud abusive voices without regard for anyone else within hearing range. They were dirty, ragged, disheveled, and smelled bad. They seemed to be the epitome of the classic "dysfunctional family."

The children all had unusual dental anomalies that needed many follow-up visits and completely stretched my dental skills. They really needed care from a specialist but they were very poor and couldn't afford it. After they left, the entire office staff was disrupted and the waiting room was in shambles.

In order to minimize the chaos we decided to appoint them when no other patients would be there, so we set aside special blocks of time for them to come in. Half of the time they wouldn't show up, and we would sit there being unproductive because their car had broken down, or they had been evicted again, or their phone had been disconnected. When they were there it was a free-for-all! They would slap each other around while they were being treated, wander around in private areas, and barge in unannounced during a busy day, as if they owned the place, telling loud distasteful jokes and asking incessant questions about nothing important. Every time they left we had to fumigate the office with room deodorizer to keep from offending the next patients. Many times when we thought they were gone, they interrupted again, and I'd have to go out to the parking lot with my jumper cables to get their car started.

It got to the point when every time I saw their name on my

schedule I was filled with dread. But there was something endearing about them—some mysterious underlying quality that intrigued me. Despite the hassles and the fact that they never brushed their teeth or followed any of our other advice, I wanted to help them. I hoped that something could help bring them out of their predicament and make their lives a bit easier.

Many of their fillings had to be redone because of the abnormal character of their enamel and they always had new cavities. It was exasperating. Several times I threatened to give up and banish them from my practice. I was tired of the failures, disappointments, and general mayhem. Finally, the deciding factor happened toward the end of that year.

A large envelope arrived for me with their name on it. I was immediately seized with a feeling of illness, knowing that it contained yet another unpleasant revelation. I was afraid to find out what. I summoned the courage and slowly opened it. Out popped the biggest and most expensive, beautiful, white lace Christmas card I have ever received. Inside, next to a smudgy fingerprint was scrawled, "THANKS."

I felt very warm inside and knew that somehow they appreciated me. I still see them, and not much else has changed, except now I appreciate them too.

PERFECTION

MOST DENTISTS HAVE certain types of patients that we are uncomfortable working with. For some it is children, for others it may be senior citizens, their mother-in-law, another dentist, or an attorney. For me, it used to be high society, middle aged, uptight women who expected perfection and who had no sense of humor. Getting a drop of water, or even worse some slobber on their perfectly made-up faces was unthinkable, not to mention doing anything to muss up one strand of their perfectly arranged hair. Just lying them back in the chair was an ordeal for me because I could see the flat spot developing on their hairdo where their head pressed against the pillow.

One day a woman who fit this description came in for a root canal. She was very nervous about it. She had never had one before and had heard all the classic horror stories and erroneous myths about how terrible root canals were. She also insisted on inspecting the instruments, the chair, and the general office environment to make sure they were clean and tidy. After she was satisfied that everything was just perfect, I explained the procedure to her and we started the work. I was already nervous because of her suspicious scrutiny, and when my usual humorous wit and charm didn't illicit any favorable response from her except a blank stare, I got more uptight. Our personalities just seemed to clash so I just silently did my work.

At that point in my career I allowed three appointments to complete a root canal filling on a molar, and I started to dread the thought of spending that much intense emotional time with this lady. She sat rigid and quiet in the chair and occasionally glared at us if she was jostled or we made too much noise with the suction. I resolved to do the best job I could and get it over with quickly.

When the third and final appointment arrived I was happy. So far the treatment was proceeding well. This was the appointment when we would fill up the root canals and then be finished. I tried a few attempts to lighten up the atmosphere, but she preferred to keep it very cool and professional. I'm sure she was very uncomfortable being so far out of her element. I don't think I quite matched her picture of what the well-heeled dental professional should be like. I worked mostly with children so I dressed casually and goofed around a lot. We were geared to be open and laid back. Nevertheless, I still wanted to do a good job for her and make a positive impression at the same time. I think she would have preferred more privacy and starch, but she had been referred to me by her friend who gave me a good recommendation so I think she felt obligated to see it through.

I explained to her that we would fill the hollow spaces inside the roots with a material called Gutta Percha. It was a natural occurring sap-like substance that oozed out of certain trees in Southeast Asia and it was the consistency of a rubberized gum. We would heat it up so that it would flow evenly and while it was still warm, pack it into the tooth so it would seal up all the little internal nooks and crannies. I informed her that the process of heating it caused an odd rubber-like smell, sort of like someone was burning car tires in her neighborhood, and not to be alarmed by it. It was just part of the sophisticated technology of today's dentistry. She glared coldly at me and nodded that she reluctantly understood.

As I put her back in the chair, I noticed that today she was especially well groomed. Her nails and makeup and clothes were perfect and her hair was all poofed up with extra hair spray. She was going to a luncheon right after her appointment and was in a hurry. I started feeling nervous all over again.

We used a mobile cart to hold all the dental instruments and it was positioned directly behind the head of our prim and proper patient. We were using plenty of alcohol soaked gauze sponges to wipe and sterilize the instruments and our heat source was an alcohol-burning torch. We were passing the Gutta Percha and the instrument tips through the open flame and placing the warm material in her tooth. Sure enough, it really smelled like a smoldering inner tube, but she sat absolutely still, looking straight ahead.

Unexpectantly, by mistake, an alcohol sponge got snagged on the opposite end of my instrument and I dragged it through the flame. It immediately turned into a little bluish fireball and it fell down on the instrument tray, lighting the paper liner on fire. I quickly attempted to smother it with my gloved hand but the heat instantly melted the latex onto my skin and scorched me painfully. I instantly recoiled like a cat coming off of a hot tin roof. Within seconds the fire spread to the pile of alcohol gauze and we had a flame burning eighteen inches high and a foot behind the patient's extremely flammable head. There was no smoke, but the ashes from the paper were going up with the heat and starting to slowly drift back down like black snow. The dental assistant was shocked but remained calm and quiet and frozen in place. The patient was totally unaware that there was anything amiss.

It was unbelievable! I remember one detached moment when time seemed to stand still and I appeared to be viewing the whole event from afar. I saw the unmistakable conclusion that in seconds the fire would ignite the patient's hair! The moving pictures of that scene playing itself out in my mind were terrible to behold. I snapped out of it and quickly rolled the cart back away from the lady's combustible coiffure. When I turned around I saw that my 12-year-old son Joe was standing in the doorway watching. He had come to wait at the office after school. Without speaking a word, I was able to communicate to him through my frantic eyes. I picked up the burning plastic tray and silently tossed it to him. He caught it, and in one continuous motion put it in the sink, turned the water on, and doused the flames! He then nonchalantly walked out with a smug smile on his face.

The patient was oblivious to the near tragedy and continued lying there in her corpse-like state. I apologized for the intensity of the heat and the annoying acrid odor and told her we were almost done. The x-ray revealed that we had achieved a perfect result on the root canal filling. The patient was relieved that were we finally finished and spent a while readjusting her hair in the mirror before she left. We were all thankful that she even had hair at this point.

When the front door closed behind her, the floodgates of released tension opened up and we just sat there laughing, congratulating each other, and giving thanks. In the background we noticed that Elvis was on the radio singing, "A hunk a hunk of burning love." It was too bizarre and yet it was just perfect!

CHAPTER 9

Dental Anomalies

STUCK!

ONE DAY A MAN BURST THROUGH THE FRONT DOOR OF the clinic in a panic! He was frantically pointing at his mouth and mumbling incoherently. He kept repeating the same frenzied nonsense over and over again but nobody could understand him. Finally someone gave him a piece of paper so he could write down what he was attempting to say.

He had been working on a craft project at home and was gluing some pieces together with super glue. He took the cap off of the tube with his teeth and some glue squirted out, instantly bonding his jaws tightly together. He was unusually disturbed by his situation and was exceedingly agitated and irrational about his future. He seemed convinced that it was a permanent condition that would shortly prove to be fatal! We managed to calm him down a little bit and reassured him that everything would be all right.

When I examined him I realized that since the glue was

clear, I couldn't see where he was stuck together. His teeth were cemented so snugly that using the drill was impossible because it would cut away all the adjacent enamel. Besides, I would be just randomly guessing where to start. He saw the look of concern on my face and started to get animated again. I decided the best way to solve this was to use a wooden mallet and a miniature chisel, starting at one side and working my way around, systematically chiseling in between each tooth until all the invisible adhesive was split apart.

I got his permission, but as I proceeded with my plan I noticed that his facial expressions fluctuated between surprise and sheer terror with each rap of the hammer. I was about half way around and nothing positive seemed to be happening but I continued on this route since this was the only idea I had. Suddenly, with one whack, his mouth snapped open and out flowed a continuous stream of excited conversation of relief and gratitude. He had been convinced that he was doomed, never to eat or speak again, and that his death was imminent from his mistake.

He was so excited to be freed up that he started telling us his whole life story which evidently had been flashing before him and was still very fresh in his mind. He was a real talker, and chattered on and on about everything under the sun. He wouldn't shut up, and spoke so rapidly that we couldn't keep up with his dizzying dialogue. He was as difficult to understand now as when he first walked in with his self-imposed "lock-jaw!"

After thanking us for the thirtieth time, he headed for the exit. We were all relieved that the problem had been solved. Using his mouth was obviously very important to him. As he walked out of the door, still happily jabbering away, I reminded him that his teeth were very useful as tools for chewing, but not for doing craft projects.

UNSTUCK!

A DISTRAUGHT MOTHER called the office one afternoon about her daughter. They needed to come in right away! She had had an accident at home and something was painfully wedged in her teeth. When they walked through the front door the problem became obvious and ludicrous. Hanging from her mouth was a nylon rain jacket. She was in a hurry to go to a soccer practice and to save time she quickly pulled the coat on over her head instead of unzipping it first. In her haste, the zipper tab jammed in between her two front teeth. No amount of pulling or prying at home would free it. Now the tearful young girl was beside herself with fear, embarrassment and discomfort.

My training in oral surgery had prepared me for deftly removing impacted wisdom teeth and broken off root tips, but not raincoats and zippers. Her mother had already tried to cut the zipper away from the surrounding material but gave up at the protest of her daughter. Now we had a shredded jacket, a bruised ego, and a highly unusual dental problem.

I anesthetized the area and with a surprising amount of difficulty finally got the zipper unstuck. The disposition of the girl brightened up considerably then, but she was still upset with her mother for ruining her coat. She made me promise not to tell any of her friends what had happened to her soccer team warm-up jacket.

I've had problems with stuck zippers before. Some were harder than others to resolve, but this one is perhaps the most memorable. Besides, it gives me one more reason why I don't like coats.

A NATURAL REMEDY

MEETING NEW PATIENTS is always an occasion for delight and excitement. There are so many unique and interesting things that people can share with you. Extraordinary things that you've never heard about before can be quite commonplace to them.

One such case involved a young woman from the Philippines. She had just moved to the States and needed a dental examination. At first I only saw her from a distance, but I noticed that she was stunningly beautiful, with smooth brown skin and a vivacious smile. Something seemed a little odd about her teeth but it didn't register what it was until I got a closer look.

When I sat down to do the exam I saw that she had something protruding from the back sides of her two upper front teeth. They were like strands of shredded straw sticking down about 1/4 inch below the front edges of her teeth. These flimsy, fibrous wads were poking out from holes that were cut into the backs of her teeth. I had never seen anything like this before and I tried to disguise my astonishment. She smiled proudly when I asked her what they were.

She explained that when she was younger she had fallen and injured her front teeth which subsequently became abscessed. The local dentist performed root canal therapy on them in order to save them, and used tiny bamboo sticks as the filling material! This treatment had been completed seven years before. I was startled at this revelation and marveled that it was actually working. The x-rays showed normal healing. There was no pain or infection and she was functioning normally.

Root canals were supposed to be performed under the strictest sterile conditions to prevent rejection and to insure proper healing. The bamboo was working perfectly so far, but it flew in the face of what I knew to be suitable for long-term success. Besides, the two twigs hanging down in front detracted from her beautiful smile and probably snagged lots of food on its way in.

I explained to her that there was another way to fix her teeth and she agreed to go ahead with it. Several appointments later we finished the "new" method of root canal therapy. She had been extremely proud and happy before, just to have kept her front teeth, protruding sticks and all. But now she was beaming with delight, never realizing that such a perfect smile was possible. Both she and I were exceptionally pleased with our accomplishment.

I never saw her again. It was one of those brief, magical encounters with people that make life so rich and rewarding. I helped make her smile and her smile made my day.

FIX THIS!

MY ASSISTANT TOLD me that a man was coming in on short notice because of an emergency dental problem. When he arrived I observed from the next room that he was in his late 30's, good looking and well groomed, and wearing an expensive suit. I figured he was a professional man, either a company executive, a highly successful salesperson, a lawyer, or a physician.

When I eventually got over to him we chatted pleasantly for a short while before getting down to business. He was articulate and interesting, and calmly answered my small talk questions. I finally asked him the nature of his dental problem and how I could help him. (I had already looked at his x-rays and there were no obvious problems visible.) His demeanor suddenly changed into a somewhat demented mode. His body became rigid and a wild-eyed expression overtook his face.

He aggressively reached into his mouth with his left hand and grabbed his lower front tooth (the lower right lateral incisor). He started wiggling and jerking at it violently as his face turned bright red. Before I could respond, his hand popped up and he pulled that tooth right out of its socket! He threw the tooth on the floor and with a grimace that showed all his teeth, he pointed to the bleeding hole where the tooth had just been and calmly said, "Doc, I need you to fix this gap!"

I had never seen anything so strange in all my years! I was completely shocked, but I figured that the guy was crazy so I held all my emotions in check and coolly reacted, "Okay, sure, no problem."

As far as I could tell there was nothing wrong with the tooth to begin with. How he took it out like that I'll never know. All I thought at the time was to just play along and don't upset the man. If he could do that with a tooth I could only imagine what he could do to my face! I offered to re-implant the tooth, knowing that it would probably "take" since it had only been out a minute or so. But he didn't want to bother with the requisite root canal treatment or charge. He was adamant that he didn't want that tooth back in there. He just wanted me to fix the "gap," and he wanted it fixed now, once and for all. He was in a hurry to get to an important meeting!

To save time I decided to use the original tooth instead of making a new one from scratch since it fit the existing "gap" perfectly. I picked up the tooth and cut off the root so that only the crown was left just flush to the gum line. I cleaned it all out and sealed it, then bonded it back in place where it belonged, to its neighbors on either side. The patient sat totally still and was seemingly relaxed for the 45-minute procedure.

Meanwhile, I was silently lecturing to myself about how sure I was that I had gotten myself into the wrong profession.

When I finished, he looked at it briefly in the mirror and appeared to be genuinely thrilled with the results. He happily replied, "No more gap."

He thanked me sincerely, gave me a hearty and robust handshake, and left with a big smile on his face after paying me in cash double what I had charged.

I'll never forget the strangeness of that event. I enjoy unusual experiences and relish encounters with new people and the unknown, but this one was way too far past the edge. Our emergency screening protocol has become much more stringent since that day.

POWER FAILURE

I HAD PRACTICED for twenty years and the electricity had never failed while I was working on a patient. I always wondered what I would do if the power went out when I was halfway through a procedure and still needed to fill the tooth up. One day when I least expected it, it happened! I was working on a softspoken and warmhearted man who had been my patient for several years. His entire family had been coming to see me for quite a while and they were some of the most pleasant folks in my practice.

I had just finished getting him numb and was about to start drilling when—wham!

Everything went as dead as his lip. No lights, no water, nothing. (Unknown to us, a car had crashed into a power pole several blocks away knocking out the electricity for the whole area.) We waited for a while to see if the power would come back on but it didn't. He graciously accepted my sincere apology and made another appointment to return for his filling.

Several weeks later he was back and we started over again. While he was being anesthetized and during the drilling I was joking about the oddity of the previous occurrence, particularly since this day an unusually stormy wind was blowing. I was kidding about the odds of it happening again when during one of our guffaws, the lights suddenly flickered and went out. The laughter quickly turned to chagrin.

The power didn't come back on, so using a flashlight, we filled the unfinished cavity with some self-drying, temporary cement. It was unbelievable that this incredible coincidence had occurred with the same man. It was unexplainable and unintentional, but it was nevertheless embarrassing and somewhat exasperating. I'm sure it was a real hassle for him to keep missing work and continually get numb with no progress being made. But he cordially took it in stride and just shrugged it off.

He returned about two weeks later for round three on the same tooth. We started with the jokes again but proceeded more cautiously this time, standing in the hall, and then slowly making our way to the dental chair. We wanted to give every chance for the unthinkable to happen again before we started the procedure. But it was a fine sunny day with calm weather and blue skies. No hint of any impending doom.

He had just begun to sit down when the lights blinked off and on not once, but twice. It was inexplicable! We looked at each other with squinted eyes wondering which of us possessed the paranormal ability to do this magic.

I wanted to believe that he was at fault. Maybe he had previously been struck by lightning or some other freak accident had turned him into a walking human dynamo. Maybe it was some otherworldly, synergistic disturbance that only manifested itself when the two of us got too close to a dental unit at the same time. I don't know, but I swear it is the truth. Fortunately, after the two quick lapses the power stayed on and we were able to complete the restoration of his tooth. Afterwards, we marveled at the sheer improbability of these coincidental electrical disturbances.

When he returned for his biannual checkup six months later, we waited cautiously for more electrifying malevolence to befall us but nothing happened. The curse was over.

Later that same day, after he had left and we had forgotten all about it—bam! the power went out for about one hour. The official explanation was that a transformer had overloaded and blown out. I'm not so sure what to believe. We'll see what happens at his next appointment.

CRITTERS

SOMETIMES THE PATIENTS that we treat don't all share the same level of lifestyles and living conditions as we do. They may not believe in deodorants or clean clothes, or have the same grooming guidelines and personal hygiene traits that I have. Sometimes when you are working on them you realize they have fleas. You can see them crawling around and sometimes they jump off of the patient onto the doctor. I'm not that bothered by fleas because I have animals at home, too, and I know what can happen. But one day I was working on a patient who fit the flea-carrying profile. I had already seen several of them jumping about.

I became aware that one of them had somehow gotten under my mask and was crawling around in my mustache feeling right at home. I was at a critical point of the procedure and couldn't interrupt the process without having to start it all over again, so I just tried to put up with it. The tickling caused by the active little bug started to get to me, though. I tried to scratch at it with my shoulder and blow air up at it with my lower lip without any success. I struggled to maintain my composure, but I finally got to my breaking point when it started to wander up into my nose. I casually reached up and took off my mask. The curious little flea immediately leaped off of me. My flabbergasted assistant and I watched it fly through the air, as if in slow motion, and land in the patient's mouth!

We froze for an interminable second or so and watched in disbelief as the energetic bug started swimming around in the pool of moisture under the patient's tongue. The patient was listening to music on headphones and was gazing off somewhere else totally distracted, so he didn't notice what had happened. We grabbed the suction and "whoosh," it disappeared into another world. I can still picture the disturbing sight of that crazy flea trying to do the dog paddle in that puddle of drool. It looked so creepy and abnormal. Never again, I pray!

I have a great bird feeder outside the office that is in full view from all the windows. It was given to me as an office warming gift by the wonderful and talented contractor who built my current office. The patients love watching all the birds who congregate there to eat and socialize. So many birds know about the free food that I regularly have to replenish the feeder with fresh seeds. I enjoy doing this. It gives me an opportunity for a quick break and a chance to commune with nature.

One classic, wet and misty Northwest morning it was time for yet another refill. The bushes were dripping with raindrops so I tried not to brush against them too much as I slid my way between them. Five minutes later the mission was accomplished. I returned to the office and walked in to greet my next patient who was already waiting for me with the assistant.

As soon as I entered the room, both women immediately cringed backwards, repelling flat up against the walls in a reflex action of repulsion. Speechless, they both pointed at me with wide eyes. I looked down, and there, right in the middle of my chest was a medium-sized, slimy slug slithering its way up my shirt. I gently picked it off and cheerfully returned him to the dank, damp world outside.

For me, it was a memorable brush with Mother Nature. I was entertained by what had happened outside my office on my break, but I knew that for at least that day, I had lost all my credibility inside the office.

Sometimes on real hot days we leave the windows open a bit to increase the air circulation. It is amazing to see how fast a treatment room will clear out when a large bumble bee flies in and starts buzzing around. The adults leave immediately. The kids usually stay around a little longer though, especially when I explain to them that even bees sometimes get toothaches, and have to come in the back door to see the dentist.

In the late '80s there was a sudden insurgence of concern about the spread of disease in the dental office, especially with regard to AIDS. Newer and tougher federal (OSHA) guide-lines and requirements were established and compliance was mandatory. This new mandate left many health care facilities scrambling to meet the code. This was especially true as it related to the use of barrier protection. Suddenly everybody was ordering rubber surgical gloves like never before. The supply couldn't keep up with the increased demand and a worldwide shortage of latex gloves developed.

We stated getting low on gloves. Our usual suppliers were out and backordered for months, so we had to get creative. We called latex brokers all over the country and finally located a man who said he had a line on some gloves from Malaysia. We ordered a case, 24 boxes of 100 gloves each. Meanwhile, we had enough vinyl gloves to tide us over, but they didn't fit well and were very difficult to put on. We were relieved when our huge box of new gloves finally arrived.

They had a nice texture and seemed to fit well but I noticed some annoying bumps in several of them while I was using them. I didn't think too much about it initially and just simply discarded the lumpy ones for alternates at first. It was typical to have some "processing blebs" in a certain percentage of latex gloves when the molten rubber bubbled and then globbed back together to form a miniature ball. It could be a problem, though, if this little clump appeared on the end of a finger because it disturbed my sense of touch and dexterity.

After several days of getting more that my share of these stupid little nodules, I got one glove that had four of them in it. Somewhat perturbed at their undesirable frequency, I curiously examined them more closely. To my amazement, I saw that contained inside each tiny globule was a small, green mosquito! I laughed at first but then realized that my whole case was contaminated with entombed insects, probably buried alive.

I visualized the latex processing center where they had come from. Somewhere out in the vast jungle of Malaysia was a huge open vat surrounded by many excited, sweaty, local people. They each held crude, canoe-like paddles, slowly stirring the liquefied sap from the numerous rubber trees in their forest. Suddenly, their economy was booming. The precious pitch had become exceedingly valuable and was being delivered by the hundreds of gallons to be slowly heated and stirred until it was just the right consistency for cooling into the forms of human hands. Large swarms of flying insects would occasionally venture near the large pool in the vat and mistake it for a fine breeding pond. They would settle in only to be hopelessly trapped. Next stop, the United States. No visa, no passport, no immigration, no inspection.

We called the broker when we realized what had happened. He apologized profusely, gave us our money back, and offered to replace the whole case with a new one. We politely declined and found a new source. It all turned out okay, was comical in fact, but it made me wonder. How big would a ball be that was made from all the latex gloves that are discarded in just a single day in this country? How high would it bounce? Who could catch it?

CHAPTER 10

Embarrassing Moments

I ALWAYS LIKE TO MAKE SURE THAT THE PATIENT'S FACE is nice and tidy before they leave the office. We are always careful to clean off any dust, toothpaste, or other debris that would be embarrassing to them in public. It is bad enough to be numb and feel like your face is twice as big as normal and paralyzed on one side.

I had just finished a lengthy procedure on a real pleasant lady. It was the first time I had done any treatment on her and I wanted it to be just right. She was prim and proper and fairly quiet and shy.

Just before she was about to get up to leave I noticed that there was an eyelash lying on her cheek. Wanting to remove it to complete the cleanup, I lightly grabbed it with my fingers and lifted but it slipped out of my grip. The same thing happened when I tried a second time. I was worried that she would notice my fumbling fingers so the third time I really pinched it hard and moved quickly. So my surprise, and her shock, it went "pop" and she jumped with a wince. Turns out it was an aberrant facial hair growing out of her cheek. I remained silent, I didn't know what to say. I just pretended it was part of the service. I don't remember seeing her again after that appointment.

One day I was working on an attractive, middle-aged woman. I needed to do a small amount of drilling on one of her teeth. I told her that if anything hurt or was uncomfortable she should raise her left hand and I would immediately stop. She said she understood and I proceeded. As soon as the drill touched her tooth both of her hands flew up and she grabbed her breasts. I stopped and asked if the drilling was painful. She said, "No, the vibration tickles me so much I have to hold on to them!"

I tried to cover my embarrassment by blurting out, "How am I going to know if something hurts if both your hands are busy and you can't raise one?"

She responded by saying, "Well, Doc, you've got one hand free. You hold one and I'll hold the other."

I wasn't quite sure what she was referring to, but it was a curious choice of words that left me speechless! An awkward silence ensued. Fortunately, my trusty assistant was there to buffer the situation and we all laughed it off.

Having a new family come into your practice is always an exciting time, especially when there are lots of happy children to interact with. One of my favorite families got off to a rough start. The first day I saw them I knew they were special. The five youngsters were adorable and the busy mom was patient and attentive. It was somewhat hectic getting all their check-ups finished and keeping track of and explaining everything, but it was fun. An hour or so after they left, the mother called back and asked if she had left her purse. Sure enough, we found it under one of the chairs. In the confusion of rounding up all the children and their coats and things she had just forgotten it.

She told me that because of the long drive back she couldn't pick it up until the next morning. I promised her I would take good care of it and keep it in a safe place until then. That evening just before leaving, I tucked the purse inside a big drawer underneath the reception desk. I made a mental note to come in extra early to meet the lady in the morning, double locked the door behind me, and went home.

Bright and early, as promised, I returned and shortly thereafter the lady arrived to retrieve her purse. She was very friendly, lighthearted, and easy to talk to and we started joking around a bit at first. When I finally opened the drawer to get her purse, I was dumbfounded to see that it was not there. I was the last to leave and the first to return and this wasn't making any sense. I quickly checked a couple of other drawers in the immediate area, but still no purse.

The woman was convinced that I was still joking with her when I told her the purse wasn't there anymore. She continued to play along in that vein, believing I was playing a cheap practical joke. Meanwhile, I was going crazy on the inside. I was totally confused and flustered and had no rational explanation for what had happened. She kept saying in a sweet and tolerant tone, "Oh, come on now, I know it's here, you can give it to me now."

Finally, after at least five or six lame excuses and empty explanations, she accepted the fact that for unknown reasons she wouldn't be getting her purse today after all. She remained calm and congenial but hung her head and slowly walked out of the office. I felt terrible and useless. "What the heck was gong on?!" I thought to myself.

About half an hour later, a staff person from the oral surgeon's office next door came over to report that they had been robbed overnight and wondered if our office was all right. We looked around and found that one of our windows had been opened and a few dirty footprints were leading into the room from the rhododendron bushes outside. We theorized that the intruder had used our office to gain access to the entire building and on the way through had found and taken the purse without disturbing anything else.

Relieved that I had found the answer to the mystery I called the lady back and told her what had transpired. I still don't think she fully believed me 100 percent, but that was my story. Several days later a man on a nature walk found her empty purse in the woods nearby and brought it to our office for identification. When I returned it, I could tell that the nice woman finally realized that I hadn't been kidding her all along. We were both relieved. She only lost about $3.00. This unusual experience created a mutual bond of trust and the opportunity to form a positive relationship with her and her entire family that continues to this day.

Here is a piece of advice for dental personnel that I learned the hard way: don't lean on top of the chair with your arm when the patient is about to sit up. Sometimes their hair is caught under your arm and it really hurts them when they move. Other times you discover that your patient was wearing a wig!

SWIMMING WITH DOLPHINS

IN 1995, THE annual National Dental Convention was held in Las Vegas. Every year it is in a different city that has some tourist appeal and thousands of dental professionals attend from all over North America. During the three to four day event there are continuing education lectures, workshops, new product reviews, and displays and demonstrations of all the latest equipment. There are hundreds of booths with venders selling everything from apple-flavored cough syrup to zebra striped dental chairs.

They all have free samples of paraphernalia to give away that act as inducements to visit their booth. Consequently, there is always a mad rush as thousands of teeming attendees scurry from booth to booth, collecting as many free merchandise samples and literature handouts as possible. They fervently fill up their free plastic shopping bags that brightly display in bold letters some type of advertising with pounds of souvenirs that most of them will never look at again. It is a huge, whirling, circus-like spectacle that all centers around teeth.

In the evenings after the grab fest there are parties everywhere. The various alumni groups from different schools get together and socialize, remembering the good ol' days back at their alma mater. It was for one of these receptions for the University of Washington that I was honored to be asked to play the piano for background musical entertainment.

I was very excited about this opportunity because I knew that one day I could truthfully tell my grandkids, "I played the piano in Vegas at the Aladdin Hotel." Besides, I had never been to Las Vegas before. I wanted to see all the fancy hotels and the surrounding canyon lands in the four corners states.

One of my regular patients travels to Las Vegas frequently to gamble and have fun. When she heard I was going, she was eager to tell us about all the sights that Jerri and I should see while visiting. I was most intrigued when she mentioned, "You can even swim with dolphins at the Mirage Hotel."

I had always wanted to do that and was elated to know about it. It became the number one priority after arriving and picking up the rental car.

As we drove down the strip looking for the Mirage, I was amazed at how gigantic the hotel complexes were. Together with the rooms, casinos, restaurants, fancy display areas out front, and parking garages in the back, they covered several city blocks each. We found the Mirage and after several illegal U-turns we parked in the garage way in the back. I was so excited to swim with those dolphins that I felt like a little kid on the inside. I hurriedly changed into my swimming trunks and we set off to find the dolphin enclosure.

I was so energized that I was skipping, prancing, and strutting all at the same time while clutching my little towel and flapping the flip-flops on my feet as we wound our way through the maze of parking levels, hallways, elevators, and crowded casinos following the pointing arrows that said, "Dolphins."

People were everywhere. I noticed that those who weren't intently staring at the screens on their slot machines were staring at me. I figured it was because my bleach-white Seattle skin that hadn't seen the sun for over eight months was shocking to them. I didn't care. I was grinning from ear to ear, elated and eager for my exciting encounter with Flipper's friends.

After what seemed like a half a mile of walking, we finally arrived at the front of the building where the dolphin pools were located. I waltzed right up to the ticket window. The girl inside looked at me with a wide-eyed, surprised expression on her face and nervously asked, "May I help you?"

I proudly stated, "I'm here to swim with dolphins!"

With a hint of pity in her voice she responded, "Sir, we don't even let our trainers swim with the dolphins."

I was dumbfounded, dazed, demolished, devastated, and dejected. I slunk to the back of the line and moped glumly as

I leaned up against the stucco wall. For a while I considered leaving right away for home, but my mature adult brain started to reappear in my consciousness and we decided to stay and visit the dolphin attraction since we were already there. It was inspiring to view their sleek, muscled bodies up close, but it just wasn't the same as swimming with them.

When we left to return to our car, I lumbered back through the bustling casinos with my head hung low, deflated by disappointment and subdued by embarrassment. It was now apparent that, except for the showgirls on stage, I was the only one in there with no clothes on. I stuck out like a sore thumb at a hitch hiker's rally. No wonder there were so many stares. I remember the ride back up in the elevator. I stood there naked, sheepishly looking at the floor while all the other well-dressed people filed in. They all made a point of not getting too close to me. They figured that somehow I was lost but they would never know to what degree.

A FALL FROM GRACE

DURING MY TRANSITION from public health dentistry to private practice, I was offered a job as a clinical instructor at one of the regional dental assistant schools. The women in charge of the instructional program were friendly, intelligent, and totally committed to maintaining a top-notch, quality program that produced highly skilled graduates who were imminently qualified for the job market and completely professional.

They ran a very tight ship! So tight that the atmosphere seemed solemn and stifling. The poor students were afraid of their own shadows. Everyone was so serious and tense. Lightheartedness and laughter and talking above a whisper were considered substandard activities that would alter your grade point in a downward direction. The fear of having your ego trashed for making the simplest mistake was prevalent and oppressive.

Now, I'm a fun-loving guy, but I found my own self getting caught up in the formal atmosphere to a certain degree, especially after some initial attempts at being amusing got me silent looks of disdain from the other instructors. Not wanting to cause problems, I resigned myself to the situation. Besides, I was there to perform procedures on patients so that the dental assistant students could get some real-life, hands-on experience in order to perfect their skills. I could still carry on genuine, one-on-one, softly spoken conversations with them. During these non-disruptive chats, I encouraged them and sympathized with their circumstances. It was sort of like being a Boy Friday to a bunch of Amazons and their captive daughters.

The clinical area decor was stylish, with thick carpeting accented by polished linoleum flooring surrounding the bases of all the dental units. The chairs were set up in long rows to make it easy for the instructors to see what was going on in each location. I really liked the smooth floors because they made it easy and fun to scoot around quickly in all directions on my stool.

One day I was working in my usual spot at the far end of one of the rows. The dental assistant student assigned to me was flustered and more uptight than usual because we hadn't started on time. Our patient was a sweet, well-mannered lady who had been delayed in traffic and arrived 15 minutes late. She was embarrassed about the time, but I reassured her that we would still be able to complete her appointment. Just before starting, I glanced down the long row and saw that all the other students were busily leaning over, nervously concentrating on their patients. Drill in hand, I quickly scooted backwards to stretch once before assuming my posture as a dentist.

I rolled too far, too fast and the back wheels of my chair hit the ridge where the carpet met the smooth surface. I was immediately flipped backwards onto the hard floor. I landed with a loud crash right on the speed control pedal for the drill. There I lay, surprised and bewildered, still holding onto the drill which was now screaming and whining out of control, at an extremely loud and ear-piercing pitch, maxed out at its top speed of 400 thousand rpm!

The violent disruption stunned everyone in the whole room. They glared at me with fear and revulsion in their eyes, afraid that some awful retribution would fall on them because of this violation of clinic decorum.

I had trouble getting up at first and during my struggle, somebody started to snicker. Suddenly, like a dam bursting during a flash flood, months of tension and stress were released. Wave after wave of uncontrollable laugher poured forth. Tears streamed down their cheeks as they held their aching sides in hysterical fits of glee. I had accidentally pro-vided them with the perfect excuse to just let it all hang loose for a moment.

After a few mirthful minutes, they all calmed down and went back to work again. The atmosphere was still quiet and professional, but something had changed. Now the students' faces beamed with big bright smiles. Everything was okay now because I had unwittingly taken the fall for them. Yes, I was embarrassed but I was lucky because when I fell, I landed in a position that made a positive difference. It was definitely a unique and desirable position to be in.

PERILS OF PETS

SHORTLY AFTER MOVING into the undeveloped wilderness east of Seattle to be closer to my office in Issaquah, Jerri landed a nurse's job at a very prestigious internal medicine clinic in Seattle. It was where all the area's dignitaries, aristocrats, and politicians went for medical care when they wanted top-notch service and anonymity. Jerri's boss was a highly refined and sophisticated lady doctor with impressive medical credentials. She had the reputation for being a very conservative, well-heeled, straight-laced, no nonsense, everything must be in its place kind of person.

She learned that our cat had just had kittens. They were Himalayan with long, luxurious cream-colored fur, light blue gentle eyes, and chocolate brown ears and paws. It was just the kind of cat she wanted to give to her seven-year-old daughter. She made an appointment to come over to our house with her daughter to get the pick of the litter.

We were a little nervous about this because our house wasn't fancy and we lived on a rough, pot-hole laden, dead-end gravel road surrounded by untamed woods. We knew it wasn't the big city type of lifestyle she was used to and Jerri's job security might be at stake if her picky boss didn't approve of our living conditions or the way we raised our cats. We spent a lot of uneasy energy tidying up the house. We dusted and vacuumed and put out decorative knickknacks here and there. We picked up all the extraneous papers and boxes, watered the plants, and swept off the porch.

Our kittens were being raised outside, so on the day of the visit we made sure they were well groomed and free of fleas. We even had a few drops of vanilla simmering in a pot of hot water on the stove to create a rich and soothing atmosphere. We decided it would be a good idea to put our big, friendly, and exuberant German Shepherd named Lucky in the garage so she wouldn't maul the doctor or knock her daughter over trying to sniff and lick them.

About half an hour before the designated visitation time, I went out to play with Lucky prior to her confinement with the cars. We were wrestling and rough-housing like members of a wild dog pack. I finally gained the advantage and using all my strength, held her down on the ground in a friendly submission hold. I heard a noise at the back screen door and turned my head to see what it was. Lucky sensed the momentary lack of my attention and immediately bounded up with full force. It was like the recoil of a giant compressed spring! The top of her hard bony head hit me square in the nose.

The sudden pain was terrible. All I could see were little fuzzy points of light dancing around in a black background. I struggled to stay coherent. The whole front of my face was numb and I quickly reached up to see how many teeth had been knocked out. I was surprised to feel that they were all still there, but that my nose wasn't. It was resting way over on my right cheek! I knew it was broken and needed to be reset. I had had my nose broken once before so I knew what to do. Before the numbness went away, I quickly grabbed my nose and gave it a sharp twist to the left and tried to mold it into place with my fingers. When I thought I had it pretty straight I buried my head in my hands and let the blood and the tears and the pain flow. Ten minutes later I heard, "Ding dong." The lady doctor and her daughter had arrived at the front door.

Jerri let them in and I peered at them through the window from the back step. I saw that they were dressed in nylons, pretty dresses and fancy shoes like they were on their way to a posh party. They were making small talk about how rustic and quiet and out of the way our place was.

Meanwhile, my pain had subsided to a level that allowed me to function again. I hurriedly wiped my face clean on my shirt tails, tucked my shirt in to my pants, and entered the house. I acted as if nothing had happened and like everything was normal. What I didn't know was that my nose was bright red and had already swollen up into an oversized, abnormal glob. There was still a small amount of blood on my chin and my eyes wouldn't stop tearing. When the lady doctor first saw me, she got a look of astonishment on her face that concerned me. Her startled eyes literally popped wide open for a second or two. I could tell she assumed that I was the grounds keeper or maintenance man on a coffee break. When Jerri introduced me as her husband, the look of astonishment turned to one of consternation and dismay.

Up to this point, Jerri had been busily engaged in conversation with them and hadn't yet looked directly at me. Then, suddenly, our eyes met and the expression on her face turned to silent stone. She was transfixed in place and time for a few seconds, before she looked away disbelieving and speechless.

The VIP's daughter was too distracted playing with the cute little kitties to notice that something was wrong with me, but her mother kept glancing at me curiously, mentally questioning, "What is with this guy?"

The fact that tears kept spontaneously welling up, and rolling down my cheeks, and that I was still wearing my dirty, trauma-stained shirt were working against me. I know the lady thought I was probably either a heavy-duty drug abuser, a big time bar brawler, or a freakish side show anomaly. Unfortunately, I had loser written all over my face and didn't even know it. Finally, Jerri asked me, "What happened to your face?"

I explained about the mishap with the dog but it was too little too late. Jerri's boss seemed somewhat ruffled by this encounter but her daughter was delighted with the cats so they stayed a while and played, politely ate some finger cookies, and drank some tea.

During the interval, I left the room and looked in the

mirror to see what the fuss was all about. Staring back at me was a misshapen man with wet swollen eyes and a large rosy crab apple in the middle of his face. At that point I became immediately concerned about Jerri's future employment with this doctor. I pretty much stayed out of sight after that. I only reappeared when the dignified lady and her daughter were choosing their pick from the litter before going home. By the way that she handled the baby cat I could tell that the lady was uncomfortable and nervous with it. She held it out away from her like it was a dirty diaper or a spoiled lunch or something.

As she shuffled down the walk to her car, the unthinkable happened. The little kitten, evidently upset by something, let fly with a sudden bout of loose bowels. The discharge dropped down and completely soiled the lady doctor's elegant left shoe and designer hosiery! Jerri rushed out with some wet paper towels to help clean it off, but it was a foul mess. The boss lady was visibly shaken and flustered. I knew that we would need to start looking for another source of income after that.

Surprisingly, the doctor graciously took the kitten home. It was such a joy to her daughter that the freakish episode at our house was dismissed. Fortunately, Jerri wasn't, and she kept her job. There was only one bad consequence to this day. Several weeks later, one of my upper front teeth started aching spontaneously. I recognized the classic symptoms. The blow from Lucky's head had done enough damage to kill the nerve in my tooth. I needed to go to the dentist for a root canal!

CHAPTER 11

A Dentist At The Dentist

CERTAIN SITUATIONS ALWAYS MAKE A DENTIST ESPECIALLY nervous. Some of the worst are treating your in-laws or malpractice attorneys. Another one, almost equally as bad, is when you are working on another dentist. I personally don't enjoy going to the dentist that much. But when I do go, I know that the dentist I'm visiting is way more tense about the appointment than I am.

TRICKS OF THE TRADE

MY DENTIST KNOWS that I know everything he is doing in my mouth by the sound of the drill, the type of medicaments being used, and the comments being made back and forth to the assistant. I like to use this to my advantage when I go in for my checkups. I know that it says right on the top of my chart in bright, bold, red letters, "This guy is a dentist, treat him with kid gloves!"

I routinely tell my dentist's assistant, "In my office the dental assistant always holds the patient's hand for comfort." I can usually succeed in convincing her that I expect the same treatment. When my dentist finally walks into the room, there I sit with one, sometimes two young ladies compliantly holding my hand, unable to get any of their other work done in the office. We always have a good laugh over this because the joke seems to work every time. I enjoy this type of tomfoolery because it acts as a stress breaker for me.

I don't know why I am so uneasy about going to the dentist, but as soon as the automatic chair starts reclining me upside down and backwards, I start feeling a little anxious. I feel like I have no control over what will happen to me or my body. It is similar to, but not quite as intense as being abducted by aliens, forced to lie inverted on a cold metal table with blinding bright lights shining in your face. All you can see when you look up are pairs of big eyes staring intently down at you from over the top of strange masks and plastic shields. Muffled voices are exhorting you to hold perfectly still while peculiar-looking sharp instruments are probing you. Every time I have this experience, I have immediate empathy for my own patients. I marvel at why people so readily volunteer for this, especially when they have to pay for it. I resolve to make my patients as comfortable as possible during their stay by minimizing their uneasiness and maximizing each individual's value and self-worth.

MEMORIES

I CAN STILL remember what it was like when I was a kid going to the dentist. In those days, the dentist stood on his feet all day and the patient sat almost upright in the chair. I recall being fascinated by the belt-driven mechanism of the old drill whirring away above my head. I liked to watch the belt, which was just a thick cotton cord, going round and round over the complex system of pulleys and springs. There was always at least one place on the cord that was fraying. It looked like a small white ball of fuzz. I enjoyed following it as it raced around, loop after loop. Every so often a small piece of fluff would tear away and come drifting down like an ill-propor- tioned snowflake. I loved it when that happened. I always hoped that the string would break so no more drilling could be done, but it never happened while I was there.

The worst part for me was when they clipped my bib on. I always believed that the chain that connected the bib clips together was hooked around the back side of the chair, tautly tethering me to the head rest. I was completely paranoid about moving because I didn't want to choke myself or tear the paper bib. Another unpleasant thing was trying to spit into the porcelain bowl that was next to the chair. There was a tube inside that squirted water around to wash it clean, but some- times it wasn't working. It was so dehumanizing trying to expectorate in there when one whole side of my face was numb. My lips wouldn't pucker or perform properly, permit- ting columns of drool to dribble unceremoniously down my chin. Fortunately, the dental assistant was there to help clean my face, but it was very embarrassing.

I learned a lot about being a dentist when I was a child because I spent so much time in the dentist's office getting my own teeth fixed. Every time I went in for a checkup I had more cavities. My dentist would lecture me about brushing better, which I admit I was not very responsible about. As part of my youthful independence streak, I would only pretend to brush my teeth to see if I could fool my parents and get away with something. I developed an elaborate scheme trying to trick Mom and Dad by standing in the bathroom, letting the water run loudly, getting my toothbrush wet, and spreading some toothpaste around. I spent way more time doing this than if I had just gone ahead and actually brushed my teeth. Even when I did brush my teeth I still seemed to get the same lecture and more cavities.

My elementary school was only a few blocks from the dentist's office, so when I had an appointment I would walk there afterwards. One day I was on my way down the sidewalk for yet another checkup. I was dreading the news about having more cavities when I realized with genuine concern that I hadn't brushed for several days. I really liked my dentist and didn't want to disappoint him further or receive another humiliating oral hygiene sermon. I had some leftover lunch money in my pocket, so I decided I would go to the local drug store, buy a toothbrush, and brush all the way to my appointment. I entered the store with the best of intentions and left carrying an ice cold can of cola. My taste buds had won out over my teeth. As I strolled along slurping my pop, I vigorously swished each mouthful in and out between my teeth before swallowing. I hoped that the surging action of the bubbling carbonation would have some cleansing effect.

As the dentist conducted his exam of my oral cavity, I readied myself for another dirty dental dissertation. What he said instead was, "Wow, your teeth are clean and spotless today! Good job, keep up the good work. Only two cavities this time."

Inwardly I felt so good that he was proud of me, and I felt smug that I had actually fooled an experienced professional. Using an eleven-year-old's mentality, I had accidentally stumbled on to the fact that the acidic nature of carbonated beverages will dissolve your teeth and everything on them if left in frequent or prolonged contact with them. (A fun experiment to do is to put a baby tooth in a glass of pop before going to bed at night. In the morning when you wake up the tooth will be gone, vanished, melted away.) I don't recommend that anyone brush or gargle with soda pop. You'll get more cavities than your dentist can shake a drill at. Use toothpaste, put it on your brush and force yourself to use it on your teeth at least twice a day. Floss regularly. I learned that taking care of your teeth does pay off. Don't try to do what I did because it will come back to haunt you! How's that for a stimulating oral hygiene lecture?

FIRST IMPRESSIONS

WHEN I WAS seven years old I had a huge gap between my two front teeth. It looked like the opening to a tunnel in a small-gauge model railroad setup. My parents decided it would be a good idea to close it orthodontically because it was frightening to look at. Before fitting the braces, the orthodontist had to make a plaster cast or model of my teeth. He tried to explain the procedure to me beforehand. A frosting-like goop in a metal tray would be wedged onto my teeth. It would slowly stiffen and set up, then at the right time he would remove it. The finished product would be a rock-hard, glossy white, portable plaster replica of my own teeth. He showed me someone else's models to illustrate. I was a little nervous about gagging on the goop but we proceeded. When he embedded the first tray of slimy goo onto my top teeth it smelled sweet but tasted like wet chalk. After a few moments of holding still,

I was slavering copiously like one of Pavlov's dogs, then I heard the phone ring. The nurse appeared and told the doctor that it was an important call for him. They reassured me they would be right back, and then they both walked away, leaving me alone.

I could feel the material starting to solidify around my teeth. I visualized it turning to impregnable stone just like I had seen on the example models. I could hear the doctor talking on the phone in the next room and the conversation kept dragging on and on. I fantasized with increasing dread that they had forgotten about me. By the time they got back to me, the stuff surrounding my teeth would be like concrete. It would be too late to comfortably remove the impression from my mouth without breaking off or pulling out numerous teeth in the process. They would have to chip it out with a mini-jackhammer, one piece at a time, to keep from injuring me, or call the fire department to help remove it.

I kept telling myself that they knew what they were doing, but my doubts were growing stronger every second. I sat there like a statue but I was panic-stricken on the inside! Finally, the orthodontist reappeared and I knew it was too late, but with one quick pop the tray came out slick as a whistle. No pain, no missing teeth, just a lot of wasted adrenaline on my part. The slop in the tray had turned into a slippery rubber-like mold. It was only the first part of the process. It never does get hard like the plaster that is poured into it later, but I didn't understand that. I learned complete communication of expectations is a key factor in helping your patients get comfortable with a procedure.

After I got my braces on, I was cautioned to be extra careful while playing and not to bump them, and not to chew sticky hard stuff that might bend or break the wires. Back in those days, braces consisted of a metal band that encircled each tooth. On the front of each band was a hook that the main wire was tied onto with a smaller ligature wire. It was cinched into place by twisting it tightly into a small knot. It was quite an impressive mouthful of metal hardware when fully installed.

One cold winter morning at recess I was standing on the ice of a large frozen puddle on the school grounds. I stood there minding my own business, warming my hands in my pockets, and watching the other kids slide back and forth. Suddenly, without warning, someone sliding out of control hit me from behind! Before I could get my hands free and catch myself, I fell down, hitting the ice face first. I instantly knew there was a problem. My tongue told me that everything in my mouth had been grossly rearranged and I tasted the warm, rusty flavor of fresh blood.

When my teacher saw me she almost fainted and immediately sent me to the nurse's station. Before long, I was at a dental specialist's office having my upper braces surgically removed from my gums. The blow from the fall caused all the bands on my teeth to slide up under my gums, out of sight. The orthodontist and my parents were pretty disappointed. They decided to wait until I was older and more responsible before doing any further therapy with braces. Fortunately, they had been on long enough to partially close the gap to be acceptable for an eight-year-old's grin.

When I was twelve years old and deemed adequately responsible, I started my second round of braces. After two years, everything came off without a hitch and I had a man-made, perfect, and pleasing smile. Three months later I had my infamous water skiing accident which totally rearranged my face and teeth again and seemed to point out that maybe I hadn't yet reached a satisfactory level of responsibility. From these traumatic circumstances I learned about accountability. I learned to keep my hands out of my pockets and I learned I would now be on my own financially for any future smile enhancement procedures. I also learned from the orthodontist that because of the severe trauma to the roots of my front teeth they could no longer withstand the forces of another round or braces. He said, "Within five years they will either be knocked out or fall out by themselves."

TRANCE-IN-DENTAL MEDICATION

TWENTY YEARS LATER I was a dentist and still had the same teeth I was born with. The front ones were a little crooked, but were still hanging in there. Unfortunately, all of them were chock full of fillings from my youth. Now that I had learned to be responsible, I was no longer getting cavities. Maybe it was because there were no more unfilled natural tooth surfaces to get cavities in. But as you get older, teeth tend to become more brittle and are prone to breaking when large fillings are in place. Sure enough while in my middle thirties, I broke two molars in one month. I looked up a friend of mine from dental school because he was noted for doing quality crowns. I knew that was what I needed. I told him to crown everything that looked like it might break in the foreseeable future. He tallied up eight teeth that qualified.

I wanted to get all the work done in the fewest number of appointments possible because I was very busy in my own office, it was a long traffic clogged commute to his office, and I just don't like going to the dentist that much. We decided three six-hour appointments would do the trick. My friend doubted that I could stay comfortable and hold still for that long, so he prescribed Valium for me as a relaxing, soothing, sedative. He told me to take it one hour prior to the appointment.

That morning I was working in my own office and running way behind schedule. I didn't want to take the medication while I was on duty and risk it affecting my clinical performance, so I waited until all the patients were done. Then I popped it in my mouth, jumped into my pickup truck, and hit the freeway for the 50-minute drive to my dentist's office. The traffic was worse than usual with several detours to contend with. I was racing as fast as I could, eating lunch with one hand, darting in and out of the commuter lane, weaving through small spaces between the moving vehicles, and passing stopped cars on the shoulder. I didn't want to be late and I wanted to get there before the medicine started to alter my judgment, reaction time, and perception.

It took longer than planned to get there, but no problem. I rolled into his parking lot with four minutes to spare, feeling fine. I breathed a deep sigh of relief and quickly stepped out of my truck. When my feet hit the pavement my body kept moving downward, out of control. I inexplicably collapsed into a limp pile of loose body parts. I laid there stunned for a few seconds, trying to stand up, but I was too flaccid and floppy to support my own body weight. With much effort and indignation, I literally clawed my way up the side of the pickup, struggling to reach the handle on the side of the door. When I finally pulled myself to my feet, I was huffing and puffing from the exertion. While I supported myself there, I realized that this drug was really doing a number on me. I was completely befuddled and physically inept. I still needed to walk across the parking lot and up two flights of ascending ramps to the second floor to get into his office. There was no way!

I could see his staff people moving back and forth through the window and I tried waving at them to get their attention so they could help me, but no one noticed. I considered honking the horn but I didn't think I could successfully open the

door. I decided I would just have to go for it. Slowly and carefully I lurched forward. I stumbled a few times but managed
to stay upright until I reached the railing around the ramps.
Then I grabbed on to it and hauled myself upwards, hand over
hand until I reached the entrance. It was the same action and
effort as pulling a heavy anchor up and out of deep blue still
water.

When I almost fell through the door and slumped into the
waiting room, the receptionist swiftly led me into the back
and rolled me into a dental chair. As soon as I sat down I was
relieved and felt completely normal again. I wondered how
many close calls had occurred on the freeway while I was driving, to which I was totally oblivious? It was a scary thought.

Evidently, my dental procedures proceeded unencumbered
as I drifted in and out of total awareness. By the end of the
third appointment, I was the proud owner of eight new, bright
and gleaming porcelain and gold-capped teeth. In retrospect,
I'd much rather have healthy, all natural, pretty white filling-
free teeth to chew with, but that was my fault. Anyway, these
new ones work fine and I learned a big lesson: don't ever eat
with a sharp fork when your face is still completely numb!
Other people in the restaurant are bewildered when you continually miss your open mouth and stab yourself in the chin.

Oh, just in case you were wondering, the root canal treatment on my upper front tooth that was injured by my dog
Lucky turned out just fine. It was like a leisurely walk in the
park. Even though I've done hundreds of similar procedures
painlessly on my own patients, I was a little worried about
having it done on myself. My self-preservation concerns were
needless, though. It didn't hurt a bit. I just love going to the
dentist, don't you?

CHAPTER 12

Fine Dining

I LOVE GOING TO DIFFERENT RESTAURANTS AND TRYING out their fare. Some of them I would never choose to return to. Others have become old standby favorites that I return to again and again with Jerri and friends because of the consistency of their great food, unique atmosphere, and friendly staff. Over the years several dining experiences have far excelled the usual experience.

TAKE A WOK

A VERY GRACIOUS Japanese man was introduced to me by my friend Dick. They knew each other from work. After he got to know us better, he invited us out to have a traditional Japanese dinner with him and to learn a little more about his native culture. We went to a very fancy and famous Japanese restaurant in Seattle. It was a popular place to eat so when we arrived, there was a long line of people waiting to get in. The line extended out of the entrance and part way down the block. Fortunately our friend had made reservations. We got right in and the dainty and courteous hostess showed the four of us guys to our table.

Each beautiful table was set up in exactly the same way. Ten chairs sat around a large, luxuriant, hand-polished teak and mahogany eating surface. The wood was formed into an elongated semicircle in the middle of which was a gigantic cooking wok complete with overhead vented hood and spotlight. It was quite impressive!

Since it was so busy, all the chairs were being filled from the long list of people waiting. Consequently, six more people who were complete strangers to us were brought to our table to complete the ten chair circle. What we thought was going to be an intimate and private cultural experience turned into a carnival side show assemblage of weird and outlandish characters committing extraordinary and inconceivable acts!

When we made our introductions around the table, we realized that the other six people had been waiting a long time in the bar and all of them were thoroughly intoxicated. There were three different couples, none of whom previously knew each other. There was the rich oil tycoon from Texas who was here on a business deal. He was in his middle sixties, rotund and red-faced, and continually bragged in a loud booming voice about all his accomplishments. For the evening's entertainment he had picked up a call girl who listened intently to his every word while hanging on his arm and gazing into his glassy eyes. She was about thirty, long and lanky, had a very pretty face, but didn't say too much. Her movements were unusually slow and sloth-like, attracting lots of stares from the other customers.

The next couple was the archetypal young lovers. As soon

as they sat down they became tightly intertwined like human pretzels, passionately kissing and caressing each other with abandon, seemingly in a world of their own. Apparently they didn't care or notice that they had a captive audience for their disconcerting display. Every once in a while they would come up for air, say a few things, change position, and go back at it. They were both twenty to twenty-five and very handsome people. The man hardly said anything, but the woman made the point several times that she was an aspiring young opera singer. She wanted to do a sample performance for us but we thought witnessing the making out was the least disruptive of the two evils. We told her, "Later, later you can sing."

The third couple were celebrating their 47th wedding anniversary. They were both very large people in their early seventies. They were old beyond their years and were the most inebriated of all. They both chattered unceasingly to each other at the same time without ever hearing what the other one was saying. Sporadically, one or both of them would start laughing hysterically for no obvious reason. It was as if they were trying to outdo each other in the shrillness and irrelevance of their boisterous guffaws. It sounded like the cacophonous cackle of two crazy witches watching over their boiling pot of toil and trouble.

After the introductions were completed, the three couples immediately ordered more cocktails and chased them down with swills of sake. Within minutes, all six of them were best friends. Somewhere in their over-indulged dimension they undoubtedly recognized each other as long-lost soul mates.

The four of us felt like complete outsiders watching a science fiction drama unfold. It was entertaining to say the least, but also humiliating to the max. We watched in silent dismay. Before long, the hooker was lying down across the laps of the other five people, squirming around below the edge of the table, being tickled and passed back and forth like a bean bag.

We didn't know why. The laugher got louder and more uproarious. It was obvious that the noisy scene was disruptive and annoying to the genteel and proper atmosphere of the restaurant. The four of us sat there speechless, enjoying the adventure but wanting to hide at the same time.

The Japanese staff were gawking at our table in mortified disbelief, whispering among themselves, trying to figure out what to do. They evidently decided to get us out of there as quickly as possible by hurrying with the dinner process. They quickly took our orders and soon our chef appeared at the center wok to prepare the food for our meals. He spoke no English and exemplified the traditional grace and honor of his culture. He was highly skilled in the culinary arts as well as being a fantastic showman. He juggled his knives and pots and pans and sliced and diced the vegetables and prawns and chicken at the same time with such skill that it seemed inhumanly possible. Food and utensils were flying through the air, behind his back, and up over his head. The food all landed in precise little rows on the hot wok and the utensils fell neatly into the pockets of his apron or were deftly caught at the last moment only to be sent airborne again. It was a fantastic show.

The expensive food sizzled on the wok and the bright spotlight shone down from above to highlight all the remarkable gymnastics of this wonderful artist. Just as the delicious smelling steam rising from the food signaled that it was ready to serve, there was a short break in the action. The young lover lady took advantage of the moment and suddenly stood up, deciding that now was the appropriate time to sing. Wanting to make believe she was on stage, she reached up and grabbed the spotlight, twisting it toward herself so the light shined on her face. The light abruptly broke off at the base and startled her. She let go and it dropped down onto the wok, shattering into a million pieces!

We couldn't believe our eyes. The chef was stunned and looked like he was going to cry. Enough elegant food for ten people was completely ruined! The chef sadly scraped all the shard-laden sustenance off into a waste can, completely cleaned and re-oiled the wok, and returned to the kitchen to get fresh provisions. The darting glances and puckered faces of the other employees displayed their sincere displeasure. Our six table mates were oblivious and blotto by now but they still expected another full performance by the chef when he returned. I'm sure he had received more orders from the management to get us out of there as fast as possible. He still prepared the food with lots of flair, but much more quickly this time and with a forced smile on his face. I had to admire him for his pleasant perseverance.

The meal was wonderfully delicious! The four of us loved it and tried to savor each of the scrumptious morsels. The other six hardly noticed. They continued to carry on with their cackling and cuddling, loud distasteful jokes, and even louder lunatic laughter. They made a mess on the table, spilling their drinks several times while toasting senseless scenarios. At one point the old lady started to choke in the middle of her hysterics. I started reviewing the Heimlich maneuver in my mind and waited for her to turn blue. Fortunately, a wad of rice broke loose and spewed out, adding to the festive atmosphere, much to the delirious delight of her new-found friends.

Finally it was over! The Texan and his date left first, staggering out, arms around each other. Then the young lovers took their leave, their hands firmly embedded in each other's rear hip pockets. The older couple lingered just a little longer and then the husband got up first and slowly strolled forward to pay the bill at the front counter. His wife laboriously struggled to her feet and waddled an uneven trail to catch up with him.

Just as she got to where he was standing near the entrance, she stumbled and fell to the floor. She laid there like a large beached whale, ponderously rocking from side to side, moaning and groaning loudly, and holding her sides. It was an ugly sight. The people still waiting to be seated stared in disbelief, a look of wonder on their faces. The Japanese people who ran the place were completely crushed. She completely blocked the path to the door. The only way to get in or out was to step over her heaving body. Very poor advertising on a busy night.

Her husband tried to get her up to her feet but he was in no shape to do so. The wails only got louder. A group of three or four tiny Japanese waiters tried next, but they didn't have the muscle to pull her up far enough. The people eating at the nearby tables were pretending not to notice the shameless display, so the four of us walked forward and manhandled her up to a wobbly standing position. We got her and her husband leaning on each other for mutual support and helped them out the door into the curious crowd. We watched them for a short while, weaving their way toward a blissful 48th year, and wished them luck.

We returned to the cashier's counter and sincerely apologized for the rude behavior and troublesome disruption of our drunken, undignified dinner partners. The nice people graciously understood. We complimented them for their artistry, their fine cuisine, their patience, and their hospitality. We gave them a very generous tip and left with smiles all around. They were happy to see us go, and we had an unforgettable, cross-cultural dining experience.

HORS D'OEUVRES

IT WAS ONE of those crazy days that happens sometimes in a busy dental practice. Lots of emergencies, phone calls, and important questions to take care of in addition to the regular demanding schedule. I was frantically playing catch-up all day, had no time for lunch, and left late in a rush to get to a very important dinner engagement. After three years of being a nurse in a hospital psychiatry unit, Jerri was leaving to take a new position in the emergency department. This had been her first job out of school as a registered nurse and she had endeared herself to the patients and staff in the psychiatry department. They were throwing a huge goodbye party and dinner in her honor.

I tried so hard to get there on time but to no avail. Heavy traffic and wrong turns got me even more discombobulated. When I finally found the place and walked in, the party was in full swing. I was sweaty, frazzled, and disheveled but no one except Jerri seemed to notice my arrival. About 20 people were sitting around a huge rectangular table in a very elegant, upper-class restaurant. They were all heavily engaged in a combination of social prattle and professional psycho babble.

There were more utensils and glassware at each place setting than we have ever had on our whole Thanksgiving table! The waiters were all dressed in fancy Far Eastern robes with a white towel draped over one arm and wore large, brightly colored velvet turbans with a giant glass jewel in the middle of their foreheads.

Relieved to be there at last, I sat next to Jerri at the head of the table. No one was sitting to my left and Jerri was absorbed in responding to questions and comments from her side of the table. As I listened and watched, I felt like a solitary island surrounded by a sea of shrinks. I finally started to calm down from my hectic day and noticed that I was extremely hungry.

There was no food on the table yet. Evidently the dinner had been pre-ordered and the restaurant was waiting for everyone to arrive before serving anything.

The yearning of my stomach was powerful! I tried to ignore it by focusing on the exquisite accouterments of this five-star palace, the first I had ever eaten in. Long-flowing silk tapestries hung everywhere and valuable artwork adorned the walls. Tall slender candles lit the tables and the dim light cast a medieval, surreal quality to the scene. Every time a costumed waiter walked by, I was jolted back into my famished reality. All I really wanted was just something to eat.

At last, it came! The sheik-like waiters were putting little gold dishes in front of each person, just beyond the dessert spoons and the rosebud decorations. They were filled with little delicious-looking cubes. They shimmered and glistened in the shadowy light. Mmmmmm, an appetizer of sorbet or chilled tofu, I surmised. Not exactly prawns or chicken-wings like I had hoped for, but anything would do. Since this was a very high-brow place, I would have to adapt to the lifestyles of the wealthy and cultured aristocrat.

No one else seemed to care about the ornate little hors d'oeuvres being placed around. They just kept right on talking and sipping their drinks. I guess no one was hungry except me. I knew it would be rude to start eating before the guest of honor but I couldn't help myself. They were all having a great time anyway, and all I wanted was just one little bite to tide me over to the main course.

When no one was looking, I quickly reached out with one of my many forks and snagged the corner of one of the tiny cubes then promptly stuck it in my mouth. Anticipating some splendid, succulent sustenance, I started chewing. The taste suddenly hit me all at once and it was terrible! Very sour and bitter at the same time, like something was totally tainted.

Fortunately, it was just a tiny piece and I swallowed it hesi-
tantly. I theorized that I had gotten hold of a bad piece of
food, or this was such a gourmet specialty that the spices and
seasoning must have been extra concentrated in that one little
part. I knew that by some coincidental quirk I had picked the
only bad-tasting portion. I was sure that the rest of it was
scrumptious.

I waited for a minute or two and then slyly tried again.
This time I speared a whole cube, making sure it was on the
opposite side of the dish from where I had gotten the first
piece. Again, I prepared myself for a delicious delight and
popped the whole thing into my chops. "Chomp, chomp."
Oh my gosh, it was horrible! Miserable! A ghastly and gross,
pungent flavor rang out in my mouth. It was much worse and
more intense than the first bite. "How can anybody eat this
awful swill?" I thought.

I kept chewing, trying to find the good part, but it just got
worse. I swallowed about half of it but couldn't force the rest
of it down. I knew my face had contorted into an automatic
spasmodic grimace and I was afraid someone would notice. I
glanced around. No one was looking. I grabbed my artistically
folded linen napkin and shrewdly spit the rest of the foul mess
into it. I drained the remainder of my water glass to dilute the
intolerable taste on my tongue and then pleasantly sat there
with a slightly crooked smile on my tortured lips. I felt mildly
disturbed, realizing that I wasn't cut out for indulging in the
rich and exotic fare of the upper crust of high society. This
stuff tasted way worse than caviar!

A few minutes later the waiters reappeared, carrying shiny
chafing dishes on small stands. They set them over each one of
the little gold, appetizer bowls, and lit the glimmering cubes
inside on fire. The little bowls were the burners, and the glossy
cubes were the fuel. Suddenly with incredible dread I realized

I had just been eating jellied wood-alcohol, a well-known poison! Would I die? Would I go blind? Would I instantaneously suffer some debilitating and excruciating abdominal distress, causing me to double up, retching uncontrollably? How embarrassing! Maybe I would just simply pass out without warning. I whispered to Jerri what had happened and she decided that we needed to ask someone in the restaurant if this had ever happened before. Maybe they could tell us what to expect.

We explained the situation to the head waiter and his face turned ashen, making the large green jewel on his forehead look even more brilliant. He said in a heavy accent, " We look after you."

He disappeared into the kitchen and soon another waiter stuck his head out from behind the hanging curtains and began pointing at me. He walked over and stationed himself right next to me. He stood there at attention, silent like a palace guard, dressed in his yellow silk tunic and pajama pants with matching slippers that turned up at the toes. His face remained emotionless and every so often he would lean way over and look directly into my eyes for signs of any toxic twitches. He remained there at his post for the rest of the meal.

Although I was plenty worried, nothing unusual happened to my stomach or my eyes. I enjoyed a fine, full course dinner with my personal attendant at my side. The only thing that was a bit curious was that none of the other guests from the psych ward seemed to even take notice of this unusual scene and all the exclusive attention I was getting from my little friend in the turban. I guess their professional training prepares them to always maintain a poker face when confronted with even the most bizarre circumstances. Anyway, now I know why etiquette and table manners are so important. Never start eating before the guest of honor. It could save your life!

⌒   ⌒

HOLDING THE BAG

I WAS INVITED to a big engagement party. It was for my best friend Dick and his fiancee. They planned to have the celebration held on Dick's birthday. It was a big deal! It would be the first time that the members of the two families had ever met each other. They had made a lot of careful arrangements for a good time. They were nervous and hoping that everything would go just right and that all the prospective in-laws would get along and enjoy each other's company. Decorum was expected. A formal atmosphere in an extravagant new restaurant was chosen to make sure that everything remained socially acceptable.

I arrived at the restaurant on a classic wet and rainy Seattle night. I put the birthday present I had brought for Dick inside an old grocery sack so the rain wouldn't spoil the ultra fancy wrapping and ribbons as I walked in from the street. I was glad that I had dressed up because the restaurant was unbelievably ornate and posh. From the outside it looked like one huge solid piece of crystallized glass. The walls were glass, the door was glass, the tables were glass, even the chairs were glass. You could see through everything. It was somewhat intimidating at first. I felt like my every movement was on display and that all the fragile furnishings would immediately shatter at the slightest bit of clumsiness. I softly sauntered over to the large gleaming table that was reserved for our group, carefully placed the paper bag with the present in it under a chair, and gently sat down.

I was a little early so I gazed around at my shimmering surroundings while waiting for the rest of the party to arrive. Mirrors were everywhere, adding to the false sense of solidity.

Huge crystal chandeliers glittered from the sparkling ceiling, and little specks of bright lights reflected from every surface. There was a ton of glassware on the table. Hand-blown decanters and goblets were delicately positioned between old-fashioned silver serving trays. The place settings were made up with exquisite hand-painted fine china, each one a piece of art. The utensils were imported "old world" silverware with little three-dimensional scenes sculpted into the highly polished handles. There was an unmistakable atmosphere of dignity and seriousness about the place. The staff was dressed in starched, pure white uniforms and maintained an air of strict sobriety and correctness.

Finally all the guests had arrived and were sitting around the imposing table. I had never met most of them and was the only one present who was not family or family-to-be. I adopted a low profile (which is very difficult when I am around Dick) and just sat back to listen to the conversations unfolding as the two families got to know each other. The mood remained polite and friendly, warm and controlled. It was exactly what they wanted. Every once in a while someone would mention a wild escapade that Dick had been involved in. Invariably, it had included me, but this wasn't my party so I remained reserved and supportive. I didn't want to draw undue attention to myself by being the unconventional extrovert that I usually was around Dick. I could tell that several other members of the group had it in them to cut loose and party hearty. But I didn't want to do anything that would get them started and ruin the dignified ambiance. However, I could feel a growing internal urge welling up in me to do something out of the ordinary.

It was a great celebration! The food was wonderful, the talk free and flowing, and people were beginning to get acquainted. The honored couple displayed a glowing look of satisfaction. For dessert, the staff brought out a large birthday cake topped with blazing candles and sat it in front of Dick. He blushed and blew and most certainly got his wish because the flames extinguished all at once. Then it was time for the gifts. I leaned over and took mine out of the grocery sack and handed it down the table with all the rest. The relatively sedate climate was maintained even during the gift opening interlude. There were a couple of gag gifts but all were tasteful and proper.

I could tell that my friend Dick was feeling the strain of having to be so gentlemanly and gracious. We were so used to just goofing around when we were together. This wasn't natural and I was feeling the tension, too. I wanted to play a joke or do something to act as a stress breaker just between the two of us.

Finally, someone suggested that we all retire to the bar for a drink. Everyone got up and started heading in that direction. I was still dazzled by the opulence of this lavish and fragile place. As I got up to leave I wondered what to do with the paper sack under my chair that looked so out of place. It would be rude to leave it behind. Suddenly, it hit me! This was it. I would fill it up with an assortment of expensive dishes, goblets and silver and nonchalantly take it over and give it to Dick, just to see what would happen. He would be left "holding the bag!"

I waited until everyone had left the table and then I started choosing the best of the best from the dinnerware left behind. Several elegant plates went into the bag, followed by a fine cup and saucer set, some dessert dishes, a wine goblet or two, and a bunch of silverware with emphasis on the larger serving forks, spoons, and carving knives. Just as I was loading the last few pieces in the sack, I glanced up for a second and got direct eye contact with the head waitress who was standing in the kitchen, 60 feet away, watching me through all the glass. From the look on her face I knew immediately that she thought I was trying to steal all this stuff. I looked back down quickly and pretended not to notice, acting totally innocent with a wry little smile on my face. I could feel her continued gaze on me as I finished the process. With everything carefully stacked inside, I rolled down the top edge of the bag, picked it up, and carried it off like an oversized sack lunch.

Dick was standing in the midst of the party group still waiting to be seated in the bar. I arrived at his side and just as I presented him with his "gift," the suspicious waitress showed up. She was accompanied by a big, burly cook, and a serious looking security man wearing a three-piece suit. I hadn't planned on getting caught doing this and at first I pretended not to have anything to do with it, denying any involvement whatsoever. I wanted the prank to go ahead as originally planned. Of course none of the guests, including Dick, knew what was in the bag yet. He thought the "gift" was a belated birthday present until the security man suggested that he open the bag and look inside. I'll never forget the collective gasp that came from the concerned onlookers when the contents were revealed. I could see the curious and questioning glares darting from eye to eye amongst the prospective in-laws. Dick gave me a stern and knowing glance as well.

Tension filled the room. The troops were getting restless and the security team did not understand and were not amused. At that point I decided I had better fess up. Suddenly I became the center of attention. The trick had backfired and now I was the one caught holding the bag. I awkwardly told everybody what I had been up to. That it was all just a harmless prank between life-long friends. After several times through the same story, the bewildered restaurant staff finally acquiesced and went back to work. The relatives were astonished at first by the boldness of my action. But upon further reflection, it served to demonstrate the trusting brotherly bond that existed between Dick and me.

I could sense that this event had acted to totally endear Dick to the hearts of his prospective relatives, and had made me look like a total idiot. It had also been a catalyst to loosen everybody up. There was a satisfying relaxation of constraint. Maybe the alcohol in the bar had something to do with it as well, but now the cat was out of the bag. The premises and pretenses were gone. The two families proudly displayed their authentic personas and they blended together well. They were happy, contented, and pleased, and I think they were particularly relieved that I wasn't a permanent member of either one of them.

FREE DRINKS AND MORE

WHEN WE WERE in college and still dating, Jerri invited me to the school's annual Tolo dance. A Tolo meant the women traditionally invite the men and arrange and pay for the evening's dinner and entertainment. We double-dated with another couple and went to a popular waterfront restaurant to eat after the dance. When we arrived, it was well past the regular dinner hour, so only about a third of the tables were occupied. We got a nice window booth overlooking the water and everything was just great. We were nineteen years old and not used to such extravagance.

The gals were wearing beautiful and expensive gowns and we guys were wearing rented tuxedos. Including dinner and the dance it would be a high-priced evening for our dates. As poor college students, it was difficult to afford something like this. Jerri and her friend had planned carefully to manage the finances for the evening to insure that we all would have an extra fun and memorable time. We guys were happy and lucky to have such caring and gorgeous dates.

We sat at our table admiring the view, talking and laughing while going over the menu and deciding what to eat. At one point I looked up to observe our waitress clearing one of the nearby tables. I was amazed to witness that while she carried the tray filled with dirty dishes back to the kitchen, she hurriedly slurped down all the remaining cocktails with a straw. At the time this act seemed totally uncouth to me, yet somehow practical. (Now it just seems totally uncouth.)

I told the group what I had just seen, but they wouldn't believe my repulsive story. I swore it was the truth so we all decided to secretly watch our waitress to see if she would do it again. Sure enough, after clearing the next table down, she finished off two more drinks on the way to the kitchen. It was a disturbing display, especially for our dates who had been told that this place was known for its cultured and romantic atmosphere. Suddenly, the place was starting to feel more like a dive and improper sanitation was becoming an issue. It became part of the sport for the evening to watch our waitress and keep score of her free liquor intake while we were talking.

When she came to take our orders she seemed pleasant enough but a little blasé about things. It was like part of her mind was somewhere else and she was existing only partially in each place. A few minutes later another foursome of older people were seated in the empty booth immediately adjacent to us. The same waitress eventually took their orders, too. This time there was a noticeable wobble in her gait that wasn't there previously.

We forgot about her after a while as we sipped our colas, ate our bread, and talked about college life, homework, and the future. All of a sudden a huge crash and clatter erupted from the kitchen! It was the sound of multiple plates smashing to the floor, the shattering of glass, the metallic tinging noise of silverware bouncing around, and the twanging of metal serving trays rebounding from a serious fall. It was a college tradition that if we heard a dish break in the cafeteria we would all clap. In this case there was so much noise and apparent destruction of property that everyone sat there quiet and stunned. We wondered if our waitress had somehow been involved. A few seconds later she emerged through the swinging doors with a bright red face and a scowl that seemed to answer our question in the affirmative. We felt sorry for her now.

She eventually brought out our food and the orders for the people next door at the same time on a mobile cart. It appeared that she was using the cart to lean on like a walker to hold herself up with rather than for the convenience of transporting the dinners. After she served the meals we realized that some of us got the wrong orders. We heard the people next door grumbling and discovered that some of the food had been mixed up between the two tables. Some of us had already started eating off of the wrong plates so it wasn't as simple as just swapping back and forth to get the correct dinner.

Unfortunately, our waitress was too soused by this time to understand what the problem was or how to solve it when we called her back over. Several people at the other table reordered, but ended up getting the wrong food the second time as well. By then everyone else had already finished their meals. It was a rough night for them.

It worked out fine at our table, though. We traded food around so that all of us had something tasty to enjoy. I'm sure it was somewhat disconcerting for our girlfriends because the evening didn't go as smoothly as planned. But it was great fun to be out with them on this kind of date, and it certainly was memorable! It just didn't seem right though for them to have to pay full price for it. We were too young and innocent to complain, but we decided we would probably never come back to that place.

Fifteen years or so went by and we changed our minds. We decided to go back there just for fun to celebrate the anniversary of when we first met. It was still a popular place, and finding convenient parking was difficult. We finally walked in, a little late for our reservations, and checked with the hostess. She seemed perturbed about something and flaunted a sourpuss attitude. We ignored it and went to our table. We couldn't get a window seat because they were all reserved for larger parties. But we did get a nice booth just for two that was comfy and private. The interior had been remodeled since our last visit which disappointed us somewhat. We were hoping for some familiar remembrances of yesteryear.

With a glass of wine we toasted and reminisced about the good old days. We laughed about the drinking waitress, wondered what had become of the couple we double-dated with, and talked about our wonderful kids, our dental office, and our dreams for the future. We marveled at how the time had passed so quickly, acknowledged our accomplishments, and made plans for what we could do better.

I think we were kind of hoping for something unusual to happen while we were there but everything seemed pretty plain. Even the food was unremarkable. The only thing exceptional was the good company that we shared. While we were eating, a young couple came in and sat at the next table. They reminded us of what we must have been like 15 years earlier. I noticed that they only ordered appetizers and soft drinks. After sharing a "chocolate decadence" dessert we left, paid our bill, and toured the waterfront scene for a while before returning home.

Two days later we got a call from the restaurant. The grumpy hostess was on the phone. She explained that we had been given the wrong bill for our dinner. It had been mistakenly switched with the young couple next to us. We still owed them $17.21. If we didn't pay it, it would come out of her own pocket. (I remembered thinking that the bill seemed pretty reasonable when we paid, but I never bothered to check the tally.) I wondered if they would have called us with the same amount of courtesy and offered us a refund had we overpaid.

The hostess reluctantly agreed to send us a copy of our bill and we sent her the money a week later. The whole experience left us feeling quite amused. It made our 15 year reunion complete. We were glad to see that the unsophisticated and outrageous ghost of the wasted waitress was still there. It had only changed form. We decided we would probably never go back. We'll see.

"Tongba"

WE WERE STAYING high in the Himalayas at 12,000 feet. Jerri and I had walked into a remote village to do volunteer medical and dental care. It was quite primitive compared to what we were used to in the States. The buildings were constructed with hand-shaped stones chinked together with mud and straw and held in place by hand-hewn wooden frames. There was no electricity, no phones, and no heat except for a small metal bucket under our table that was filled with hot coals and glowing embers taken from the wood burning, open stone hearth in the kitchen area. We were an eight day walk from the nearest road, and two days from the nearest rustic airstrip. We were in heaven. This was Sherpa country! In my opinion they are one of the most friendly, sincerely gracious, and hard-working people in the world. We relished this opportunity to be there, working and living with them in their community.

We were at the foot of Mt. Everest in Nepal to teach disease prevention and to help take care of emergency medical problems. I had been there two years earlier to see the mountains and the highest point on Earth and had fallen in love with the people. I vowed I would return to help and here I was. I was so thankful to have Jerri along this time. Her emergency room nursing experience was a valuable asset and sharing the indescribable culture of this magical land with her was a dream come true.

One evening after a hard day's work, we were resting in our host family's home, sipping hot tea, and warming our toes under the table. The owners came in from their cooking chores in the kitchen and sat down next to us. They explained that they had a special local treat to serve me called "tongba." By this time I had restricted my dietary intake to fried potatoes and mushroom soup since the other local foods just didn't appeal to my palate. So I was hesitant at first. Then they told us that they wanted to serve me tongba to honor and thank us for our service to their family and community. How could I refuse?

I learned later that to be served tongba is a rare and extraordinary honor. It is laborious to prepare and the ingredients are hard to come by. Millet seeds are harvested and brought up by porters from the lower valleys. The seeds are soaked and then placed in a dark, dank, and cool location to ferment for six to nine months. It is a traditional drink reserved to honor and acclaim visiting dignitaries, politicians, members of the royal family, and other VIPs.

When I graciously accepted their offer, our host and hostess happily hurried off to prepare the delicacy. They returned with proud smiles and a tall, metal 20-ounce cup. They ceremoniously placed it before me. I looked down in the dim, kerosene lantern light of the room and saw quite a sight!

The fermenting millet seeds had been dug out of their

hiding place and piled into the cup so that they overflowed the rim. It was a mass of small black specks contained within a thick film of gelatinous slime over which grew a dark green lawn of fuzzy mold. I immediately winced on the inside but kept a smile going on the outside. Some rice was sprinkled over the top for a blessing, and then the kitchen boy brought in a kettle of hot water and poured some over it until the level of liquid came right up to the top. A hollow, metal tent stake was then placed into the mix to be used as a straw. Now it was time for me to drink.

A crowd of delighted faces eagerly waited and watched as I leaned forward. I could barely force myself to put my face down that close to the hairy green fungal ooze. But I did. I took a little sip and prepared for the worst. It was lukewarm and slightly bitter but not too bad. It wasn't something that I wanted much more of, but it was acceptable. I swallowed and smiled broadly and saw the satisfaction gleaming from the eyes of all of our wonderful new-found friends as I accepted their special favor. For politeness I decided to take one more sample. I also wanted to drink just enough so that the level of water was down below the surface of the floating goo. I figured that if it was just out of sight then it would look like I was really enjoying it and no one could tell how much I had drunk. Meanwhile, I could just sit there looking satisfied, pretending that my glass was half-finished.

My plan backfired. Every time the kitchen boy came back around he would refill my cup back up to the rim and I would be forced to drink it back down out of sight once again. I surely didn't want to appear disrespectful. I loved these people and I knew that they sincerely honored Jerri and me. As a matter of fact, I never knew the meaning of Love until I came here and experienced it Sherpa style! They look beyond your physical form with reverence and honor to that spark of Divinity that dwells inside each one of us. This universal and genuine atmosphere of unconditional love was powerful, soothing, and addictive. It was one of the main reasons I came back— to get some more of it, and to learn how to take it back home, and share it with others.

The more I drank, the more I noticed a taste like nutty licorice. I started to like it! The steady supply of hot water continued to flush the alcohol from the fermentation process down to the bottom where the hollow tent stake picked it up with full force. Soon, a warm, gentle glow started to spread through me, starting at the center of my being. I indeed felt honored by these people and honored to be here in their presence giving what I could to them. There were beaming faces all around and everything was just perfect. I was smart enough not to drink too much and I experienced a great truth, "Even if something looks terrible on the outside, it doesn't mean there isn't something wonderful to find on the inside."

After all, this was the land of "Namaste," the traditional greeting and attitude that every person receives here from everyone else. Namaste means, "I honor the Divinity in you," or, "I respect you for who you are."

I liked it much better than just saying, "Hello."

Tongba and Namaste—what a fine dining experience!

Music Lessons

BOTH OF MY PARENTS LOVED MUSIC. MY DAD WAS A FAN of cowboy music and Lawrence Welk, while my mom preferred classical music, especially works by Beethoven, Chopin, and Tchaikovsky. Our home was constantly filled with the strains of these melodies which emanated from the polished, wooden radio and old 78-speed record player console that stood in our living room. Mom and Dad were serious about passing their passion for music on to us kids. This was especially true of my mother who had visions of me becoming a virtuoso concert pianist or a famous symphony conductor. So when I was seven years old, I began taking piano lessons with earnest. They purchased my first broken down, upright piano for $10. The hammer action and the strings were a shambles, but with the help of a fine craftsman and tuner the old piano was restored and became very functional as my first musical instrument.

I had to practice every day for an hour. I hated it at first! It was especially bad on weekdays, because as soon as I got home from school and had my snack, I was required to go straight to the basement to play all the scales up and down several times, plink around here and there, and rehearse the little one-page songs I had been assigned by my piano teacher. Meanwhile, I could see all my neighborhood chums through the window having a grand time playing games and rough-housing out in their yards. I wanted to be out there with them, participating in the fun. But alas, it was always do, re, mi for me.

As time went by, I grew to adore my piano teacher. She was a sweet and gentle lady who believed in me. She was always soft-spoken and kind and I wanted to do my best so that I could please her. With consistent practice and recitals, my skills increased. By the time I was in junior high school I started getting some recognition for my talent. This really bolstered my ego. From that time forward, I put my heart and soul into music and began to thoroughly enjoy it. In addition to classical piano soloing, I played in every type of musical group I could find, including chamber music, Dixieland, pep band, full orchestra, and rock and roll. Those were some of the best of times—being on stage, back stage, and under the stage; setting up equipment or packing up for the night with your best friends. Playing music and feeling that thrilling, tingling sensation when all the musicians were in sync, the music was spontaneous, and the audience was entertained and electrified was what we lived for!

I performed with various groups all the way through dental school, sometimes for money but mostly for fun. Since then, I've continued to play as solo entertainment for parties, providing enthusiasm and ambiance for them and continued thrills and amusement for myself. Over the years I've had some wild and wacky incidents happen in and around the music business. Here are a few choice examples.

~~ ~~

PUNCH DRUNK

WHEN WE WERE in high school, our four-man dance band combo, "The Centuries," got a regular job playing for a catering service. It was a good deal because every time they catered an event we got to provide dance music for it. It included all the free food we could snag and a little spending money on the side as well. We performed for firemen's balls, political rallies, anniversaries, New Year's Eve parties, club socials, county fairs, company picnics, talent shows, dinner cruises, and horse's birthdays. Most of the parties we played at were for adults. We were too young for and not interested in drinking at the time, so in our innocence it was fascinating, educational, and sometimes quite challenging to deal with the effects that booze had on our audience.

One night we were playing in an overly crowded bar for a social club dance. It was a semiformal affair. Everyone, especially the ladies, were dressed in their finest outfits. So many people were jammed in they could scarcely move around on the dance floor. Each couple was restricted to a small space that just barely allowed them room to turn in a tight circle while dancing. It was like human bumper cars in slow motion. Despite the congestion, the crowd was friendly, relaxed, and romantic. They wanted all the lights to be turned off and kept requesting slow songs. It was so dark that we couldn't read our music so we had some candles brought over and placed them around us for illumination. It added an extra warmth to the atmosphere. Unfortunately, it was a little too much for some of the dancers.

Many of the people had drunk so much that the only reason they were out on the crowded dance floor was to hold each other up! One couple in particular was dancing right in front of the piano. The tall man was dressed in a dark, pin-striped business suit. He was silent and tipsy and seemed almost incoherent. His lady partner wore a long sleeveless evening gown and held on to him for dear life in perfect, close-dancing position. I could tell she was also feeling no pain because as they very slowly twirled to the music, her out-stretched elbow would leisurely linger just above the flame of one of the burning candles. After a few moments of singeing stillness, she would gently flinch and lightly swat at her arm as if a fly was bothering her. This action caused her to move away from the flame's influence and she quickly returned to her cheek to cheek stance with her partner. She seemed completely oblivious to the proximity of the candles and the cause of the burning irritation.

This same scenario repeated itself over and over again upon every successive rotation of the clutching couple. Sometimes her arm passed through the hot fire for many seconds at a time without her even responding to it. Other times she would quickly glance around, searching for the invisible menace that was teasing her, thinking it was another dancer nearby who was pinching her. In between songs I tried moving the candle to different places, but as the two swayed to and fro, her arm would always find the searing flame, sometimes twice in the same undulating circle. After several songs of seeing this endless drama of eternal torture, I knew that it was bothering me more than it was hurting her. It was comical in a way and sad at the same time. I finally blew out the candle and played on in the relative darkness. They were too tanked to tell the difference anyway. I just wondered what that lady would think had happened when she woke up the next morning with a hangover that extended all the way down her right arm?

As the evening wore on, the dance floor throng thinned

out a little and the pace of the music picked up. We were banging out some good old-fashioned rock and roll and the crowd was kicking up their heels. The band members were getting hot, sweaty, and thirsty, so the caterer brought us a huge punch bowl filled with ice cubes floating in rose-colored tropical fruit juice. There was nowhere else out of the way to put it except on top of the tall upright piano. I had opened the hinged top of the piano earlier so I could hear myself better over the volume of the amplified instruments. The large punch bowl just barely fit on the open edge of the lid.

One slightly inebriated guy in the crowd was complaining that the music was too loud! He still wanted soft and slow but the rest of the room wanted to boogie now. He kept stumbling over, right in the middle of the songs, yelling at us to tone it down. Finally, after repeated failed attempts to get his way, he got mad. He came over, reached up, slammed the lid on the piano shut, and stormed off! Apparently, he was unaware of the presence of the punch bowl, which tumbled down into the piano, spilling about a gallon of sweet liquid everywhere inside. Well, the show must go on, so I quickly stood up on the bench, removed the unbroken bowl that was keeping the keys from working, and resumed playing without hardly even missing a beat. Of course, all of us were completely shocked and worried about getting into trouble for damaging the piano, but we still had more than an hour to go on our entertainment contract. It seemed that no one else had witnessed the incident so we kept at it, saving our best stuff for last.

In the middle of the next song I noticed that the viscous solution was starting to seep out between the keys. My fingers got tacky and my performance speed slowed down as the keyboard grew gummier. Occasionally, two keys would stick together, making our simple dance tune melodies sound like free-form jazz riffs. Also, some of the soft felt hammers were saturated and started making a dead "thunking" sound instead of a melodious ring as I played. I continually wiped my hands on my pants to de-glue them, but that only added to the confusion. We coyly smiled, rolled our eyes at each other, and continued on. The beat and tempo remained the same, but the sound and style of our music was altered for the rest of our set. The crowd didn't know the difference though and kept on dancing. When it was all over, they chattered happily and laughed loudly as they filed out, meandering their way back to their cars.

We cleaned up the sopping mess the best we could and lingered for a while discussing the craziness of the night, eating cookies, and waiting for all the drunks to clear off the road before we left for home. On the way out we told the intoxicated manager about how the punch had been spiked into the piano by one of the patrons. He didn't seem to mind too much. I guess he wasn't ready yet for quite such a sobering thought.

As we got older, our music got bolder. During practice sessions we started improvising and playing more of our own original songs. Later, we just made them up right there at the gig. It was always difficult to predict what was going to happen. Sometimes we would lock into a tight and exhilarating groove, taking the audience soaring along with us. We could do no wrong and the crowd screamed for encore after encore. At other times we would be doing our best just to keep the audience interested, much less out on the dance floor. There were even a few times when we had to dodge eggs and other foreign bodies that came flying randomly out of the darkness. They were undoubtedly thrown by disgruntled party crashers who found out we were from a rival school. I know it couldn't have been a comment on the entertainment value of our music.

There was even one time when a thug carrying a club was waiting for us in the back alley behind the stage where we had just finished a three hour show. Our "scab" musical performance had left him so cold that he was hot under the collar. He wanted to get his money back and all of the rest of ours by beating it out of us! He said, "There is no place left in the world for non-union musicians."

Fortunately our bass and Hawaiian guitar player was much bigger and more imposing than he. The confrontation ended non-violently with a war of words and a barrage of colorful expletives. We ended up telling the two-bit hoodlum to go home with his club and beat a drum instead of people. The fact that we only got paid $6 each that night made the whole experience even more scary.

~~ ~~

ORGAN TRANSPLANT

BY THE TIME the 70's rolled around, you weren't cool unless you had an organ in your band. Jim was a friend of mine in another band called the "Embalmers." (Their business card said they played "fluid music," and they hauled their gear around in the back of an old hearse.) He was selling his beautiful Hammond A-100. It produced the perfect, punchy, rock-style organ sound that was popular for the era. I took over his payments and taught myself how to play it. Meanwhile, he was using his money to buy up several huge, theater-style pipe organs that were for sale on the West Coast. They were extremely fashionable when they were used to provide live action sound tracts back in the heyday of silent movies. Now they sat unused and forgotten, collecting dust and tarnish behind the old and heavy curtains that were hanging back stage.

Jim was a one-of-a-kind character, a mechanical genius

with a never say die attitude. He spent several years combining parts and pieces of these old and ornate mammoths. He rewired and upgraded the electronics in the main console, beefed up the output on the compressor, retuned and reorganized hundreds of pipes, and completely rebuilt the entire system into one colossal traveling pipe organ. He billed it as the "World's Largest Portable Pipe Organ!"

It was transported in a customized truck and trailer rig driven by my friend Dick, who was a professional truck driver at the time and also played lead guitar and sang in the band. As I recall, it took about 24 hours to set up the whole thing once it arrived at a site. I helped them out as much as I could because they were my good friends and I was totally fascinated by the success and adventure of this amazing undertaking.

When the organ was fully assembled it was a monument to Jim's mastery and ingenuity and it was a magnificent reminder of the monolithic music makers of the past. There were ranks upon ranks of gleaming brass and silver pipes. The tallest bass tibia pipe stood over 35 feet above the ground. To the right and left of the center console, huge pneumatic chambers filled with smaller pipes were elevated up on the trailer beds to produce a resounding stereo effect. The giant shutters on the front of them popped open with an arousing rush of wind when the volume was turned up. You could feel its awesome power pulsating inside your chest!

The console itself was bright white with red felt and beautiful wood trim. It contained a full pedal board, five full manuals, and a vast array of stops, buttons, switches and knobs that would intimidate even the most experienced modern airline pilot. Playing it was like trying to tame a wild beast, like attempting to control a giant, fire-breathing dragon on a four-foot leash. It was a thrill that I took advantage of whenever I had the chance. It made me feel like I had unbelievable power in just my fingertips.

Behind the scenes was a different story. It was a frightening, jumbled maze of heaving air hoses hanging over two-inch
thick power cables that were dangling like vines in a jungle.
There were trap door access panels and crawl spaces tucked in
the midst of rickety scaffolding and stacks of backup staging
supplies. Drab and dusty black canvas hung here and there to
hide the chaotic view from curious onlookers. Everything was
swinging and shaking to the sound of the roaring, industrial
power generator, the rumbling energy surge of the air com-
pressors, the hissing of air escaping from a myriad of small
leaks, the clicking and popping of the pneumatic levers and
hinges, and the robust blast of the music itself! It was like
being inside a mad scientist's version of a king-sized Rube
Goldberg contraption. The amazing thing was that it all
worked.

During the performances, Jim dressed like the phantom of
the opera. He often made his grand entrance by swinging
down on a rope, landing perfectly on the console's bench then
immediately starting to play. He was self-taught, played by ear,
and had an impressive repertoire of cover tunes and originals.
He didn't read music very well, though, so he asked me to help
out on gigs when that was required. My biggest thrill came
when he asked me to play for the first Russian-American
hockey game to be held at the Seattle Center Coliseum. It was
Christmas season 1973 and I accompanied a 50-member
choir singing carols to the fans before, during, and after the
game. The acoustics in the immense concrete and steel building were overwhelming. Playing the gigantic pipe organ that
loomed over me and listening to the harmony of all those
voices booming and echoing through the place was a definite
holiday highlight and religious experience.

WEDDING BELL BLUES

AFTER A WHILE I got pretty good at playing the organ and I started filling in for the church organist where I attended worship services. When he moved away, I became the regular organist while the church council searched for a professional choral and music director to take his place. I was in college now and the extra money was very handy.

In addition to practicing with the choir and attending all the services and special programs, I played for all the weddings that occurred at the church. For this, of course, I was paid separately by the bride's family. I played for dozens and dozens of weddings, learned lots of new music, attended all the rehearsals, and got a free dinner once in a while. It was a great job with the exception of one particular incident.

I was hired to play for a large and lavish wedding. I didn't know either of the families, so when I showed up at the wedding rehearsal I was an outside observer. I noticed right away that there was an unspoken but unmistakable high level of tension between the two families. The bride and groom seemed okay with each other but the rest of the group wasn't meshing well at all. A cloud of resentment and stress was thickly suspended in the air. It seemed that one wrong word or offhand comment could trigger a spontaneous fist fight at any moment. I didn't know what the problem was but it was a spooky, suspicious atmosphere, so I politely passed on my invitation to the dinner afterwards.

The next day at the wedding I fully expected that something disturbing or unanticipated would occur and I was ready for it. I sat at the organ watching all the people come into the church. The organ was at the rear of the sanctuary and faced away from the altar toward the choir loft in back. In order to see what was going on up front during the ceremony, I had to turn my head around and peek over my shoulder a lot but I was used to it.

This was an extravagant, military-style wedding. All the service men were dressed in their high-collar, stiffly starched, white dress uniforms, and the women wore Southern-style full gowns with extra petticoats for added fluff. When the wedding party entered, they marched down the aisle under an archway of silver swords crossed above their heads by spit and polish soldiers. It was a grand spectacle but the tension was still there. The mothers of the lovely couple had dour looks on their faces and I saw some darting glances across the aisle that were filled with steely daggers. I played all my musical parts satisfactorily and waited with nervous anticipation during the service.

When the minister finally said, "If there is any one here who knows a reason why this marriage cannot proceed, let him speak now or forever hold his peace," I quickly pivoted all the way around on the organ bench so I could see who would stand up first. I put my arm down across the full keyboard for leverage and balance and instantaneously an earsplitting, discordant, "BLAAAAAT!" erupted from all the loudspeakers in the church. In my excited expectancy I had mistakenly kicked the volume pedal full on instead of to off.

Everyone in the church jumped about two feet! It startled the wits out of them and me. There was a shocked, dead silence afterward that lingered incessantly. No one dared to speak now. The unnerving, blasting blare of the organ had spoken volumes and had temporarily burst the taut balloon of blame and discontent that hung over the room. After a long mournful moment of disquiet, the minister thankfully resumed the ceremony. I wallowed in my own private sea of chagrin and embarrassment until it was over. Afterwards, I disappeared quickly, glad that I didn't know anybody there and feeling fortunate that I had received my payment in advance. Hmmm, I wonder if that couple is still together and what their family reunions are like?

SYNTHETICS

WHILE IN DENTAL school some friends and I formed a new group called the "Arbor Band." The sound of pop music was drastically changing with the advent of electronic synthesizers. They produced the most captivating reverberations and undulating wave forms I had ever heard. What's more, they could fairly accurately synthesize the sounds of all the other known instruments. One player could sound like a full orchestra now and could carry the entire keyboard with him under his arm. Compared to the four men required to lug around my heavy Hammond organ this was much more convenient and efficient. The only drawback was that synthesizers were expensive.

I was enchanted by them and set about learning as much as possible about how they worked. I read all the literature, took classes, and hung out at music stores playing with them. I wanted to have my own but it just wasn't in our budget. Then I had a bright idea. I offered to trade dental work to the managers of several music stores in exchange for baby-sitting their electronic keyboards in my home over the weekends. Two guys took me up on the offer. I worked after hours fixing their teeth and improving their smiles and then showed up at their stores on Saturdays at closing time to have my pick of instruments for the rest of the weekend.

It seemed so absurd and incongruous to be driving around in our $200 rattle trap and rusty old Rambler with a shiny new, state-of-the art $6,000 synthesizer resting between the protruding springs on the torn and ragged seat beside me. I would stay up all night learning the instruments inside and out, creating new sounds and recording innovative music. It was a sweet deal!

Several years later, I was finally able to purchase my own. After that I became a keyboard junkie of sorts. Trying to keep pace with the explosion in electronics technology was a daunting task, but I gave it my best shot. I slowly assembled a small home recording studio with acoustic, analog, and digital gear. It's a great place to go to relax, be creative, and have fun. It's probably not exactly what my mother had in mind, but I can truthfully say now, that I am the conductor of my own electronic symphony orchestra.

SHOW MAN SHIP

AFTER OUR ROCK and roll band started performing live, my father offered one piece of advice that he repeated many times. He would always say, "Remember, showmanship is nine-tenths of the show!"

He had been a successful saxophone player in the big dance bands of the 30's, so I took his advice to heart. We tried everything to put more showmanship into our act. We were already doing flashy costume changes between sets in junior high and high school. We had our own professional graphics imprinted on our instruments and choreographed our routines. We borrowed huge speakers and amplifiers, setting as many as possible up on the stage without even plugging them in just so we looked exciting and really cool. When the social revolution of our generation hit in the 60's and 70's we took it one step further.

Black light posters and viewing rooms were the rage then, so we decided to capitalize on that. We started wearing day-glow makeup on our faces and using banks of fluorescent black lights for staging. It was an eerie and memorable special effect. It was showmanship to the max! All the audience could see were our teeth, and our painted faces dancing around in the dark to the beat of the music. Sometimes we even painted our fingernails bright day-glow pink or orange so the audience had an extra thrill watching them fly over the invisible instruments. As time passed, our makeup became more intricate and extensive. We were always experimenting with it and the lights to achieve the optimal effect.

One night Jerri and I were having dinner with Dick and his wife at their home. Dick was still a guitar player but now we were together in the same band. We started talking about what we were going to do for our next gig. We decided we should try some brand new face paint designs and get some input about them from our wives before the performance. We went all out being creative and before long we both had eccentric and incomparable day-glow faces.

I flaunted yellow spirals on my cheeks over a cascading background of three-dimensional green, orange, and white. My ears and eyes were bright pink, topped off by brilliant blue glasses and mustache. Dick was more a fan of solid colors with designs over the top. His base color was speckled metallic gray, just like the tin man. He accented it with squiggles, lines, squares and dots of every conceivable color in the rainbow. We looked like a couple of primitive tribesmen in war paint ready to rumble. We were delighted with the results. Our wives were supportive but less enthusiastic.

Both Dick and I had been enthralled by boats and boating since we were children. We were especially drawn to older cargo ships, freighters, and cruisers from the 40's and 50's. There was a certain mystique about the deep, dark, diesel smelling secrets of the engine rooms, the massive anchor chains, and the giant pulleys and gears. Everything about them seemed ten times normal size! How could these titanic steel tubs float, much less weather the storms of the open ocean? Where did they go when they drifted out of view below the horizon, and where did all those passageways, hatches and stairways lead to? It was an intriguing mystery, which we wanted to be part of.

While applying our makeup we were talking about boats and I remembered that I had seen a new bunch of old ships tied up at the marine scrapyard on the east side of Lake Union several days before. We decided it would be fun to go over there and take a look at them after dessert. The girls decided to stay at home and gab while we went sightseeing.

It was very unusual for anyone in those days, even performers, to be wearing face paint, especially grown professional men. But music was something we did after our day jobs were over, and our gaudy day-glow faces were part of our act. We were so used to being in public all painted up that we didn't give it a second thought. Just as we were leaving for the ship yards, Jerri humorously called out through the closing door, "Don't call us if you get stopped by the police!"

Arriving at the docks just as the sun was setting, I parked Black Beauty by the side of the road and we walked across a large open field to the water's edge. There were six glorious and rusting old relics lined up, all tied with three-inch thick manila ropes and steel cables to enormous concrete stanchions on the beach. These tired-out marine workhorses and sojourners of the sea captivated our spirits. We slowly worked our way down the shore line, stopping in front of each vessel, carefully scrutinizing them from stem to stern. We "wowed" and "oohed" and "ahhed," fantasizing about being the captain or one of the crew. Where had they been? What had they seen? Who did they know? We daydreamed in reverent revelry about these things and more.

By the time we reached the end of the line, it was completely dark and we were standing in a low point in the rolling field. We were about 250 yards away from my car, but from our low-lying vantage point it couldn't be seen. Slowly strolling back across the field, we ascended a little mound and were astounded at the sight before us. My car was ablaze with bright lights. It was surrounded by police cars! There were five squad cars, two canine units, and one paddy wagon clustered in a tight circle. Each one had all of their lights turned on full boar. It was a sea of high-beam glowing headlights, blinking crimson taillights, spotlights shining off in all directions, and the whole area was awash in the deep, penetrating brilliance of their strobing, blue emergency flashers. What a sight! It looked like a crowded crime-scene from a low-budget, made-for-TV police drama—except this was really happening. We wondered what was going on, and if by some chance we were involved?

At that moment, a growling roar startled us from behind! A speeding police boat came charging up the channel next to the old ships. It turned on its dazzling searchlight and started scouring the area where we had been standing only minutes before. We surmised that they were probably looking for us. Suddenly, the searchlight beamed out across the field. Without thinking, we reflexively dropped flat onto our stomachs in the waist high grass. As the blazing beacon swept back and forth just above our heads, it reminded me of several prison escape movies I had seen.

Lying there facing each other, feeling slightly amused and very alarmed, we started having a muffled conversation about what to do next. Dick and I hadn't done anything wrong, but hiding there in the tall grass certainly made us look guilty of something. The police search team hadn't seen us yet, but we knew eventually they would find us. We decided the best thing to do was to stand up and let them see us walking along nonchalantly, minding our own business, innocent and unaware of any problems. The only thing that might look a little strange was our painted faces! I knew that maintaining a positive mental attitude about our appearance was crucial so it would work in our favor instead of against us. The best way to accomplish this was to decide that it was a "good" thing, not a "bad" thing. With confidence and the chant, "This is a good thing, this is a good thing" repeating in our brains, we stood up.

The instant we got to our feet the searchlight turned off. They didn't see us! So far, our positive thinking theory was working. We began walking back toward my trusty Rambler and the cluster of incandescent patrol cars that had converged on it. As we approached the brightly lit scene, we could see police scurrying back and forth, talking on radios, writing on note pads, and just waiting for something to happen. It became obvious that they were blinded by their own lights and couldn't see outside their perimeter into the surrounding blackness. We could see them, but they couldn't see us.

By the looks of their wide-eyed, dropped jaw expressions, they had a rather sudden and startling surprise when our multi-colored glowing faces abruptly appeared out of the dark, only a few feet from them, gleaming more vividly than ever in the brilliant lights! Before anyone else could speak, I said to the group, "I hope we're not the ones you guys are looking for."

They quickly and professionally frisked and handcuffed us, read us our rights, loaded us into the backseat of a squad car and whisked us away to the main downtown police station. At that time, the infamous Ted Bundy was unidentified and still on the loose in the Northwest. The police were on highest alert looking for him and weren't in the mood for humor from a couple of suspects.

On the way downtown we learned the shipyard had been robbed the night before. The night watchman on the dock was extremely uptight, and when he saw us park and walk toward the ships he was sure we were the thieves coming back to finish the job. He called the police and was charging us with the crime. We professed our innocence to the two cops in our car. I could tell the senior officer believed us, but the other guy was a rookie and was trying to make a "federal case" out of the whole thing. He was particularly perplexed and dumbfounded by our face paint. It just didn't fit into his conservative, small-town upbringing that grown men would paint their faces just for fun. There had to be a more sinister reason for it and he was bound and determined to get it out of us.

When we got to the precinct he kept drilling us over and over again about the robbery, trying to make us admit to it. He hounded us incessantly about our makeup. I could tell that it troubled him on a deep psychological level and that he was trying to reconcile the real reason for it in his own soul. He finally gave up and summoned the seasoned watch commander who came in, surveyed us briefly, and left after he declared, "Looks like a damn good disguise to me!"

His comment didn't help our case and only refueled the rookie's quest to get the truth out of us. I told him he could verify our story if he would only talk to my wife. I was entitled to one phone call so I dialed the number and he got on the line. When Jerri answered, he explained to her that he was officer "so and so," and that her husband had been arrested. Before he could go any further, Jerri assumed that one of my friends was playing a joke on her, especially since she had told us not to call her if we were stopped by the police. She laughed, and hung up on him! That only confounded the officer even more and wasted my one and only phone call.

The "this is a good thing" mantra was still repeating in my brain but it was getting quite a bit weaker and more desperate now. I pleaded with the officer to let me call Jerri one more time and let me talk to her for a minute. He could listen in. Wanting to satisfy his burning curiosity, he finally relented and I convinced Jerri that this was for real! Then the officer quickly grabbed the phone, and asked the burning question, "Why are their faces painted?"

With no coaching from me, Jerri repeated the simple truth, "Just for fun. They do it all the time."

With a pained expression of inner turmoil and frustration, he turned us over to his partner and walked away shaking his head and muttering, "Just for fun, just for fun."

The official jail photographer came in and took a color picture of us standing together. They detained us a while longer and then let us go to catch a taxi so we could retrieve my car out of the impound lot. Before we left, they informed us that the shipyard's night watchman was pressing criminal charges against us. We would have to settle the whole thing in court!

On the day of the trial we sat respectfully in the courtroom, watching the concerned-looking judge study our photo from the police station. She called the night watchman to the stand to testify first. He immediately began to rant and rave and was so inflammatory, inconsistent, and irrational that after five minutes the judge called a halt to the tirade and dismissed the charges against us as being unsubstantiated. She then turned to us and said, "I find you not guilty of any crime, but I think you are guilty of exercising poor judgment in this case. To guard against this type of disturbance in the future, this court declares it illegal for either of you to appear in public with painted faces, at any time, except on Halloween and New Year's Eve. Case dismissed!"

To this day that unprecedented injunction still stands on the books. Such was the justice of the 70's. We were relieved and jubilant. The reprimand against us was fair and an unexpected ending to a crazy drama. We felt righteous, amused, and thankful at the same time. It was a win-win situation. The judge was right about the judgment. My dad was right that, "Showmanship is nine-tenths of the show," and continuously chanting, "This is a good thing," was a good thing to do.

We celebrated with Chinese food for dinner that night and

I fantasized that my fortune cookie would read, "Wise man says, 'First you must show man ship, then he will buy it.' "

MUSEUM PIECE

LONG AFTER THE days of playing in rock and roll bands were over, I was still entertaining. My role was to provide pleasing background music for social events. My instrument of choice now was the grand piano. I loved the magnificent resonant sound of the seven and nine-foot-long models. Their reverberations filled the room and were the perfect way to enhance the atmosphere of a party. I learned that the touch, feel, and voice of every piano was different. It was a challenge discovering their individual personalities and tailoring the music to augment the character of each different instrument.

For this reason I promised myself never to pass by a piano without playing at least one tune on it. It is an opportunity to use my skills to soothe and entertain the listeners and it is a chance to communicate in a pleasurable way with a lovely music-making medium. When I have the ability and chance to add to the positive vibrations of my environment, why waste it and walk away? Whenever I see a vacant piano I force myself to sit down and play because it demonstrates to others what is possible. Something worthwhile and unexpected always happens when I do.

One weekend I was helping Dick cut up some large trees that had blown over in a storm. They were on the property of one of his mother-in-law's friends. She was a very gracious and spry widow whose busy social calendar always kept her on the go. She needed assistance keeping her property well-groomed and in good order, so Dick helped her with some of the repairs and upkeep. It was a rainy and blustery day but with chain-saws blaring, we were having a great time cutting, splitting, and hauling wood and burning up all the brush and branches in a huge fire that was blazing away in the driveway. It was a fine mix of testosterone, adrenaline, and gasoline. The kind-hearted lady was gone for the day, but she had invited us to come inside and rest, eat lunch, and warm up if we wanted to. She even told us to help ourselves from her refrigerator and bar.

By early that afternoon we were wet, tired, dirty, and hungry. The fire was smoldering under control so we went inside and took her up on her offer. While we relaxed in the kitchen eating our sandwiches and having a drink to loosen up our sore muscles, Dick told me a little about her history. She and her husband were independently wealthy. They had spent their early years traveling around the globe, sight-seeing, having adventures, and collecting souvenirs. In their later years they became patrons of the arts and provided lib-eral financial support to help underwrite the local arts com-missions and symphony. They were well-known for hosting elaborate parties and fund-raisers at their home. The most accomplished classical musicians in the area came there to per-form and entertain for these galas. Now that her husband had died, she still maintained her social ties but there were no more parties. The fine old house and its contents slumbered in undisturbed repose, sheltering its memories and treasures of days gone by.

I got up to use the restroom. As I walked down the hall I glanced into the adjoining rooms on either side. What I saw there fascinated me. On the way back I decided to do a little exploring. This place was like a museum! There were several large rooms filled with the wonders of the world. The floors were covered with thick, exquisite, hand-woven carpets from the countries of the ancient Far East. The walls supported pigmented tribal masks and stuffed wild animal trophies from numerous safaris, and original oils and water-colors from old masters. Antique chests were draped with rich tapestries and hand-carved, hardwood bookcases were filled with dusty manuscripts, maps, and charts. Every nook and cranny held a previously unforeseen relic. Dick joined me in the reconnaissance and we wandered from room to room in absolute wonder. A full set of medieval armor hung in one corner of a room that had a leopard skin rug on the floor, fragile-looking Chinese vases sitting here and there, and life-sized, aged acupuncture charts pinned to the walls.

We eventually came to stairs that descended into the basement. Not wanting our magnificent treasure hunt to end, we climbed down into steadily growing darkness. At the bottom we groped around for the light switch and flipped it on. It was the ballroom! The acoustical tiles on the ceiling and walls enclosed a large open dance floor and performing space. Down both sides hung decades of pictures of bygone symphony and dance companies and at the far end of the long, elaborate room stood a large and elegant concert grand piano. It was covered with a thick, quilted, custom-fitted blanket. On top of it were stacks and stacks of old newspapers and magazines that had been collecting there for years. The piano bench was piled high with full orchestra scores and old music books. It was love at first sight! I knew I had to play it.

Between the piano and the wall stood a marvelously ornate telescope. It was a beautiful heirloom of ground glass and polished brass. It sat on an exquisite wooden tripod with tall festooned legs. It was an imposing and delicate piece with its topmost, gleaming reflector mirror standing seven feet from the mahogany floor. We started clearing off the mountains of papers and mounding them up around the legs of the piano and the telescope. We slowly removed the cover for probably the first time in ten years and revealed a magnificent black satin Steinway built in the 1920s. I was thrilled! I propped the lid open part way and began to play a quiet and reverent classical piece. Each note sang and rang out with breathtaking clarity. The sound was vibrant, full-bodied, and resonant. It was the richest instrument I had ever played. I was so enamored with that keyboard that I didn't want to stop playing it. I wanted to play all the songs I knew.

I eventually exhausted all of the classical pieces I knew but I remembered an old tune that Dick and I used to play years before when we were still rockin' and rollin'. Its upbeat tempo and boogie style were probably unknown in the entire previous history on this refined and venerable master instrument. I was hoping I wouldn't offend its spirit and cause it to rebel. I was playing hard and we were both bopping around dancing and singing along. We were remembering the routine of the good ol' days and redoing it with flair.

Suddenly, out of the corner of my eye I saw something moving. Our raucous vibrations had toppled one of the newspaper piles which in turn displaced one of the supports on the tripod. The telescope was falling over! The end of the lens was crashing down toward the center of the black satin finish of the piano's lid. We were riveted in place, watching with horror as it fell in slow motion to interminable doom. Simultaneously we both dove at the plummeting spectacle. We caught it at the last possible second and stopped its momentum. When I looked up, the heavy glass dangled only a half-inch above the pristine silky sheen of the Steinway's priceless wooden body.

The fright of this extremely close call snapped us back into our senses. We marveled at our good fortune, relieved we hadn't caused any damage. In one more split second a real tragedy would have occurred. Irreparable physical, emotional, social, and historical destruction would have happened. It would have changed a lot of lives for the worse. Maybe that stately and peaceful old piano was rebelling after all? We quickly and carefully put everything back the way we found it and got the heck out of there! We brutes belonged outside breaking up dead trees, not inside a fancy house playing rock and roll on a museum piece!

I've had many music lessons over the years. I learned a lot about life and living from them. The importance of being on time, how to accompany a friend, the proper way to settle a score, what to write notes for, when to remain silent, when to do an encore, not being afraid to sing your song, and the importance of playing a little bit every day. The lessons weren't my idea, but I'm glad I stuck with them. They've served me well.

CHAPTER 14

The Great Outdoors

MOST OF MY life I have lived on quiet, dead end streets next
to the woods. The only exception was the ten years I lived in
various parts of Seattle while completing my college education. I grew up climbing trees, making camps in the ferns,
damming up creeks, falling into cold lakes, tripping over
hidden roots, finding camouflaged animal dens, bushwhacking on my own through unknown territory, and sitting alone
in the still, wide open spaces, listening to the sounds of nature
that surrounded me. I wanted to be like Tarzan, swinging
through the treetops and talking to the animals. I wanted to
race through the dense forest on silent feet like the great
Native American warriors did, unseen and unheard. I wanted
to be a mountaineer and ascend the great peaks to the top of
the world.

I practiced these skills every chance I got with the encouragement of my parents. They taught me the basic survival
tools for being a successful outdoorsman, including how to
swim, ski, climb, and fish. The group of kids I hung out with

were into the same thing. We spent most of our time playing in the water or hiking in the woods. Our quest for adventure grew. We always wanted to hike further, climb higher, and camp in a more secluded place than the previous trip. This ever-upward spiraling intensity for derring-do continued well into adulthood. For a while, even after receiving my doctorate in dentistry, I was more comfortable being in the woods than sitting chairside, fixing cavities. But there were a few defining moments that put into perspective just how well I had acclimated into the grand scheme of the great outdoors.

THE POWER CIRCLE

DICK AND I decided to go for a little conditioning romp in the hills. We were climbing Silver Peak, a 5,603-foot talus-covered summit in the Southern Cascades. It was fairly easy going, meandering through stunted evergreen trees and manicured marshy meadows. The only strenuous part was the last 200-foot scramble to the top over steep, loose shale.

Along the way, I told him about a book I was reading detailing the rites and rituals of native indigenous peoples throughout the world. I was particularly fascinated by the explanation of how some cultures used a "power circle" to influence the weather. The spiritual leader of the tribe would draw a circle on the ground with special shapes and sacred designs in the middle. Somehow he could use this configuration as a medium to alter the atmospheric conditions in his local area to induce rain, wind, or thunder at will. There was an illustration of one in the book.

Gasping and heaving, we reached the summit and sat down to eat our lunch, dangling our legs over the edge of the

1,500-foot sheer drop to the alpine lakes below. We sat there catching our breath, admiring the view and joking about life in general. The subject of the power circle came up again. I noticed a level area in the rocks off to the right of our route. It was about 25 feet below us, 15 feet in diameter and filled in with loose sand.

I climbed down and drew my own rendition of a power circle in it with a stick. I wanted to show Dick what I was talking about and it also served notice that we had been there. It was like scratching your name on the side of the clubhouse wall.

I filled the large circle with several smaller concentric circles, drawing the tiniest one right in the center like a bull's-eye. Then I randomly added some squiggled lines, odd rectangular shapes, and designs in a Southwestern-style motif. I returned to my perch, we chuckled at my creation, and then forgot about it. The spectacular vista of the adjacent mountains quickly diverted our attention. Transfixed by the immense beauty around us, we drifted into silent contemplation and time passed by unnoticed.

My rapture was interrupted by a low moaning sound. Dick heard it too as it grew louder and louder. Soon it was roaring like a freight train and was coming from around the corner of the vertical wall we were hanging over. We couldn't see what it was, but assumed it was a low flying jet whose pilot was on a thrill ride through the valley. The volume and character of the noise kept increasing and became unnerving and spooky. We strained to visualize its source and solve the mystery. Suddenly, it darted out from behind the corner, into view! It was a small but intensely raging cyclone, bouncing along the side of the wall about 40 feet below. It was buzzing along voraciously like the Looney Tune's cartoon version of the Tasmanian Devil. It seemed to have a life of its own and scared the hell out of us! It tore small rocks and bushes from the side, creating minor avalanches and plumes of dust. We grabbed onto the rocks for dear life and watched in awe as it advanced in our direction.

Its lateral motion stopped, then it lingered for a second and started climbing straight up the cliff face. It hopped up over the top edge and danced across the flat area where the power circle symbol was drawn. The ferocious howling and growling of the miniature twister was almost deafening now. The tornado hovered slightly above the design as it moved along and then touched down in the exact center of the bull's-eye. Instantaneously, there was a tremendous swooshing sound! The whirlwind spontaneously exploded to ten times its former height, billowing up a colossal column of swirling sand that surrounded us, totally obscuring our vision! We huddled there in the dust cloud listening. There was nothing to hear now except a sudden, eerie silence. All was calm.

Sitting on the invisible edge, we waited for our hearts to stop racing and our breathing to stabilize. The dust slowly settled and drifted away. When we could finally see the ground again, the sandy patch below us was like a smooth slate wiped totally clean! No sign of the circular diagram remained, not even the faintest hint or remnant. The power circle was gone, totally gone! Our hearts started racing again. Had we just witnessed a mere coincidence or was it something more? Had we awkwardly stumbled into a realm of the supernatural or was it just synchronicity at its best? Did the medicine men, witch doctors, and shamans have inside knowledge about the world, or were they just old folk tales and myths? All I know is that we were spooked, so we left the summit of Silver Peak for the solace of the lowlands, vowing not to fool with Mother Nature until we learned more.

SAND FLEAS

WE DROVE ALL day to get to a hidden cove on the east side of Vancouver Island. We performed our patented "slap launch" of the 10-foot aluminum boat, flipping it 180 degrees, bow over stern, from the top of the truck canopy into the frigid salt water of the Inside Passage. The loud, rivet-jarring, metallic splash was our signal that another adventure was underway. Exuding mirth and excitement, Dick and I quickly latched the small outboard motor on, threw our gear in, and headed out for the open water. The sun was getting low in the sky and our plan was to spend the night on one of the many small islands that dotted the horizon, then spend the next three days exploring the area and living off the land.

After droning along through the fresh air and smooth water for quite a while, we noticed that the islands didn't seem to be getting much closer. As the daylight began to fade, a slight feeling of alarm tingled through me when I realized by how much we had misjudged the distance. Upon finally reaching the first islet at dusk, we made another disturbing discovery. There was no beach! The entire islet was ringed with 20-foot high vertical rock cliffs. There were no landing places anywhere! We went on to the next one.

The same geological features kept repeating themselves over and over. Each island was like a stone fortress, resisting access to the sculpting action of the relentless tides and anything else that floated by. We were stymied by this predicament but not completely undone. In the gathering darkness there was one more large black void just visible against the backdrop of the horizon sky. We sped toward it at eight knots. This island was larger than the others and was our last hope for landfall. Upon arrival, we began slowly circling, scouring the shoreline with our flashlights, looking for breaks in the vertical topography. To avoid dinging the prop and adding to the adventure, we turned off the motor and pulled ourselves along the cliffs with our hands, using rock outcroppings and embedded pieces of driftwood for leverage.

I could feel the subtle pangs of desperation starting to stir as we drifted into a quiet little bay. Then, miraculously, there it was—a beautiful sandy beach. It was large enough to camp on, sheltered, contained adequate firewood, and provided easy access for island exploration in the morning. We hooted jubilantly, heartened by our good fortune and surprised by the echoes of our shouts resounding from the surrounding bluffs. We beached the boat, dumped our camping gear on tarps in the marsh grass above the high water mark, and began building a fire on the sand below.

When the fire was blazing away and ready to cook on, I returned to the tarps to retrieve my utensils and a frying pan out of my pack. While I was standing there in the dark I thought I heard the sound of gentle rainfall pelting the plastic of the ground cover. A wide brimmed cowboy hat protected my head and I felt nothing when I reached out my hand to check for rain, so I curiously shrugged my shoulders and returned to the fire. Ten minutes later, I returned to my pack for my water bottle and a can of spaghetti. This time there was no mistaking it. I definitely heard the sound of rain falling on the plastic tarps. I removed my hat to look up and feel the shower, but not one droplet of precipitation hit my face as groups of stars twinkled above me through large holes in the clouds. I was perplexed by this dichotomy. A slight shiver of fright and dismay coursed through my psyche. I silently walked down to the water's edge and peered at the surface, looking for tiny rings of ripples that would confirm the rainfall. There were none.

All of a sudden I thought I might be going crazy. I crouched down to warm myself by the fire and shyly asked Dick if he thought it was raining. He looked at me and just started laughing, no doubt thinking I was launching into one of my illogical joke sequences for which I was famous. The satisfying feeling of the warm food was punctuated by a few sips of brandy. Soon the depth of our conversation turned my mind to other thoughts and I felt more at ease.

Sometime later, I went back to our pile of gear to blow up my air mattress and roll out my sleeping bag. This time I could hear the sound of a complete downpour as I approached, but felt nothing coming from the sky. I was completely confounded and unable to remain quiet about it any longer, so I called Dick to come over and help me decipher the mystery. He could hear the loud pitter-pattering too, but when we shined our flashlights on the tarps we saw nothing! Then we decided to look underneath. We slowly lifted up one corner and there to our astonishment were thousands, no millions of sand fleas haphazardly hopping up from the ground, hitting the underside of the polypropylene, sounding exactly like rain. They lived in the sand around the roots of the grass that grew just above the high tide line. We had unknowingly thrown our bedding down on top of their home. They had all come outside to protest our invasion and disrespect for their privacy.

The sight and sound of so many of them jumping around like that was unnerving, repugnant, and unacceptable. There was no way that either of us was going to lie down and sleep there with them, so we reluctantly moved our camp site out of the nice soft grass down onto the wet sand of the beach. We picked a location that was closer to the fire but still a safe distance back from the water's edge. With the stars forming our ceiling, I crawled into my warm sleeping bag and laid back on my full air mattress. As I drifted off to sleep I felt so glad that I was still sane, it wasn't raining, and we had discovered the teeming swarm of sand fleas in time. I was ready for the adventure of tomorrow.

Hours later, in the dead of night, I woke up. I was very

drowsy but I knew something wasn't right. I opened my eyes and tried to focus them on my pitch-dark surroundings. Slowly my vision locked on, and to my absolute horror I realized I was surrounded by water! I froze in terror! The tide had come in and we were going with the current, floating out to sea. I knew that any sudden move or shifting of my weight would immediately dump me into the cold, dark water of the Sound. I could feel a gentle bobbing at my feet as baby waves rolled under me. Off to my right I saw that Dick was still within reach and still asleep. I knew I must wake him up before he rolled over and submerged. I gently and softly called his name not wanting to startle him into a jerk. I knew the revelation that we were floating out in open water would be enough of a shock to him. In a comatose voice he finally uttered, "Huh!"

I quickly said, "Dick, don't move and stay centered on your air mattress! We're floating!" Then, I felt something hit my back! Fearfully, I pushed down firmly but cautiously with my hand. It was solid. It was the beach! Vastly relieved, I slowly sat up and saw with fully accommodated eyes that indeed the tide had come in and surrounded us with water but just barely. The edge of the shore was only 18 inches above my head. We weren't floating after all, but from my groggy and prone perspective it appeared we were in the middle of an expansive sea.

We climbed out of our somewhat soggy beds and unenthusiastically moved them back up to the fringe of the grass where the sand fleas were waiting for us. We rolled up in the plastic ground cover and wrapped it tightly over our heads, risking asphyxiation, and listened to billions of bugs dance the night away on top of us, as they joyfully tried to gain entrance into our dens. The noise they made sounded just like rain.

We spent the remainder of the night in a fitful and fretful state, waiting for dawn, afraid to open a space big enough to see if it had come yet. At last it was confirmed. The sun was up. It was a glorious sight as I squinted out through a crack between the covers. Backlit by the sun, a whole line of tiny spouts erupted randomly down the beach as hundreds of butter clams siphoned their breakfast as high tide retreated. Throngs of sea birds sang good morning and dove into the water fetching minnows. An occasional sea lion's head would pop up, eye us curiously for a moment and then disappear beneath the waves. We were in the midst of a crush of life and life-forms all going about their daily business in the most merry way. It was a fantastic experience just being immersed in their world. Even the sand fleas seemed friendly this morning.

We realized that they were our welcoming committee. It was exactly what we were looking for. It was a rough start making the transition into their world, but we were successful. We learned how to live off the land and had a wonderful adventure doing so.

GROUP ENCOUNTER

ONE OF THE best parts of having outdoor adventures is sharing them with your friends. Over the years, a ragtag bunch of male groupies formed who shared the same common zeal for off-trail bushwhacking, random roaming of the hills, finding creative camp sites, and climbing steep stuff just to see what was on the other side. Because of our work schedules it was rare that all of us could get together at the same time for the same trip. When we did, the unexpected always happened.

We were fortunate enough to get six of us together for a week-long trip to the Enchantment Lakes in the Stuart Range of the Cascades. I was the designated driver, elected to transport us to the trail head in my old-style, family-sized station wagon. The central meeting and pickup location was the west side of the parking lot in a big shopping mall just north of Seattle. I was the first to arrive and kept driving in circles around the area until one by one the rest of the team showed up. We continued to play follow the leader in a five-car caravan that serpentined through the empty stalls and around the parked cars, using them like buoys in a slalom course. It was great fun! When a parking lot security van finally appeared, we quickly stopped in an open area, positioning each of our cars perfectly between the painted lines. As if on cue, we all jumped out of our vehicles at the same time. The motley crew consisted of: Crazy Larry, Looseman Dan, Tim Terrific, Kurt The Flirt, Captain Dick, and myself, sometimes referred to as Shinn Bone.

There was much shouting and laughter accompanied by boisterous but good-natured shoving, jostling, and joking as everyone hurried to stuff their tents, boots, packs, and sleeping bags into the back of the station wagon without leaving any important items behind. At the same time the race was on to be the first to jump into the car and claim the most desirable and comfortable seat for the long, tightly crammed commute to the mountains.

My place behind the wheel was secure, so I helped organize the gear in the rear compartment while the others clamored into their places, clutching their individual bags of goodies and snacks to eat along the way. Everyone was wound up into hyper mode. It was a chaotic scene of happy turmoil and confusion. The whole car was loaded with male hormones surging out of control. By the time I got in, they were rocking the car side to side and bouncing it up and down. I feared a mechanical breakdown right there in the parking lot. Meanwhile, the security guy stayed in his van, cautiously observing us from a safe distance.

I slid into the bucking driver's seat next to Crazy Larry who immediately offered me a delicious looking, dark brown and gooey bite-sized lump. He held it out and said, "Here, do you want some of this?"

I love chocolate fudge, so I hurriedly grabbed it and tossed into my mouth while simultaneously trying to shut the door, start the engine, and fasten my seat belt. I mashed it around in my mouth with my tongue for a second or two before realizing that something was horribly wrong. I spasmodically lunged back out of the door and fell into a spontaneous gagging, retching, spitting, coughing and choking fit! What ever it was, I couldn't get it out of my mouth fast enough! The rest of the guys were equally doubled over with hysterical laughter, but only Crazy Larry knew what had actually happened. On the way into the car he had scraped off a wad of grease from somewhere underneath and was holding it on his finger tip. I'm not sure whether he meant for me to eat it, or just mess up my hands with it. Either way, he didn't say. After all, he was called Crazy Larry for a reason.

After an extended bout of vigorous spitting and using half of my water bottle to rinse out with, we were under way. No harm done. We completed two hours of true male bonding consisting of continual hilarity, free-flowing one liners, plenty of put-downs, and macho tales of past heroic deeds. Then we turned off the highway down the dusty and rutted road to the trail head. Fifteen bone-jarring, whip-lashing miles later we were there.

Our arrival was later than planned, but no problem, we had plenty of time. We cheerfully worked our way up the lower valley, stopping at all the bigger streams to play and quench our thirst. It was obvious we wouldn't get to the lakes before dark, so we ambled along, savoring the sensory input from the immense evergreens that surrounded us and the glimpses of majestic mountain peaks that teased us through breaks in the trees. It was still pretty early in the season, which insured that we would have the place to ourselves, avoiding the hordes of hikers that would follow after the weather stabilized.

Several pockets of melting snow invited wild and raucous free-for-all snowball fights. After all the yelling, running, throwing, ducking, falling, and rolling, we were huffing and puffing like tired-out steam engines going up a steep grade. We decided to call it a day and camped in a sheltered clearing nearby. That night we sat around the warm fire, watching the orange and yellow flames reflecting off the faces of our friends sitting across from us. One by one we crawled into our bags and went to sleep.

The next morning we awoke to a crystal clear, crisp blue sky. We packed up quickly and headed up without any breakfast. Using the map, we blazed a shortcut across the rocks and arrived at the lower lakes by noon. The beauty was stunning and unforgettable. The sun was hot. It was a perfect day. Above us loomed the towering pyramid of 8,440-foot Little Annapurna. Its rocky summit gleamed in the sun, calling down to us to come up for a visit. We couldn't resist. We decided to race to the top. The last man up had to cook dinner. We threw off our packs and started running for the first steep section. It was every man for himself! All the boasting of the last 24 hours put our egos on the line.

The weather was so warm that several of the guys had stripped down to only climbing boots and shorts. I always carry a knapsack full of survival essentials just in case of an unforeseen emergency. Today was no exception, but I was annoyed with my decision because it seemed to be slowing me down. I figured it was one and three quarter hours to the top and about an hour or so back down. I decided to shorten my route by staying in the steeper section of the rocks and avoiding the snow field on the more gradual but longer main slope. The extra adrenaline boost of the contest, coupled with free climbing up the steep chutes and scrambling over the loose boulders was totally exhilarating! I was fearlessly maneuvering through challenging obstacles that I normally would have never attempted. I hadn't had this much fun in years!

About two hours later I breathlessly jogged up the final gentle slope to the summit. Crazy Larry was already there waiting for me, but I was second, followed closely by the Looseman. The other three were scattered about five to ten minutes below us. We stood there transfixed by the sight before us. It was our first view over the ridge crest to the other side. Hanging in the western sky was the blackest, thickest, meanest looking curtain of storm clouds I had ever seen. Even though the sky above us was still clear and blue, it was obvious that bad weather would be upon us soon. We lingered long enough to get a group photo at the top, then we headed back down.

Crazy Larry took off like a shot and raced ahead. I grouped up with the Captain and the Looseman. Tim Terrific and Kurt the Flirt started to lag behind. Ten minutes later we could hear rolling bellows of thunder from behind us. The interval between volleys began to shorten. We still had a long way to go. We were traveling down as fast as we could, using the snow fields to glissade on, but the tempest was gaining on us. The wall of clouds shoved up over the ridge and the sky darkened. Just before we got to the flats it started to hail a little. Then suddenly there was a flash of lightening that lit up the whole sky and electrified the atmosphere! It was quickly followed by the deafening sound of the sky splitting open. Out poured a barrage of ice pellets the size of marbles. They stung like nettles! The hat and nylon windbreaker from my knapsack gave me some protection, but I was worried about the other guys who had nothing.

The storm continued to intensify. When I looked back, I could just make out the silhouettes of Tim and Kurt running willy-nilly back and forth like panic-stricken chickens, heads lowered, looking for shelter that didn't exist. There was another loud flash and the rain of ice suddenly doubled. Tim and Kurt disappeared into an opaque void behind us. In just a few minutes the air temperature plummeted from 75 to 40 degrees. We reached the plateau and started running down toward our packs, passing Larry who was already hauling his pack back up the hill to find some cover in the rocks above. He had more than the usual crazed look in his eyes. He refused to stay together with us and kept going. I remember wondering if I would ever see him again.

The pummeling from the torrent of hailstones was unbelievably painful. They were pounding our backs and heads from above and ricocheting up from the rocks and battering our faces. I was thankful that I wore glasses which protected my eyes, but it still was impossible to see any more than three or four feet. Luckily we stumbled upon our packs and pulled out a large polypro tarp and wrapped it around us. With the blind leading the blind, we scampered back up a few feet and crowded into a cleft between two huge boulders. The storm raged on.

For the next 45 minutes the nonstop booming of thunder threatened to rupture our ear drums! Continuous brilliant lightning strikes, brighter than burning magnesium, hit all around us sending a heavy scent of ozone to our flaring nostrils. There was so much electricity in the air that every time we moved, little jolts of static trapped under the tarp would crackle and cause our hair to stand on end. It was all we could do to protect ourselves from the hail and melt water that was streaming over the rocks we were hiding under. We hurriedly pulled on warm clothes from our packs and waited for Kurt and Tim to pass by on the way down to their packs. They never made it!

When the frontal edge of the storm finally passed by, the

intensity lessened a bit. Several inches of ice pellets had accumulated on the ground and the warm radiant energy stored in the rocks was melting them rapidly. Zillions of tiny rivulets were coursing downhill, collecting in the low points and flooding all the troughs and trenches formed by the uneven terrain.

We cautiously returned to the cache of packs to see if Kurt and Tim had somehow gotten to them without us seeing them. We found their two solitary packs, right where they had dropped them, marooned in a shallow grassy basin, filled with 14 inches of melt water. All of their belongings were soaking wet! With a genuine visceral concern for the welfare of our friends, we grabbed the dripping bags and set them out on high spots to drain. We then realized the awful truth. Our two comrades had endured the entire cloudburst and icy onslaught bare-skinned, wearing only boots and hiking shorts.

We fanned out in the cold air and sleet and began searching behind and under every natural shelter as we worked our way back up to where we had last seen them alive. While shouting their names and straining to hear a response over the retreating thunder, I felt a frantic feeling welling up inside. I silently prayed for their safety and struggled to quell the fear of finding them dead. I selfishly dreaded the consequences of having to explain the tragedy to their families and was feeling responsible for the whole mess.

I suddenly saw something moving up ahead. Just visible through the chilly mist, the two of them were slowly lumbering toward us, bare chests heaving in the wind. We joyfully embraced! They had thankful smiles of rescue and survival on their faces but were shivering so badly that they could barely speak. They managed to say they were okay, but I knew better. We lingered for a while searching for Crazy Larry but he was nowhere to be seen.

We retrieved our packs and quickly spread out the plastic

tarps over the tops of the three-foot high dwarf evergreens that sprouted between the rocky slabs. We tied the corners down and crawled underneath. Both Tim and Kurt seemed to lose whatever spunk they had left after finding that all their clothes were wet. We shared our dry clothes with them and laid them down on insulated sleeping pads. They refused our offers of food, lying there muttering incoherencies and wanting to sleep. Their lips and fingernails were turning blue.

I was the only one with medical training and knew they were drifting into a hypothermic coma and would never wake up if we didn't do something soon! I alerted Dick and Dan to the emergency. They started heating up our enclosure and making hot soup with three butane cook stoves going full blast. Meanwhile, we were crawling around on our hands and knees, buffeting and rubbing Kurt and Tim, refusing to let them fall asleep. We laid on each side of them under a sleeping bag, sharing our body heat and forcing them to drink hot liquids. They protested, weakly pushing us away, insistent that we leave them alone, but we kept shaking, cajoling and feeding them, not daring to let them close their eyes.

Slowly they started coming out of it. Eventually they sat up and started gulping down hot oatmeal and tea. An hour later they were pink, laughing, and almost back to normal, seemingly unaware of how close they had come to making a fatal decision.

Now our attention turned to the fate of Crazy Larry. He was up there somewhere. It would be dark soon. Could we find him in time? We left the cozy confines of our shelter and headed back up the incline, searching again. It was still raining lightly and the dirt between the rocks had turned to mud. We came across what seemed to be a slight hint of a trail of lone boot prints leading upward. We'd lose it for a while, then find another muddy cleat mark inspiring us upward even further. Carefully scanning the slopes, there was no sign of a tent or any response to our constant yelling. Alarmed by how far above our camp we were and the quickly dimming light, we gave out one more collective scream at the top of our lungs before heading back down. Standing there in the silence, we heard nothing except the soft murmuring of the evening breeze moving through the convoluted landscape.

Pangs of grief and desperation filled my gut, threatening to swallow up all my confidence. Then I heard the faint sound of a muffled voice somewhere close by. It was within 50 feet of us but came from an invisible source. With much gratitude and exhilaration we followed the sound, eventually finding Crazy Larry. He was in his sleeping bag and had slid himself down into a hollow beneath a large dead log for protection. He was completely covered with thick mud; reasonably warm, but miserable. He was unwillingly to move from his mucky den, not believing that we had anything better to offer him down below at our campsite. It took much arguing and convincing to get him to climb up out of his beastly bivouac. As we stood around cheering him on, his crazy stubbornness subsided and he reluctantly came with us.

Before long, all six of us were back together again, reveling about in the most luxurious, makeshift plastic enclosure I have ever inhabited. Four feet tall at the highest, it was our own secure little world, filled with hot food, comfortable beds, positive vibes, and good friends who were elated to still be with each other.

The next morning broke clear, warm, and bright. We spent the rest of the week exploring every nook and cranny of this fantastic, fairyland kingdom of alpine lakes, wide open flower filled meadows, stark jagged peaks, and ice covered ponds. We were in paradise. We watched as a myriad of fish chased our lures through the crystal clear pools. We basked in the sun and hiked to our hearts' content, never ceasing to be amazed by the beauty of Nature around every new corner. We enjoyed each other's company immensely. Everything was much better than we expected except for one other little rough spot.

Looseman and I decided to free climb neighboring Prusik Peak for a thrill. We slowly shinnied and squirmed our way up the steep 75 degree pitch using our bellies for purchase. The smooth granite slab on our route offered very few niches for finger or toe holds. As we climbed higher, I bemoaned our decision and prayed for an easier way back down when I knew that gravity would team up with our inertia, working doubly hard to pull us off the wall.

After reaching the ridge crest, we traversed across just below the knife edge and finally found an easier-looking way down. Little scrubby bushes provided more anchorage than on the way up, but it was still very steep. The struggle to hold on and lower ourselves was so taxing that we could only descend 15 or 20 feet at a time before stopping to rest. At one of these stops I was clinging to the precarious pitch, willing to give anything to be back home sitting on my cushy living room couch! I was contemplating my next move when Dan gave out a yelp.

He was just slightly above me and to my left, turned around, with his backside squatting against the hill. He had unwittingly slid over a yellow jacket's nest! When I looked up at him, a swarm of bees was angrily buzzing out of their hive right between his legs! The sudden impulse to escape their menace overrode our fear of falling. The panic-induced charge of adrenaline helped us scurry and scamper down that perilous face like sure-footed mountain goats. We didn't stop until we reached the bottom where we breathlessly surveyed our damage. Miraculously, other than a few scratches, scraped knuckles, and bruised egos, we were all right. Even though Dan was wearing cutoffs he only suffered one bee sting. Were we hard-core, awesome mountain men, or was this just another lucky break? Was this further proof that guardian angels were nearby, ready and willing to protect us in our folly?

It's more difficult than ever to get together now, but when we do, we celebrate and always hearken back to the thrills, chills, and spills of our group encounter in the Enchantments. Each of us has his own favorite memory of that trip, but we all agree that the best part was the comradeship. Sharing good times together is one of the best things Life has to offer. None of us knows how close we came to being permanently separated by death because of our innocent and gleeful zest for Life on that trip! We were young then, and tended to just laugh it off. But as the years go by, its significance is starting to sink in deeper and deeper.

A Change Of Heart

I THREW MY trusty old boots in the trunk and we were off for another adventure. Three of us were leaving to explore the southwest corner of Mt. Rainier. Since we were bored with hiking on trails, this trip would be off-trail bushwhacking all the way. We planned to follow the Mowich River up from the lower valley to its source, the Mowich Glacier. We were in tip-top condition, had enough food and essentials for an extended stay in the wilderness, and carried a U.S. Geological Survey topographical map to keep us headed in the right direction.

Dick, Dan, and I parked the car in a thicket of young alder saplings at the end of an obscure, dirt side-road that lead off of the main highway. We shouldered our gear and scampered down the clear-cut ravine, crawling over, around, and under hundreds of discarded logs, fallen trees, and slash piles. It was a strenuous trek that included a few stumbles and some not so graceful falls. But the sun was out and we were full of vim, vigor, and anticipation of a grand venture into the unknown.

After about 1 1/2 miles we reached the river right where it intersected with a beautiful little quick-flowing freshwater stream. Dropping our packs and grabbing our water bottles, we spread out in three different directions to search for the crispest-looking oxygen-rich waterfall to fill up from. On my way I discovered a completely intact snake's skin. It had been recently shed by its relatively large owner and was still mummified into a perfectly coiled ghost of a real serpent. I carefully picked it up and took it back to show the guys.

When I returned to the packs, Dick was there but Dan was still off somewhere at a secret spot, guzzling cool liquid from the stream. Dick and I marveled at the intricate detail and realism of the snake's skin and then carefully set in down on Dan's pack in perfect striking position. Looseman Dan was a good-natured, soft spoken and gentle kind of guy with a love for nature. He had strong legs and a reputation for being somewhat gullible, which we exploited from time to time. We sat on a log nibbling cookies mischievously anticipating his return.

Dan soon reappeared carrying his overflowing water bottle and a bag of trail mix. With his back toward his pack, he sat on a rock facing us, munching away on nuts and raisins. He didn't see the snake. We chatted pleasantly as if nothing was amiss, but Dick and I were busting up inside with hysterics. We could hardly contain ourselves or keep a straight face, especially when making eye contact. Minutes went by with no relief. Choking back a chortle, I finally asked Dan if we could take one more look at his map. He slowly turned toward his pack to fetch it from the top-zippered pocket. Out of the corner of his eye he suddenly caught sight of the coiled viper and his whole body instantly flinched, reflexively levitating about one foot straight up into the air while still remaining in a sitting position!

His animated overreaction caused Dick and me to shriek

out loud in unison. We howled mercilessly with glee and amusement, stopping just short of shedding tears. Dan was graciously amused at the ingenuity of the gag but didn't share our belly laughs and guffaws. When we finally settled down, we apologized to Dan for the thousandth time since we'd known him, reshouldered our packs, and started to follow the river up the grade, everyone in a party mood.

The underbrush along the sides became so dense that it was easier to hop from rock to rock in the riverbed. We continued on this way for hours, crossing and recrossing the milky white torrent of glacial meltwater and silt that tumbled down the hill from the giant mountain hiding somewhere in the fluffy clouds. As we continued up, the angle of the incline increased and the river grew narrower, deeper and faster. It was extreme fun, finding our way, picking our own individual routes, leaping across raging rapids, shouting to each other over the roar, and getting wet when we slipped or didn't quite clear the churning gaps over the cascade!

By late afternoon we were still unscathed and jubilant. We were all alone in extremely wild country at the confluence of the north and south forks of the river coming from their respective glaciers somewhere above. A huge, wedge-shaped spine of forested rock rose up between the two rivers, keeping them apart until they rounded its prow where they crashed together in an immense, curling, standing wave. We carefully traversed the north fork, climbed the moss covered rocks to the top of the central spine, and walked into the woods on the floor of a towering, pristine forest. We set up camp on a soft bed of centuries of fallen needles from the surrounding giants of magnificent, old growth cedars and firs. What a place! It was deep, dark, and silent except for the muted rushing sound of the rivers below us. It was filled with the ancient wisdom of bygone ages. The reverence that it commanded reduced our happy talk to whispers and quiet wonder.

Early the next morning we decided this would be our base camp. We would leave our heavy packs and tents here and reconnoiter the whole area by day, returning to sleep at night unless we found a more desirable camping place farther up. We set off in our climbing boots, carrying ice axes and lightweight knapsacks that contained food and some basic survival gear.

It was easy going with little, if any, underbrush in the dim light. It allowed us to move freely in any direction. We felt like ants passing between the massive trunks of these colossal titans. We followed the ridge to the left, paralleled the north fork, and noiselessly passed a herd of grazing elk and several white-tailed deer. Two hours later, with the river now far below us, we came to an immense vertical rock wall that blocked our further progress. It rose 80 feet straight up out of the ground and was covered with slippery moss and tiny ferns dripping with dew. At the top were many rocky terraces spanning out in step-like stages. We scouted back and forth along the base of it looking for a route up. Only one steep little chute looked doable, but even it was pretty questionable. There was no other way and it was too early to turn back so we went for it!

We held on with our fingernails and clawed our way up the slick passage. It was actually easier than it looked and we were elated when we reached the surefootedness of the terraces above. We continued exploring over hill and dale, through mysterious-looking canyons and under delicate archways of huge fallen trees. I was exhilarated and feeling invincible! I was one with Nature.

We kept climbing, always working our way to the highest part of the ridge which was getting narrower and narrower. In the increasing altitude the trees became smaller and smaller. We finally found ourselves in a vast expanse of densely packed, fiercely resistant sub-alpine firs. They were no more than seven feet tall, but their stiff prickly branches blocked our view, swatted our faces, and slowed our progress to a crawl. Their limbs and trunks were all twisted and splayed out in every direction from the heavy blanket of seasonal snow that stunted and mutated their growth. As we labored through the almost impassable jungle, we felt like hobbits on an extended odyssey in a strange and mysterious land.

It was easier to stoop down and slink along beneath the thick, vibrant green boughs in the needle-free zone of tangled roots and bare stalks. We traveled this way down through a U-shaped valley, finally ending up on top of a hillock on the opposite side where the trees thinned out a little. I popped my head up to look around. In the not so far off distance was the gleaming, dirty snout of the North Mowich glacier! The sight of it energized us. In double-time we breathlessly raced to the edge of the forest so we could see it in its entirety.

It nestled in an immense, rocky, and almost barren gorge that had been scraped clean by generations of this slow-moving wall of ice which was now slowly retreating back up the mountain. Like a giant omnipotent dozer blade, it blazed its own trail through the landscape, leaving behind a deep impressive scar. It was covered with patches of dirt, loose rocks, and dark sections of colored lichen. Its face stood 60 feet above us with a chocolate brown cataract gushing out of its mouth. In its wake on either side rose stupendous cliffs of terminal moraine, centuries of debris that had been dug up and carried down from above, pushed aside and stacked up along the route. Above and beyond was the lofty summit of the massive mountain itself. We were overwhelmed by the majesty and massive scale of the scene and thrilled to be in the presence of such unspeakable power! The cracking and groaning of the moving ice, the crash of small avalanches falling down its flanks, the growl of the rapids, and the pounding of heavy boulders rolling downstream all added to the mind-boggling experience.

We ate our lunch sitting there in the midst of it all. With

my senses wide open, I yearned to capture its entirety. I surveyed every detail carefully with my eyes and became particularly intrigued with a spot about 350 feet above on top of the wall of moraine where it flattened out. There was a glimpse of an emerald green glen filled with elf-like perfect trees. It was in stark contrast to the pencil lead, gray color of the surrounding walls. I fantasized that it was a mystical place filled with fairies, crystalline waterfalls, and elegant, fragrant gardens buzzing with beautiful butterflies. I knew no human had ever been there before so I had to get up there and touch it to see if it was true. A fabulous treasure waited above, begging to be explored.

I pointed out the object of my wondrous vision to Dick and Dan. They were intrigued, but not nearly as much as I. Finally I convinced Dan to come with me to check it out. The 350-foot pile of moraine was a chaotic concretion of compacted silt and rocks ranging in size from sand pebbles to boulders as big as cars. The bottom started at a 65-degree pitch and then steadily steepened to 90 degrees vertical about two-thirds up. The last 15 to 20 feet overhung slightly backwards, defying gravity and forming the final barrier to the undercut lip of the land of enchantment that enticed me upward.

The only climbing gear we had was our boots, our wits, and our ice axes. We counted on using the picks on our ice axes for cutting leverage into the sandstone-like texture of the exposed earth to help us manage the steepest section. Full of confidence, we started up the wall. To avoid hitting each other with loosened rocks, we took slightly different routes, converging on a gap that broke through the overhanging, verdant-laced edge so far above our heads. The first 200 feet were relatively easy and exhilarating climbing, maneuvering up, over, and around the obstacles trapped in the mounded soil of the glacier's furrow.

When I reached the vertical section, I needed a little more

security so I grabbed my ice axe and swung it hard to embed the pick into the surface for anchorage. "Whap!" It was like hitting a slab of cement! The ice axe bounced off sideways, causing my knuckles to bash into the rough surface. The action surprised me! I tried again, swinging even harder into several different spots, but to no avail. It was so hard that the pick wouldn't penetrate far enough to stick. All I got from the exertion was a bloody, bleeding hand and a fragile feeling of fear welling up inside. The ice axe now became an unwanted hindrance hanging from my wrist strap, clanging against the concrete as I slowly pulled myself up toward my worthy goal. It was so steep now that I had to continuously maintain a three-point stance to hold on and keep from falling. I even mentally activated the magnetic energy of my solar plexus to help glue me to the side with my stomach. It was scary, but so far so good.

Finally I reached a spot about 25 feet below the overhanging shelf. I stopped to rest and gather my grit for the last challenge. This had been a much harder climb than it had appeared from the bottom. Sweat stung my eyes as I breathlessly sucked in clouds of dust and gasped at the swirling air. I could barely see through the cake of mud that had accumulated on the perspiration-laden lenses of my glasses.

While I was holding on for dear life, Dan appeared from out of a rocky chimney on my right. He emerged slightly above me and stopped to rest on a protuberance several feet beyond my outstretched hand. We talked for a minute. I could tell he was as harried as I was about the extreme exposure. We decided that he would go the rest of the way to the top and then I would follow to insure that I wouldn't be in the way of any rocks that he kicked loose. I watched him deftly pick his route up and over the ridge crest. He disappeared out of the taxing vertical world into what I imagined was an oasis of lush green, relaxing and luxuriant flatness.

Now it was my turn to reach the promised land. My next possible handhold was about nine inches above my reach. I knew I would have to lunge for it. This was the crux move on my chosen path. After that, it was relatively smooth sailing to the top. I slowly transferred all my weight to my right foot, summoned up all my courage, breathed in deeply and violently leaped upward with all my might. Suddenly, there was a sickening and terrifying feeling! Something was wrong! I had come loose from the wall, but instead of moving up, I was out of control, sliding down! My ice axe slid up between my chest and the wall acting like a sled as I groped around for a grip. Miraculously, after what seemed like an eternity, my hands caught onto two baseball sized stones. I clung to their slippery, half-round shape with my fingers and frantically tried to get my feet underneath me. My left knee was barely touching something, but my right foot just wouldn't cooperate. I quickly looked down to see what was the matter. To my dismay I saw the awful truth. The sole on my right boot had torn loose when I jumped. It had peeled all the way back to the heel, and was flopping around uselessly, preventing me from establishing any kind of solid foot hold. My mind started racing!

I hung there, feet dangling. I couldn't believe it! How could these boots fail me? They were hand-picked and given to me more than 15 years before by my friend, Jim Whittaker, the first American to reach the summit of Mt. Everest. He was one of the world's best mountaineers and my hero. An expert boot cobbler had recently told me to get rid of them because the stitching was getting rotten and unsafe but I didn't believe him. I had gone everywhere in these boots. They had come to me from a mountain god. They were magic!

It would only be a short matter of time before the muscles in my hands and arms gave out. I would plunge over 300 feet, dash into the rocks below and die. I wasn't afraid of death. My life would continue on in an even more glorious plane than here. I wasn't afraid of feeling pain when I crashed into the ground knowing from my previous water-skiing accident that at the moment of impact, I would just go numb. Rather than feeling fear, my prevailing emotion was anger. I was furious and enraged that I had been so foolish, so reckless! I was too young to die. Two little boys and a lovely wife waited for me at home and I wanted to be with them. They deserved a father and husband who was present to watch them grow and mature. It was my responsibility to participate in their lives, sharing and nurturing the success of their future. Now, I realized how badly I had screwed up and how I had totally let them down.

Over and over again I yelled for help, both out loud and silently, inwardly. There was no response. The gusty wind blew my voice away from anyone that could hear. I figured Dan was basking in the pleasure of an enchanting Garden of Eden just above, in a completely different world than mine oblivious to my plight. Time was running out. I couldn't believe it was going to end like this!

Desperately hanging on, looking up, and waiting for the inevitable, I saw Dan's inquisitive face suddenly appear over the top edge. His carefree look of delight quickly changed into a somber grimace of concern. With renewed confidence, I told him I was in trouble and needed a hand. Without hesitation, he quickly backed out over the over hanging earthen cornice, accidentally unleashing a volley of rock fall that whistled by me only inches from my face. I would like to think, had our roles been reversed, that I would have the guts he had. To recommit himself to that terrible, more than vertical, rotten pitch took real courage.

He got back down to the protruding platform he had rested on previously and reached down to me. We clasped arms and he pulled me up far enough so I could get my left foot onto some solid support. That was all it took, but it saved my life! I reassured him I could make it now, so he returned to the safety of the flat land on top. I followed after him. With pure adrenaline, I propelled myself up to the platform, quickly gulped a couple of deep breaths, and then kicked and crawled my way up behind Dan.

I flopped up over the edge onto a grass-covered blanket of safety and sat down with absolute relief on a large boulder. Within seconds my beleaguered arms took on a life of their own, spasmodically twitching, jumping, and waving around in space like they were trying to reject my body. After 20 minutes of being on autonomic auto-pilot, my overwrought muscles finally settled down enough so I could feed myself.

After a snack, we did what we had risked our lives for. We explored the alluring new world. It was just as I thought it might be: beautiful, pristine, and majestic; a perfect solitary haven for mountain goats and out of the way, off-trail adventurers. There was so much to see—unlimited possibilities for new discoveries and stunning vistas. But somewhere deep inside tugged an unresolved, nagging feeling that disturbed my complete immersion into this paradise. It blunted the sharp edge of this thrilling discovery and haunted my fleeting thoughts. I knew it had something to do with my near-death experience. I tried to ignore it.

After about an hour, we reluctantly decided it was time to return to the valley floor and reunite with Dick. We descended along the edge of a large, cascading waterfall. The eons of falling water had eroded the moraine, exposing gigantic granite blocks that tenaciously clung to the cliff. It was stupendous exhilaration worming our way down through that maze of suspended projections of potential energy. We hoped that the extra weight of our relatively tiny bodies wouldn't be just enough to topple the tons of stone that had been patiently waiting for centuries to fall. It was sure-footed, but insecure climbing. We slowly tested each step, listening intently for sounds of separation and avalanche. As we got lower, the danger lessened and prompted us to move faster and faster.

At long last we reached the rugged valley floor and recounted our escapade to Dick, who had witnessed my "trouble" on the wall and was happy that he had stayed behind. We explored the mud-covered body of the glacier, peered into its deep blue crevasses, and dared each other to jump across the raging tumult of the river pouring from its mouth. We squeezed as much exploration and adventure out of the allotted daylight as possible, then headed back down toward base camp. The way back was just as exciting. With no trail to guide us, we purposely took a new route, investigating several beguiling gullies, hidden hollows, and knobby knolls.

But ever since my death-defying grip on the wall forced me to review my life's priorities, a disquieting background of emotional discomfort was distracting me. What was it? Self doubt? Fear? Guilt? I wrestled to keep my internal brooding subdued, but the closer I got to camp the more it dominated my thoughts. Finally, lying in my sleeping bag, in the deep, dark void of the powerful and all-knowing forest, I spent a sleepless night exploring my innermost thoughts as they erupted to the surface of my mind.

I was overwhelmed with gratitude that my life had been spared. I knew there was a reason for it. I didn't want to disregard and lose it. I had been given another chance. I vowed to be worthy of this priceless gift. I could feel the unmistakable divinity in the Great Spirit of Nature that surrounded me. I wanted others to realize its presence too. I resolved that my first order of business would be to share my outdoor experiences with my family. I would quit going off on my own and tone down my thirst for extreme adventure to a level where Jerri, my sons, Joe and Mike, and I would share the exuberance of Life in the wild together. I rededicated my life to this pursuit.

After unraveling and reorganizing all my discordant thoughts into clarity, I felt better. I realized that the anger and guilt that flashed through me while dangling above death and grasping the wall had been bothering me deeply. All of us are connected to Life by only the most tenuous thread and it is up to us to make the most of it. And so there, hanging on the brink, I had a change of heart. I would take a divergent direction, a new unexplored route where there were no established trails. Things would be different now. No more solo attempts at reaching the heights. The raising of family became my quest. We would rope together now and wherever we went it would be a peak experience.

GOING DOWNHILL FAST

FOR SOME REASON when I took my family out into nature all my outdoor expertise seemed to disappear. When I attempted to demonstrate and share my wilderness prowess things backfired. On the first hike with my boys I was showing them how to identify and follow animal trails. We were walking through a long forested box canyon just east of Snoqualmie Pass. In the process of a rollicking snowball fight deep in the woods, I lost track of the animal path that led off of the main trail we had been on. We were lost! It was the first time it had ever happened to me. We searched and searched for the skinny little route that ran through the bushes but we couldn't find it. Thick brush and brambles surrounded us. I realized it would be fruitless and dangerous to blindly grope our way through miles of this choking forest while hoping to spot the trail. Besides, it would take so long that it would be dark before we got there. I tried to remain calm, cool, and collected and in control of the situation. I didn't want to show any obvious concern that would scare the boys.

Our only option was to cross down to the river that was gushing through the ravine below us and follow it out. I remembered that it intersected the main trail about two miles downstream. It would provide an infallible and faster access to our exit. As we carefully rambled down the bank toward the sound of the river, the scrubby undergrowth tore at our exposed arms and legs. It was tough and troublesome going but the boys handled it well. The sharp, whiplike vegetation grew densely packed right up to the edge of the river, forcing us to wade in the water to avoid further lashing punishment. Scratched and bleeding, we stepped into the icy torrent.

It was so cold that it stung our wounds and hurt our feet. We could hardly stand it! But after a while, we got so numb that it deadened the discomfort from our minor cuts and lacerations.

We continued shuffling along in the rapids over the slippery river rocks, holding onto each other and moving downstream like a human chain. I used a long-pointed stick to help stabilize us, but in some places the water was too deep or fast to safely negotiate. We also encountered several large waterfalls. In these areas we had to reluctantly return to the abusive chaos of the bordering jungle and fight our way through, returning to the water as quickly as was feasible.

It was a long, freezing trudge but I knew we would make it. My confidence infected the boys and their brave determination inspired me in return. They were just little guys, barely seven and nine years old. Finally, in the distance I recognized familiar landmarks that were in the area where we had crossed the river on our way in. Hallelujah, we found the trail! We were so stiff from the frigid water that we couldn't hike very fast. It was dark half an hour before we reached our parked car.

Fortunately, we had brought several flashlights along for just this sort of unplanned occurrence.

All in all, it was not the type of experience I was hoping for on our first outing, (or ever for that matter) but it turned out okay. We learned about staying calm, being prepared, and paying attention to our surroundings. The best part was that we learned these things together. It was to be the first in a long series of great bonding events to come. When we got home, I took some good-natured ribbing about my "bungle in the jungle" from the family. Dad, the so called wilderness expert, had gotten lost! But we eventually found our way and survived. I was still their hero. That night Jerri and I decided that we should look for another recreational pursuit for the boys until they got a little older. We chose downhill skiing.

We signed them up for snow skiing lessons and got them outfitted for the upcoming season. The four of us went to the ski shop, filled with anticipation and had great fun trying on boots, fitting skis, and sizing poles that we would rent for the winter. I decided this would be the perfect time to take up skiing myself. I had fond memories of skiing a lot with my Dad when I was a kid, but that was at least 25 years ago. Those were the days of the old leather, hobnail boots, wooden skis, and free-heeled cable-release bindings. Modern equipment was drastically different. After picking out a nice pair of used skis, new bindings, and matching boots, I sat down on the fitting bench and tried on the new high-tech plastic boots to make sure they fit properly. I was surprised at how rigid and stiff they were, not at all like the flexible leather of yesteryear. The salesman assured me that this "state of the art" equipment would guarantee me a stellar performance on the slopes. I took his word for it without trying them out any further.

It was slightly less than a hour's drive from our house to the ski area at Snoqualmie Pass, but we got up extra early on the first day of lessons to make sure we arrived on time. We piled into the station wagon with all our gear and braved the ice-covered roads and crazy, impetuous drivers. We passed several cars that had somehow turned over or skidded into the ditch. Seeing these misfortunes reminded us to be especially careful to avoid our own mishap. We arrived safely and parked on the snowy shoulder across the main road from the ski hill.

With much fussing about trying to get dressed and organized in our cramped quarters, we hurriedly got ready. Sitting out on the tailgate, I put on my new boots, goggles and gloves, while pretending I was a hotshot ski expert. With my cool outfit and flashy equipment I knew I looked the part, at least until I attempted to cross the street. Figuring I would just dart across between the oncoming cars, I leaped out into traffic carrying all the skis. Frantically, I found myself standing there virtually immobilized! My feet and ankles were locked up so tightly in my new boots that I couldn't walk normally. It was a real-life version of a nightmarish dream when you're trying to move quickly, but despite using all the effort you can muster, you're stuck in thick, invisible molasses, frozen into extreme slow motion.

I couldn't move out of the way fast enough. The nearest cars coming in both directions locked up their brakes and began sliding on the ice while I moved across in front of them at a snail's pace. The drivers' honking and bewildered expressions indicated that I had been recognized as a complete novice instead of the pro I was trying to portray. Several of the cars barely missed hitting each other, ending up partially sideways in the road. I played dumb (I'm sure it was evident anyway) climbing part way up the opposite bank. Then I turned around to face the curious stares of the rest of my family who were still patiently waiting on the other side for the traffic to clear.

Then we reunited, found the kids' ski instructors, introduced ourselves, shared some encouraging words, planned when and where to meet for lunch, and that was it. They were off.

We watched with some trepidation as our precious little boys boarded the chair lift and were swept away, finally disappearing into the fog near the top of the mountain. The look on their faces bespoke lots of exhilaration mixed with a tinge of apprehension. When we could see them no longer, Jerri left for the warm comfort of the lodge to read while I began my assault on the snow.

SNOW SWEAT

I WAS A pretty good skier in my youth and I didn't need lessons. I would pick up where I had left off. Just to make sure I still knew what I was doing, I opted for a preliminary run on the intermediate rope tow before heading up on the big chair. Slowly tightening my grip on the rope as it sizzled through my gloves, I grabbed on. Whoops, it nearly pulled me over on my face! Struggling to retain my balance, I flailed around and barely made it to the top. It wasn't the most graceful ride, especially for a grown man, but it was early in the morning and few people were around to see. Standing on the edge of the slope and confidently pointing my tips downhill, I mentally picked a spot at the bottom where I would stop and then shoved off. In seconds I was skimming along quickly, rapidly picking up speed. I was absolutely thrilled by the sensation and realized that I was totally and utterly out of control. I couldn't turn, couldn't stop, and my ego wouldn't let me fall. Fighting to stay on my feet, I finally skidded to a stop 300 feet below where I had planned to. I stood there perplexed about what could have gone wrong. It never was this difficult before!

As I strained to pole myself back to the rope tow for another go at it, I told myself, "I can do this." All the other skiers were just gracefully floating down the hill, turning at will, having a great time. I was going to do that too.

Before the morning was over I had effectively shut down the rope tow several times by falling in a useless heap half way up the track, blocking the way for everyone trying to ride up after me. I had wrung my neck on the bright orange safety-netting that secures the area underneath the chairlift. Unable to stop in time, I had run pell-mell into the back of the last person standing in the lift line causing a giant chain reaction. In dismay I watched as more than half the line went down like dominoes, creating a huge, tangled mess of bodies, ski equipment, lane-divider ropes, and unconstrained cursing. At that point I headed for the lodge.

It was one of those rare winter days in the Cascades. The sun was bright and balmy and the cloudless blue sky was intense and sparkling. Many people were eating their lunch outside in front of the lodge, soaking up the warmth and working on their tans.

When I saw the crowd, I knew I still had a chance to redeem myself. None of them could possibly guess what a basket case I was up on the hill. I strode up confidently on my skis and stopped right in front. I intended to expertly stab my skis into the snow and coolly strut into the lodge just like all the rest, but as I stood there smiling, I realized I wasn't sure how to unfasten my fancy new bindings to get my feet loose. Theorizing it was just like the old style where you had to bend down and pull up on the lever, I turned, twisted, and stretched, trying to reach around behind myself and grasp the release while fighting to maintain my balance and my dignity. It was all I could do to barely touch the back of my binding without falling over. I hooked my fingers under the edge and pulled up but nothing happened. I did it again, this time harder.

The extra force contorted me backwards too far. I felt a sudden and loud pop in my chest as a rib cartilage tore loose from my sternum. "OWww!" I yelped as I grabbed the sharp pain in my chest and crumpled to my knees in the snow. I heard a collective gasp as several of the curious onlookers in my audience checked to see if I was having a heart attack! I reassured them saying, "I'm okay, I just pulled a muscle or something." As I knelt there trying to recover, a real skier shooshed up and stopped beside me. He calmly placed the point of his pole into an opening in his bindings and with a casual little flip unlocked them. Before I could take another deep breath he was out, done, and gone. I sheepishly followed his example and meekly wandered into the lodge to find Jerri and meet the kids.

My chest was sore for more than a year, but during that time I got better at skiing. The boys really loved the sport and excelled at it. One day, I decided I was good enough to throw caution to the wind and really go for it! I started at the top of the hill and deliberately went straight down with no turns. Going faster than ever before, I was in control but teetering on the edge of disaster. I was thrilled, and proud and that I was actually skiing like a pro. The blazing speed, the rush of cold air, and the feeling of accomplishment pumped my ego sky high. It couldn't get any better than this! Suddenly from out of nowhere, a skier streaked past me like I was standing still. How could anyone possibly pass me? Amazingly it was a little kid flying down the mountain. Then I realized it was my young son Mike racing down to meet his brother, Joe, who was waiting at the bottom. I couldn't believe my eyes. Trying to go even faster, I hollered at them to watch me. When I caught up with them I breathlessly asked, "Hey guys, did you see me skiing? How was I doing?" I expected some well-deserved praise.

In unison they responded matter-of-factly, "Dad, you ski like a girl."

Well, maybe that was praise, but I interpreted it differently. It spurred me on to keep at it, to push the envelope, to get better. As the years went by, I improved to intermediate status while they both grew into great skiers. They eventually became ski instructors, inspiring the youth of the next generation to follow their joyful tracks down the mountain.

Skiing was a good decision.

CAR CAMPING

IN THE SPRING and summer when there was no snow in the mountains, we looked for other outdoor family pursuits. "Let's go camping," I said. I had been camping all my life and was undaunted by this prospect. It would be fun to teach the kids how to put up tents, build fires, sleep outside under the stars, and how to use your wits to stay comfortable and safe while living outdoors.

To eliminate the effort of backpacking, we decided to go by car, and camp along the way. Our first destination was Glacier National Park. With exciting anticipation I drove all day, trying my best to ignore the occasional squabbles that erupted from the restless kids in the backseat. We finally arrived at the park entrance to find signs saying, "Sorry, Campgrounds Full." I couldn't believe that it pertained to us, but the ranger at the gate assured me that it did. He directed us to a privately owned camping area about 18 miles back up the highway. Unenthusiastically, I turned around. We turned into the site a half hour later, just before sundown.

The manager told us we could pick any available spot for

$12. I was incensed that we had to pay that much, especially when the area was just a gravel-covered field with no trees or privacy. We would have to camp right next to people on either side in a wide open parking lot! To top it off, if we wanted a camp fire, we had to pay extra for the firewood. This was highway robbery!

I had always camped for free. I chose my own locations in secluded little glens, next to beautiful, babbling brooks with wide open views of magnificent scenery in the middle of untrampled wilderness. Only my closest friends, Mother Nature, and I were there. As far as I was concerned, this stupid place didn't even count as a camp site. This was not what we had come so far to find. My family was worthy of better! I drove off in a huff, back toward the park, muttering under my breath and vowing we would find a righteous camping spot for the night. Motoring along slowly, I watched for side roads or turnouts that would provide access to the woods, but none panned out to my liking.

Soon it was pitch dark and the kids were tired and hungry. This combination of circumstances gave our search a heightened sense of earnestness. When we passed a couple of rustic looking motels with their "vacancy" lights still on, the kids whined and Jerri wondered out loud if we should stop, but I was determined to camp.

A few miles later at a bend in the road, I detected a clearing off on the other side. It was difficult to see in the dark but we turned into it. The headlights showed that it was flat, large enough to park in, and a safe and quiet distance from the highway. It wasn't exactly what I had in mind, but it was out of the way and had trees on either side. It would have to do!

We gently rolled to a stop and immediately began putting the kids to bed. It was so late and dark we decided it would be easiest to just eat and sleep in the car. The front seats in our Rambler folded down neatly to meet the back seat, creating one large, fairly comfortable slumber room. After a quick bite to eat, we got the kids tucked in with cushy blankets and pillows. Surprisingly, they settled down quickly and started softly snoring.

Jerri and I got situated and laid back to relax, letting our lower legs stick out underneath the dashboard. We whispered silently in the night. I could feel the tension of the long drive and the anxiety of the last few hours of frantic exploration draining out of me. We were cozy and warm. A few stars twinkled through the windshield and I marveled at how quiet and peaceful it was. Nothing could be heard except our breathing and the nostalgic echo of a train whistle faintly sounding somewhere, way off in the distance.

Time passed. Jerri was asleep and I was floating off into my dreams when I heard the train whistle again. This time it was a little louder. I love to watch trains. They kindle something pleasurable in me from the memories of my youth. I pulled myself upright with the steering wheel and peered into the blackness for signs of moving lights. But there was nothing. The inky void remained silent and still. I watched nothing for a while, then laid back down to snooze. I was lightly drifting in and out of repose, dreaming of riding the rails and feeling the low rumbling vibration of the iron wheels turning beneath me. Then I realized, "Wait a minute! I'm awake! This is real!"

I sat up with a start. There was a distant roar like a freight train was coming. I could hear the engines chugging and churning. Then I saw the single, solitary, bright light bouncing along through the trees. I could tell it was moving at a high rate of speed by how the long light beam danced and flickered through the forest. It was heading in our general direction but at 90 degrees to us. It would pass by about a third of a mile to our left. I tried to wake Jerri to tell her a train was coming but she was too drowsy to care. I would have my own private and special show.

Suddenly, without warning, the locomotive came charging around a sharp bend, heading straight for us. The blinding beacon shone directly in my eyes, rushing toward me. Before I could blink, the most awful and deafening blast exploded from the whistle, shattering the air. The ground shook violently. Panic stricken, high frequency screams erupted from the kids and Jerri. Our little poodle dog Mickie howled and piddled on the seat. I prepared to meet my maker. Within seconds it was upon us, too noisy to hear and too close to see! It streaked by us like a screeching, elongated rocket, filling the windows with a metallic, high-speed blur and filling us with stark terror! It was racing along at over 50 miles per hour and took more than 45 seconds to pass. The car shook and shuddered, jarring our sensibilities and severing our contact with reality. It was a jolt to my nervous system that I'm sure did permanent damage.

When the caboose finally flew by, it quickly disappeared into the darkness. Iron horse, Doppler echoes followed after it, slowly fading into the distance like a fleeting dream. The atmosphere in our car was frenzied! We laid there stunned and panting. I could hear my heart thumping wildly inside my head. We realized that physically we were okay, but mentally we weren't sure. It took well over an hour for all of us to settle back down enough to sleep. In the meantime, we talked about how fortunate we were to survive such a close call, how we were overloaded with exhilaration and fear when the train came busting out of the night, and what a swell, safe, and secure camping place I had chosen.

The next morning at first light, I got up to survey the scene. I had unknowingly parked with our front bumper less than five feet from the unseen tracks. I've always enjoyed watching trains go by, but this one was ridiculous! I thanked my lucky stars that we hadn't rolled any closer and I prayed for help in being a better scout and finding a "real" campsite for tonight.

We drove into Glacier Park early that morning and had a wonderful family outing exploring our stupendous surroundings. We hiked down steep trails, crossed rickety logs over rushing streams, sat in the spray of a magnificent waterfall, and picnicked in a fragrant, flower-filled meadow. All the while we were watching out for bears. There were bear warning signs everywhere, and plenty of pamphlets offering advice on bear confrontation safety and survival. I was somewhat worried, but I had come across bears in the wild before and they had always run the other way.

We retired to the campgrounds in mid-afternoon. It was a good thing because we got the last campsite available in our area of the park. We worked together setting up our old canvas umbrella tent, blowing up air mattresses, starting the campfire, and getting dinner ready around the picnic table. From several campsites away, I could hear a park ranger talking on his 2-way radio about a rogue bear that was roaming the area. It was boldly stealing food, picking through garbage, and terrorizing campers. The rangers were obviously concerned and trying to determine the bear's whereabouts. As evening fell, the ranger came over to warn us not to leave any food or garbage in our tent and to keep our dog tied up for safety.

I couldn't help but notice that directly across the access lane from our tent was a full garbage container that was overflowing its smelly contents onto the ground. At least another foot of trash was lying around the base of the can. I was concerned that this would be an attractant to bears, but figured the rangers had it all under control. After cooking pocket bread for dinner and smores for dessert, we bedded down. Jerri and I placed the boys between us and tied Mickie to the tent wall next to me. Tired from the day's vigorous activities, everyone fell asleep almost immediately, leaving me to listen to the soft breezes and the chirping crickets, and to ponder tomorrow's itinerary.

Suddenly I heard a crash and a clatter coming from the garbage pile. The haphazard noise was accompanied by occasional snorting sounds. It was obvious that a large wild animal was pawing through the litter, looking for food less than 35 feet from our heads. I froze with fright, petrified by fear. I didn't know what to do except lie there very still, hoping that no one would snore or make any other strange noises. I listened intently to every sound, my auditory senses peaked to the max! For 15 or 20 minutes the rummaging racket went on. Then it abruptly quit. I strained to hear what was happening next. I detected the rustling of soft padded feet walking in our direction. Then the side of our tent caved in slightly as the big lumbering beast brushed by outside with only 1 millimeter of material between us and him! I could hear him breathing as he passed. Fortunately, he kept right on going. I heard him walking off through the brush.

What relief! It would have been so easy to claw through the thin canvas walls and eat our family and dog for dinner. The tension slowly faded away and I started to relax again, although I kept one ear tuned for any other animal sounds. I rolled over and with horrors discovered I still had half a bag of chocolate covered peanuts lying next to me. What an oversight! A bear could smell this a mile away. I wrapped it up tightly and stuffed it into my coat pocket. I didn't have enough courage to get up, go outside, and lock it in the car like I should have. Just as I was about to fall asleep I heard footsteps again. He was coming back, probably for the peanuts.

As he got closer and closer, panic welled up inside again, tying my stomach into knots. My heart was racing as my breathing slowed to almost nothing. I waited and watched in our shadowy, cloth enclosure. Suddenly the flimsy fabric next to me collapsed inward, forming an obscure outline around a long snout, only two feet from my face. I could easily hear it rapidly sniffing the air. I prayed that our dog wouldn't wake up and start yapping wildly out of surprised shock and complete dread like I was enduring. I could feel every pore silently oozing cold sweat and my own throat was constricting, threatening to choke me. I wanted to yell out, but didn't.

After what seemed like forever, the beast backed off. He returned to the rubbish pile and resumed raking through the refuse, ransacking the remainder of my reason. I listened to bottles and cans being scattered about for a while, then decided I couldn't stand it any longer. I had to catch one glimpse of this fearsome creature before it was too late. Ever so carefully I emerged from my sleeping bag and very shakily crawled across the tent floor to the back wall. Right in the center of it, facing the commotion, was a small transparent window of insect-proof fine mesh, covered with a canvas flap hanging down on two draw strings. From a kneeling position I gently tugged on the cords, slowly raising the flap.

I peered out through a narrow slit and was completely shocked at what I saw!

It was a dog! A harmless, silly old dog scavenging in the night. I was instantly at ease and laughed at how I had just spent the last hour in complete torment and utter anguish, my imagination filled with ghastly, grizzly bear attack scenarios. Jerri woke up and saw me looking out. She asked, "What's the matter?"

I responded, "Oh, it's okay honey. I just thought I heard something, but it's nothing."

I told her what really happened the next morning, but I kept it a secret from the kids. My skillful and fearless frontiersman image had already suffered enough. We had a fantastic time on the rest of our vacation. Although we saw and experienced the very best of what nature has to offer, we never did see any bears.

THE CLOUD

ONE SPRING MIKE and I hiked up to Summit Lake, which sits high above Steven's Pass in the Cascades. Our plan was to rendezvous with two other friends at the lake and do some camping. It was quite a haul getting up there, but we made it with a minimum of complaints and plenty of sweat. When we reached the elevated plateau that holds the lake, we found numerous deep pockets of snow still hanging around from the winter pileup. It made finding our friends harder than we expected. There were several sets of random boot prints going hither and thither and no answer to our calls, so we picked a track that followed along the shoreline and pursued it.

We went up an over dozens of snow mounds, occasionally breaking through the thin crust into the rocks and bushes below. It required lots of exertion and care to avoid stepping through the fragile snow bridges and not to injure our lower extremities when we did. We stopped often to catch our breath. Each time I detected an odd static-like background noise. It sounded like the faint humming of large, electrical power transmission lines nearby. I kept looking around for them, expecting to see tall, metallic towers or shiny silver wires showing through the trees, but saw none. It was probably just the sound of my throbbing heart pulsing in my ears. I shrugged it off. Finally our war whoops attracted some attention. Yells were coming back to us from the far end of the lake. Fortunately, we had guessed correctly and were heading in the right direction.

Eventually, with much exuberant and overt hullabaloo, we joined up with Dick and Steve. We all shouted and danced around like a bunch of cowboys coming to town after a long cattle drive. The two of them already had a nice campsite picked out. Firewood was gathered, bed rolls were laid out and fishing poles strung and baited. After the homecoming celebration settled down, Mike and I spread out our gear and then we all tromped down to the lake to hook some dinner. During the quiet moments, I continued to catch a fishy, whispering ring in the wind. It was that same dim, humming drone I heard before. I asked the guys about it. They heard it too, but there was no obvious explanation for it.

It was a delightfully warm, sunny day. The snow that fringed the lake was melting away quickly in the heat. The placid water looked so fresh and inviting I wanted to dive into it. I knew it would be cold, but I was a veteran of such antics. Long ago I had made a personal pact to never let cold water ruin a good swim. Besides, I was just dying to explore a small enticing island of grass-covered granite about 75 feet out. I peeled down to my shorts and slowly waded out, letting the icy liquid creep up on me inch by inch. I stopped often, allowing each newly submerged section of my body to chill out into relative insensibility. When I was almost chest deep, I dove in and swam. The sudden shock ached strongly in my throat, but I put it out of my mind, making a big show of briskly kicking, splashing, and porpoising out to the islet. I jubilantly heaved myself up onto the rock and dried in the sun. One of the best things about swimming in cold water is getting back out. Your whole body tingles with exhilaration. You can feel every individual goose bump as it shivers and quivers, vibrating the moisture loose from each tiny hair as it struggles to evaporate the coolness and recapture some warmth.

As I sat there in that phase I heard a large splash from the shore. It was Mike swimming out to meet me. I was surprised he was braving the raw, wintry water. Like father like son. He climbed up on the island with me and we felt proud together as we looked back at the two others on the beach, bundled up in their insulated outer wear. It was almost like we were in a completely different dimension, observing them from a separate reality.

As I gazed back at them into the low-angled sun I saw a sight that was infinitely more chilling than the lake. It was a humongous cloud! It became immediately obvious that it was the source of the strange resonating sizzle we kept hearing in the air. As far as we could see in every direction there were trillions of mosquitoes! Backlit by the setting sun, we saw that for miles every possible cubic inch of space contained at least one flying insect! There were literally tons of them suspended in the air! The cloud continued up vertically out of sight but stopped abruptly seven to eight feet above the ground to form a completely clear zone. A perfectly flat, horizontal plane defined the bottom of the cloud below which the bugs didn't go. They evidently were doing their own thing and weren't interested in us humans. That explained why we hadn't noticed them before.

As we watched, it was apparent that Dick and Steve were still completely unaware of the massive swarm of stinging anticoagulant that hovered just above their heads. Even more mesmerizing was the fact that all these mosquitoes seemed to be murmuring and moving in unison! We could see that they reacted to the motion of the guys on the beach. We tried an experiment. We hollered to Dick to jump up and throw his arms up over his head at the same time. When he did so, the entire cloud, for miles around, instantaneously reacted at the exact same time and shifted upward an equal distance! It was as if they possessed one mind that functioned for the whole group. It was similar to the way flocks of birds and schools of fish turn and dart together in shared agreement. We told Dick and Steve to turn around so they could see what we were seeing. When they did, they were flabbergasted. Time after time they leaped into the air and every time the mosquito cloud automatically recoiled on cue.

Even more mind-boggling, we could actually hear them move! Because there was such a vast horde of tiny, whirring wings, every collective flinch of the cloud caused the frequency of their buzzing pitch to increase. Their audible vibration raised up then lowered back down, cycle after cycle as we toyed with them. It was like directing an immense orchestra full of soprano slide trombones. It was truly unbelievable that they were responsible for the tone that reverberated through the mountains! To experience so many life forms dancing and singing together in such perfect harmony was astounding. In a sense it was eerie and even disturbing that we were in the midst of so many miniature, soaring, segmented organisms. If their group-mind decided, they could readily descend on us and carry us away to devour at a later date. It would easily set a record for the world's biggest mosquito bite!

Mike and I returned to the beach and heated our bones in the glow of the crackling camp fire. We wondered what our friends flying overhead thought about the platoons of sparks that billowed up into their domain. Would they retaliate after the fire died down, and come to get us in the middle of the night? I shuddered in my sleeping bag, not from the cold but from the stark realization of the infinite scope, depth and breadth of Mother Nature. The soft and gentle cloud continued to hang over us like a blanket, watching us sleep, keeping their distance and the peace. The next morning the dance continued on. Our airborne partners stayed with us, whispering in our ears until we had to take our leave and go back down the mountain.

The great outdoors never fails to thrill me, surprise me, educate and uplift me. I keep going back for more. The kids are young adults now, and living their own lives, yet there is one common bond that continues to draw our family back together: viewing magnificent mountain vistas, skimming across the surface of a mirrored lake, braving the cold rush of tumbling waterfalls, standing breathless together on the summits of the highest peaks, feeling the living power of the crashing surf, singing songs, and telling tall tales around the flickering campfire, watching the infinite expanse of other worlds twinkling in the night, and knowing that we're part of it all. Not even death can separate us from the omnipresent, omnipotent, omniscience of Mother Nature.

CHAPTER 15

Odd Jobs And Real People

BESIDES BEING A DENTIST, I'VE HAD QUITE A FEW OTHER interesting jobs up to this point in my life and I expect to have even more before I'm through. My very first job was picking berries. On a good day I could make $3.00. The best part was being outside in the hot sun and wide open fields, competing against myself for finding the most luscious-looking fruit in the most efficient manner. I learned a lot about the farming business and the brotherhood culture of the migrant workers. It was a positive experience that propelled me enthusiastically into the labor market. I was willing to take anything I got.

Subsequently, I've worked as a landscaper, house painter, mail man, research science assistant, musician, warehouseman, college instructor, laboratory technician, general laborer, truck driver, boat repairman, and motivational speaker. Every occupation contained moments of complete angst opposed with occasions of utter delight. My general impression was that all of them were mostly just plain fun. Several circumstances, though, contained special emphasis in the odd, unusual, and unexpected departments.

THE BALER

IN COLLEGE I worked on weekends in a large grocery warehouse. I stacked and sorted crates, ran a forklift, learned how to swear from the women working on the potato-bagging line, and risked my life on the baler. The baler was a new-fangled machine designed to shred cardboard for recycling. Its central feature was a five-feet long by three-feet high set of chopping blades that whirled around at thousands of rpms. It violently tore everything that came into contact with it into jagged fragments of its former self. Along with several others, my job was to stand along side the constantly moving conveyor belt that fed the roaring, ravenous monster and pick out anything that wasn't cardboard before it reached the all-consuming blades.

The boss man was concerned about production, so every day the race was on to maximize our output number of cardboard bales. This required running the baler at maximum capacity while being careful not to overload it and cause it to jam up and shut down. (This demanded a 15-minute break while some brave soul climbed inside to unclog the mechanism.) We pushed it to the limit and beyond every day. We feverishly picked litter off the belt while standing only three to four feet from the relentless snarling grinders. It was so loud we could barely hear the guy next to us yelling. This was before the days of strict federal (OSHA) safety regulations. It was basically every man for himself. When sorting, you had to be very careful about reaching into the constantly passing pile of jumbled paper. If you grabbed a piece of string or strapping, the end of which was entering the gnashing jaws of steel, it could easily rip off a finger or hand. The worst danger was letting a glass or metal container get by us and at the last second see it drop into the terrible twirling teeth. We instantly ducked to avoid the shotgun blast of shattered shrapnel that blew out at us.

Every day was like this. It was a job with no opportunity for advancement. Interpersonal communication was nil, the stress level extreme, mistakes were deadly, and the only benefit package was an exceptionally high thrill factor. But it paid the bills and for some reason I loved it.

A MAN NAMED DAWG

I LOVE BOATS! I grew up around them. I've raced them, rowed them, sailed them, sunk them, exploded them, rebuilt them, and ran them aground. But until about 1980 I had never owned one. At an old marina on the Duwamish River I saw the one I wanted. It was a classic, 40-year-old, wooden captain's launch that was rather dilapidated but had a strong, 20-feet long, cedar lapstraked hull. Years before someone had converted it from an inboard to an outboard. It languished in disrepair and I lusted after it. I contacted the owner and after a lengthy negotiation bought it and the moorage for $500.

I thought it was a steal until I realized it leaked like a sieve! I hauled it out, repacked the seams, caulked the planking, coated the bottom with the finest copper-based antifouling paint, put a new roof on the cabin, built in some really funky, fold-up benches, and drew a big, bold smile on the prow. I named him *Webber*. He was a boy boat and was my pride and joy. I spent countless hours with salt air ruffling my hair, tooling around in Elliott Bay, exploring the river, fishing for salmon, feeding sea gulls, and having loads of mariner fun.

Because *Webber* was open in the back, he took on lots of water during the rainy season, which is about nine months of the year in Seattle. At least once a week I went down to make sure the bilge pump was operating properly and to do some hand bailing of my own. On one such occasion it had been pouring for days. No one was about. Even the old-salt old-timers were huddled down below in their live-aboards, out of sight and out of the rain. I was just finishing up when I heard a yell.

A rough-looking man stood in the downpour on the pier above me. He was in his fifties, tall and skinny, with a completely bald head that was staring down at me. I could tell he wanted to talk. He took a few steps and then inexplicably and without warning, jumped off the pier and landed with a loud bang on the slippery, uneven, and wobbly float down on my level. The tide was all the way out, making it at least a 10 foot drop. It seemed crazy and reckless that he would even attempt such a thing, much less be able to land on his feet without injury or losing his balance. As he walked toward me I observed that his clothes were drenched and plastered to his skin. He seemed unaware that a fresh gash on the left side of his skull was leaking rain-diluted blood down and across his cheek and neck. Many of his teeth were black or missing and he had a wild, searching look in his darting eyes.

He came right up to me and announced, "Most of the people around here call me Dawg."

I nodded silently, remembering I had heard some of the good-old boys on the dock talking about him.

He asked, "Is this your boat?"

I nodded again and said, "Yeah."

He replied, "I've been eying this here boat. I want to make

you a proposition. My friend is a commercial fisherman. We could use a boat like this to haul our daily catch in from the outer Sound to get it to market faster. We'll only use it when you're not using it. We'll make you a helluva deal, pay you rent or give you a cut or somptin'."

As he rambled on, my mind started wandering. The best picture I could conjure up about this "deal" was that if I ever saw *Webber* again he would be filled with slimy fish scales and smelly entrails, even after they had cleaned him out. Meanwhile, some blood from his wounded, hairless head splattered onto *Webber's* deck. In my mind, the answer to his offer was a resounding, "No way, no how," but I was struggling to find a way to say it a little more politely. For all I knew, the knock on his noggin came from an altercation between him and the last guy who had turned him down.

Before I could adequately formulate my response, he surprised me by slapping me sharply on the shoulder and saying, "What do ya say pal? Do we have a deal? All it takes is a handshake!" and thrust out his open grimy palm.

My initial instinctive reaction was to reach out and grab his hand. I leaned forward but stopped myself just in time. Every fiber of my past conditioning told me to shake, but my rational brain was shouting not to. It was all I could do to keep my trembling hand at my side. I had to mentally force it to stay put. I knew that even the slightest grazing of skin between us would permanently seal this crazy contract with no easy way back out. I stood there like a statue, shaking on the inside. This was the first time I had ever refused this friendly formality. It was very awkward.

When nothing happened, a perplexed expression replaced the eager look on his face. I blurted out some lame excuse about how I needed to think about it for a while. I told him I would get in touch if I wanted to go ahead with the fishy deal. He shook his bald and bloody head as if he understood perfectly where I was coming from and lumbered off, disappearing somewhere into the maze of vessels moored in the middle of the marina.

Upon reflection, I realized the emotional power and pull that a handshake has. Not only is it a friendly greeting, but a symbol of trust and good will, a proclamation of promise and commitment, and an acknowledgment of agreement. It is an act that can be used to define your character. It can be used to signify absolute sincerity, or it can become a ritualistic gesture devoid of any meaningful forethought. In this case it was a door that led somewhere I didn't want to go.

I only saw Dawg one more time after that when he appeared out of nowhere and angrily threatened to shoot me for trespassing. Apparently he didn't recognize me, or maybe he was just peeved because I didn't shake his hand.

TRUCKIN'

EVERY TRUCKER HAS true tales to tell of near misses, real mishaps, and highway mayhem. Life on the road for the long-haul driver is a series of open weigh stations, crowded truck stops, greasy-spoon cafes, CB conversations, customized sleepers, and diesel perfume. It's a difficult life requiring nerves of steel, quick reflexes, long hours of alertness away from home, and quick-fix, on-the-fly, mechanical know-how. It is a separate culture with its own special language, customs, and tools. I can't say that I'm an expert or a member of the inner circle but I have floundered around the fringes of the trucker's world.

I used to deliver sailboats from Seattle to Los Angeles for a friend's company. Two of us would drive non-stop to a ritzy marina in Los Angeles, help their crew off-load the cargo, stack the trailer on top of the truck piggyback style, do necessary repairs to company boats, then drive back home. We took turns sleeping and driving. It was a challenging couple of days of constant driving but I always looked forward to the fun and excitement of dealing with the unexpected events that would always happen along the way. Besides, there was a certain feeling of power that came with successfully shifting all those gears, sitting up so high that regular cars seemed like toys, and being able to see way down the freeway above all the other traffic.

We were heading south and had just passed Tacoma with a fully loaded rig. A 26-foot and two 16-foot fiberglass sailboats, a canoe, an outboard motor, the masts, and all the rigging were lashed onto the open flatbed. I was driving along wistfully when I happened to glance down at the sedan passing unusually slowly on my left. An elderly couple was inside. The woman passenger was staring up at me with a totally aghast expression on her face, as if she had just witnessed something horrible. Her wild-eyed stare captured my attention. Her husband then sped up as if to get out of our way and pointed frantically to the back of our truck. I looked in both mirrors. Everything felt and looked fine. I almost shrugged it off, but we decided to pull off onto the shoulder and take a look just in case.

At first glance everything seemed to be in order—no flats or loose tie-downs. But then we saw it. Unbelievably, the towing ball had fallen off and disappeared! The trailer was completely loose from the truck and was being pulled along by just the safety chains! The heavy steel, 2-1/2-inch-wide angle-iron support on the trailer-tongue had dropped down and was dragging along on the pavement. The heat generated by the fierce friction had melted off about a foot of it already. It was amazing! It must have been spewing out an impressive shower of sparks for miles! In only a matter of seconds, the increasing torque would have broken both the chains sending the trailer tumbling out of control and spilling tons of sailing boats onto the crowded freeway at 65 MPH. People would have died. It was a fatal fiasco that I thank God didn't happen.

It was a close call. Too close! We spent the rest of the day being buffeted by blasts of wind as hundreds of speeding cars and trucks blew past us while we refitted a new hitch and jacked the trailer back up onto it. Somewhat shaken, we returned to the factory to get a fresh start the next morning. Even though I hadn't loaded the truck, I knew that as the driver I would have been held responsible for the carnage when it flew apart. It was an unforgettable incident that always reminds me to double-check the security of what I've taken responsibility for at every stop.

My good buddy Dick called and asked me if I would be available to help him drive a truck and trailer rig back to Seattle from a truck show in Denver. Dick was a professional truck driver. I would be along mostly for comic relief. I jumped at the chance. It was always predictable that the unpredictable would happen when we were together. It would be another grand adventure. It was also early October, so I knew the fall colors would be spectacular, providing plenty of opportunities to pursue my hobby in photography along the route.

We flew into Denver about dinnertime, drove a rental car to an outlying area where the truck was being serviced, and checked into a cheap motel. My room was right next to a busy pool hall in a noisy bar. A championship billiard tournament was being played on a table just on the other side of my wall. I could hear every break, the sharks calling their shots, and the balls ricocheting around and dropping into the pockets. Just when I thought I was drifting off to sleep, another loud cheer of celebration would erupt from the neighboring crowd. To make matters worse, the men's restroom and my bathroom were the same! I had a locking door from my bedroom that led out to it. Several times during the night, inebriated patrons exiting the toilet would turn the wrong way and start pounding and cursing at my door, thinking they were locked out of the bar. It was a frustrating, sleepless night.

I stared at my clock, waiting for the alarm to ring at 5:30 AM. I tried to revive myself with a cold shower and some hot chocolate, but I was still feeling a little woozy when we drove out of town. We headed west toward Loveland Pass in a gorgeous, brand-new purple and gold Kenworth exhibition truck. The dashboard looked like a 747 console. Gauges, dials, buttons, and toggle switches were everywhere. The center aisle between the seats was extra wide and led to a super chic, rolled and pleated sleeper compartment. We were pulling a custom-built, 40-foot empty display trailer. It was all sleek and polished chrome with extra flashy "mag" type wheels and spectacular, metal-flaked, four-color graphics. The whole rig was so showy that even the hard-core truckers going the opposite way on the freeway turned their heads to gawk when we passed by. As soon as we cleared the busy metropolitan area Dick relinquished to wheel to me. It had an automatic transmission which made the driving much easier. I didn't have to worry about grinding any gears along the way.

We were pulling up the eastern slope of the Rockies toward the Continental Divide. Dick was asleep in the air-cushioned passenger's seat and I was having the time of my life pretending to be a real road warrior. As we approached the pass at 11,000 feet, I saw signs announcing Eisenhower Tunnel, the world's highest automobile tunnel. I was looking forward to plunging into the 1.7 miles of darkness at 60 MPH and blaring the air horns to give my sleeping friend a surprise wake up call!

About 3/4 miles from the entrance I heard a siren behind me. I wasn't speeding and there were no flashing state patrol car lights in my mirrors. There was hardly any traffic at all. I kept going. The siren stayed with us, getting more shrill and intense like some type of signal. I still didn't see anything wrong, but just in case I reached over and gave Dick a little shake to ask him what was up with the weird sound. I hated to wake him so soon.

He looked around for a split second and then without hesitation wildly lunged toward me grabbing the wheel. He turned sharply onto the shoulder and yelled at me to stop the truck. With him steering from the faraway other seat and me frantically working the brakes, we rolled to a stop in a cloud of dust and a spray of flying gravel. Almost immediately we were joined on either side by several small white sedans. Out jumped some very troubled men in fluorescent orange coveralls. Meanwhile, Dick and I were quickly climbing over each other, switching places, because I didn't have a valid CDL, (commercial driver's license). I had evidently already committed one serious violation. Driving without a proper license would only add to our trouble.

Dick hurriedly explained that the sirens meant we had tripped the laser sensor alarms telling us our trailer was too tall for the tunnel. I had completely by-passed all the emergency exit lanes set up for such an eventuality without even slowing down. By the time Dick realized what was happening and drove us off the road, we were less than 100 yards from the yawning entrance of the tunnel! Dick climbed down from the driver's side of the cab and cheerfully greeted the incredulous road crew chase squad. One of them had assembled a long pole and was gloomily measuring the trailer height all along the entire length of it. We finally got the verdict. The back end was one inch too high! In only a few more seconds of driving, the entire top of this extraordinary, very expensive trailer would have been brutally ripped open and peeled back like a flimsy sardine can. The west bound lanes would have been closed for hours, the truck ruined, the tunnel damaged, and hundreds of thousands of dollars later my name would be turned into "mud." Somehow, somewhere, someone was looking out for me. My lucky stars were still in my favor. I had dodged yet another speeding bullet.

By releasing some air from the pneumatic shocks, Dick was able to lower the trailer enough to comply with the legal clearance limits, allowing us drive through the tunnel and get out of there. He was nice enough to take the blame and endure all those judgmental stares from the freeway officials without saying a word. He laughed at the quirky nature of our latest memorable adventure together, and proved for the countless time that he was special—a best friend.

We spent the next three fun-filled days photographing glorious fall colors while driving through surprise snowstorms, terrific thunder and lightening displays, brilliant rainbows, and stupendous, mountain-filled, scarlet sunsets. We laughed in amazement at the majesty and beauty of it all. At night we convened in truck stops with our fellow colleagues. We ate what they ate, slept where they slept, and talked like they talked. We were thankful to be sharing with them and driving through the same landscape together. I was particularly thankful that we had been able to drive all the way through the tunnel instead of being stopped dead in our truck's tracks.

BEING A HOD CARRIER

I WAS RIDING home on the school bus from high school and overheard two friends talking about a job opening that was available. Someone in our neighborhood was looking for a kid to work for three bucks an hour! In those days that was a fantastic wage, especially for a high school student. It was unbelievable that someone hadn't already grabbed the job. I was trying to make money for college and this sounded like a gold mine. I talked to the kids before my bus stop and got the phone number of the interested party. When I asked what the job was they replied, "Being a hod carrier."

I had no idea what a hod carrier was, but I shrugged my shoulders like I did and said, "Oh."

When my dad got home that night I asked him about it. Eager to pass his strong work ethic on to me, he called to find out some more details. He told me the job was still available and that I could start in two days, on Saturday if I wanted it. It would be hard work, assisting a stonemason in building a fireplace, a chimney, and pouring a garage floor for one of our neighbors who was remodeling his house. I was elated at the prospect of earning $20 to $30 a day. I didn't care how hard the work was. Besides, I was used to working hard. I had been helping my Dad and doing yard work for the neighbors for years.

I was even more exhilarated when I found out the job was at the home of Jim Whittaker, the first American to reach the summit of Mt. Everest. He was a national hero and a world-renowned mountaineer, a man who stood larger than life. An autographed picture of him standing triumphantly on the top of the world was the centerpiece in the hutch next to the kitchen table where our family ate. Even though he lived only one-third of a mile from us, I had never met him. Now was my chance. I was thoroughly perplexed about why none of the other local kids had taken this job. To pass up a chance to earn that much money and meet someone famous was curious to me.

Early Saturday morning I nervously pedaled my bike up the road toward his house. Gathering my courage and my wits, I lingered at the top of his long driveway, not knowing what to expect. Finally, I coasted down the dirt lane to the house. It was a fine, old style cottage, perched on a wooded bluff overlooking beautiful and placid Lake Sammamish. The only person around was the mason who was already at work high up on a ladder. His name was Ed. From my perspective, he was a quiet and crotchety old man who seemed amused and mildly irritated to be having a total novice and rank amateur trying to help him. I could tell he was a consummate craftsman from the old school of hard knocks and the "do it right or do it over" era. Highly skilled artisans with his degree of practical knowledge were a dying breed. I was glad to be in his company for my own edification.

My first task was to learn how to mix mortar. He told me the proper proportions of water, sand, and cement to put together in the mortar bed and handed me the hoe. It had an extra large blade with several holes in it to help blend the ingredients better. At first I thought this was going to be a no brainer, a piece of cake. I started mixing away. It was heavy, thick and monotonous. Three hours later I was ready to die! My wrists, arms, shoulders, and back were painfully protesting every move. Every time I attempted to rest just a little and lean on the hoe, my mentor on the roof would call out, "Keep the mud moving, boy."

The only break I got was when I had to load up about 30 pounds of fresh mud onto the "hod" (a wooden trough) and carry it, off-balance on my aching shoulder up the ladder to replenish his supply of grout. I was starting to get an inkling of why nobody else wanted this job.

When lunch time finally arrived, I was extremely relieved to sit down and eat my sandwich. I still had to jump up occasionally and keep my mud moving but by now most of it had been used up. What little was left was relatively easy to rake around. While I ate, my boss identified all the different kinds and sizes of bricks, blocks, flue tiles, masonry tools, and supplies by name. I was expected to have them all memorized by the afternoon shift so when he called for the various pieces I could fetch them quickly and accurately.

After lunch I made up a new batch of mortar and began moving bricks closer to the house from the main pile. After about a hour when I was really starting to feel the soreness and fatigue setting in, he called down to me, "Bring me up two of those number one flue tiles, boy."

Number one flue tiles were the biggest ones there. They were 14x14x14-inch squared-off sections of concrete pipe about one-inch thick. They were unwieldy and weighed about 20 pounds each. I couldn't figure out how I was going to carry one up the ladder and still have both hands free to hold on with. Then it dawned on me to put my arm through the opening of one and let it hang there like a gigantic bracelet. I tried it on. It was way heavier than I expected but I figured I could make it up the ladder to the roof with it. As I climbed, the sharp edges and rough texture dug into me, painfully scraping my skin raw down to the quick as the block slid back and forth while I shifted from rung to rung. When I was just a little more than halfway up and feeling proud of my effort, Ed looked down and yelled in a disgusted voice, "No, damn it, I said two of 'em!"

Incredulously but without complaint, I climbed back down and slung the second tile over my other arm. I struggled back up the ladder, severely abrading both my bare arms, but I maintained a look of calm and composure. I must have looked like a crazy guy wearing oversized, concrete water-wings. My head finally cleared the roof line and suddenly I was face to face with Ed. He didn't say a word, but as he unstrung the tiles from my shaky arms I detected a slight but unmistakable grin on his weathered face.

My hod-carrying day continued on as such until 6 PM. I was worn out, exhausted, battered and bruised, and I hadn't seen one celebrity. Now it was crystal clear why no one else had taken this job! Fortunately, it was all downhill to my place so I draped myself over my bicycle and let gravity take me home.

The next day I was up bright and early, stiff and sore, but ready to go. I think Ed was surprised to see me again as I came skidding down the driveway. He put me to work hand digging trenches for a 60-foot long drainage line and the foundation footings for the new garage. I had dug a lot of ditches and moved a lot of dirt for my Dad over the years, so for me this was a fun and familiar diversion. I knew how to pace myself, work steadily, and maintain a constant slope. I think even old Ed was impressed with my progress after only two hours.

Later that morning, while I was digging out a large boulder, I heard the back door shut. A tall muscular man came bounding enthusiastically up the hill and leaped onto the top of the pile of dirt. I knew from the pictures that it was Jim Whittaker! He smiled, shook my hand, and congratulated me for my work. I was impressed by his stature and genuine sincerity. I couldn't believe I was actually standing next to him, talking to him. It's a powerful moment when you meet your real-live hero face to face. He talked to me like I was his equal and told me to call him Jim. I immediately respected him even more for that. His empowering charisma made me want to work harder and faster than ever before. After several minutes of rapture the phone rang and he ran inside.

I was intoxicated by the praise I had received from one of the world's greatest athletes. I started picking, digging, chopping, and slinging dirt like there was no tomorrow. Every day I worked after school and before the week was over the trenches were finished ahead of schedule. Jim, Ed, and I worked together pouring the concrete and I made some new adult friends. Ed showed me how to "work up the fat" on the surface of the fresh concrete with a "sweeper" or a trowel to get the flattest and smoothest finish. Jim continued to exude confidence and strength that never ceased to amaze me.

After several weeks, Ed's work was completed and he left for another job. He still called me "boy" but now the gruffness in his voice had been replaced with a ring of fondness. My hod-carrying days were over, but Jim kept me on to assist with other chores. I guess he really liked how I could dig! Over the next 3 1/2 years I helped him with many other construction jobs that included digging a deep privy pit for his cabin at the ocean. I remember really pouring my heart and soul into that pit.

He trusted me to baby-sit his sons and later, when Senator Robert Kennedy and his family visited, I kept the Whittaker and Kennedy children safe and entertained down at the beach while the adults socialized and talked politics up at the main house. I even got to take Mrs. Kennedy and the kids water-skiing. I couldn't have been more honored.

Every time I was with Jim Whittaker he filled my high school head with tales of his adventures in the high Himalayas, the amazing warmth and stamina of the Sherpa people, and the unbelievable exotic nature of the country of Nepal, the home of Mt. Everest. I knew that someday I would have to go there and see it all for myself. He planted an undying seed in me for seeking out adventure. He raised my self-esteem and taught me that anything is possible. I saw him do things with gusto that no one else even attempted. He was kind and gentle, and cared about the world around him. He pushed the envelope and broadened my frontiers. He was a real man!

I'm glad I hung in there and learned what it meant to be a hod carrier. The $3 an hour turned into an immeasurable fortune.

CHAPTER 16

Putting It All Together Into Smile Power

BY 1989 I HAD ACCOMPLISHED ALL THE IMMEDIATE goals of my youth. I had met and married a wonderful woman who would be my lifelong partner. We had two loving sons well on their way to manhood. I had successfully graduated from dental school and had practiced long enough to become confident and skillful at my profession. I had established a fulfilling niche in working with children and was doing it my way. I was able to make dentistry a painless experience and a vehicle for raising each patient's self-worth. I was the proud owner of a thriving business. Our close-knit family lived in a comfortable house with a beautiful yard and various cherished pets, in our own out-of-the-way corner of the woods.

It took a lot of very hard work to get there but Jerri and I did it together. In the face of frustration and failure we never gave up. We stepped back from time to time to cry some tears, mop our brows, and lose some sleep, but we always moved forward again. We knew that with the perseverance and confidence to hold on to a clear vision of our dream and the conviction to keep going for it, we would have it one day. By following this formula we couldn't fail! It is a basic law of the Universe.

But now something new was happening. I had turned 40! Mid-life crisis was hitting me hard. The restless seed of wonder from my youth was starting to germinate. What was the meaning of Life? Where could I find ultimate Truth? What other goals from my youth lay dormant, waiting to be fulfilled and accomplished? I remembered that it was "adventure" I used to dream about: climbing the highest mountains, exploring the deepest, darkest jungles, sailing the seven seas and meeting the people of wisdom in the world. I realized that if I was going to achieve these ambitions it was time to start. I needed to go for it while I was still physically able to satisfy the visions of my early imagination without any compromise.

The first thing on my list was Mt. Everest. I wanted to hike all the way in from the end of the road to base camp, just like Jim Whittaker had done. It was an objective I had carried with me for at least 25 years. I studied, trained, and arranged for another year, then left by myself for Kathmandu, Nepal.

A Day In The Hills

EVERY DAY, NO matter where I looked, there was something new, something unexpected, something unimagined. And every day the heights and depths of my emotions were plumbed by these new realities. Laughing out loud at the exhilaration and crying openly from the desolation and loneliness, I was a 12-year-old boy again, inside a 42-year-old body. I was in the Himalayas!

I had come to Mt. Everest, not to climb it, but to see it up close from every conceivable angle. It was a dream come true and the adventure and magic of it all were much more than I expected. I had already spent three and a half weeks and 200 miles walking around the base of "Sagarmatha," the Nepalese term for the highest point on Earth. But there was one more valley I hadn't explored and it promised the most spectacular view yet of Everest from the top of an 18,000-foot hill named Gokyo Peak.

I had asked my Sherpa guide named Pemba to take me there and today was the day. It would take a week to make the roundtrip and it meant leaving our group of friendly porters behind and carrying my own heavy backpack for the first time. But I was excited and felt up to the task, feeling in great shape from all the previous hiking and camping. I shouldered my pack with a grunt and we set off.

We walked to the edge of the 12,000-foot high ridge and Pemba pointed to the river that was crashing through the gorge 2,000 feet below us and said, "I meet you there. *Jaene.*" (sounds like john-ay)

Jaene meant "It's time to go." He stayed behind to talk to a friend from his village and I started down. There was no trail, just a slightly worn animal path still frosted over from the cold night. I gingerly placed each foot on the slippery, steep terrain using a stick in one hand and holding on to bushes with the other to keep from falling. I hadn't figured on doing this alone and I didn't expect the extra weight of my pack to make this much difference, but my legs were screaming at me. When I finally arrived at the river two hours later they were two sticks of quivering jelly.

I had no sooner sat down on a warm rock and breathed a

sigh of relief when Pemba appeared, pointed at the 2,000-foot high ridge across the river and said, "*Jaene*."

We slowly but steadily climbed the other side. It seemed easier than going down but still took another two hours. At the top in a broad, open meadow was the ancient village of Phortse. At the entrance gate through the 500-year-old rock wall sat a woman grinding barley into flour between two stones.

We went into one of the first houses and Pemba motioned for me to go up some rickety wooden stairs. I emerged out onto an open air balcony. I looked for a place to sit and eat my lunch amid the yak manure that was spread out everywhere drying in the sun to be used later as cooking and heating fuel. As I began to eat a side door opened and out shuffled a very old woman with the most picturesque face I had ever seen. Using sign language, I excitedly asked her if I could take her picture. She shook her head no. I think she was embarrassed by her wrinkles.

Disappointed, I continued to eat but I could feel her intensely watching me. Deciding that she might be hungry, I gave her some crackers, then some cheese, some jerky, and an apple. She silently took each offering one at a time and quickly stored them inside the folds of her cloak without eating anything and continued to stare at me. There was a hard-boiled egg at the bottom of my sack that I was saving for later but I realized that I would feel better if she had it. When I gave it to her she smiled like she knew it was there all along. She put it in her dress with the rest of the groceries.

Unexpectantly she tapped my arm and pointed at my camera, indicating that now it was okay to take her picture. They are some of my most treasured photos. I loved sharing those remarkable moments with her, communicating only with our eyes. She was a 91-year-old Buddhist monk in a land where the life expectancy was only 47. She was widely revered for her wisdom and longevity. She exuded knowledge and power, confidence, and strength. When Pemba finally came to get me, she bowed many times, thanking me and blessing my family and me. I was humbled by her grace.

Pemba told me he had learned of a shortcut to the village we were trying to reach. It meant going straight up the side of the ridge to 14,500 feet but it would save us one whole day of up and down switchbacking. I decided to go for it so we started up. Several hours later I was panting and muttering to myself, bemoaning my decision. Trance-like, I trudged along. I was bleary-eyed from the continuous exertion of climbing and constantly and carefully putting one foot in front of the other. Suddenly, Pemba started yelling, "Mountain God, mountain God!" and started jumping around wildly, pointing to the left!

I couldn't believe what he was saying and my eyes wouldn't focus on anything. I strained to see this holy apparition. Finally there it was, only 60 feet away—a Himalayan Tahr, a huge brown mountain goat standing in perfect profile against the valley floor. (Pemba's pronunciation of "goat" was different from mine. It sounded like "god" and it definitely got my attention.)

As I looked around, I realized we were tightroping across a very exposed, narrow ridge crest. I could see thousands of feet down on either side and miles ahead. There was no sign of a village. We kept on for hours and I struggled to keep up. By now I was completely exhausted and stumbled forward with almost every step. The only thing that kept me going and on my feet was the image I held in my mind of my lovely wife so very far away at home.

Finally at dusk, there it was—the village of Na. The sun was setting in my eyes, burning them along with a gallon of sweat and a few tears. I staggered into the darkness of a stone hut where I would spend the night and promptly ran head first into a large wooden post that supported the shale roof. Almost knocked unconscious, I strained to hold onto the post to keep from falling to my knees. I saw stars swirling around in my confused mind. Slowly, strange faces appeared one by one out of the darkness. As I came to my senses I realized I had blundered into a local council meeting where 15 men were sitting around a small fire. I must have been quite a sight! (Can you imagine a semi-coherent, dirty, and disheveled stranger from a completely different culture suddenly stumbling into your living room unannounced in the middle of dinner?)

They motioned for me to come in and cleared a special place for me next to the warm fire. They were passing around a bowl of boiled potatoes and dipping them into a saucer filled with some kind of creamy condiment. I was famished, so when the plate came to me I smeared as much of the sauce on the end of my potato as possible. Just before I bit into it I looked up and saw that every eye in the house was staring at me. I chomped down and swallowed. A searing wave of fire exploded in my mouth and a line of hot napalm blazed a trail to my stomach! The bewildered expression on my rookie face must have been priceless. The room exploded with laughter. Concentrated, high altitude pepper paste is very hot!

Embarrassed again, I carefully finished the rest of my potato and politely observed the meeting for a while. Then I excused myself to an adjoining sleeping area ready to crash. I laid out my sleeping bag on the straw-covered bench and crawled in. I was almost asleep when an exhausted porter came in and collapsed close by. He immediately began snoring, talking in his sleep and tossing and twitching about. He rolled into the other support post that was next to him and the roof shuddered.

Suddenly, out flew dozens of bats, flapping about wildly in the dark, running into my head and face! I was dumbfounded, frightened, and amazed. The bats finally settled down but the same event repeated itself three more times that night. I was too nervous to sleep, but too tired to stay awake. I finally drifted into a nebulous dream world suspended between two realities.

At dawn Pemba woke me and handed me some hot tea. I felt surprisingly rested and exhilarated. As I loaded my pack I marveled at the wonder of this great adventure. I was ready for yet another glorious day in the hills. Pemba looked me in the eyes, smiled and said, "*JAENE!*"

SAVING A LIFE

I HAD BEEN a tourist in Nepal now for over a month, camping in tents, and staying in teahouses and family lodges. One morning I was startled to hear a child crying. I suddenly realized that despite the challenging living conditions here, I had never seen or heard any children crying, not even babies—until now.

Curious, I followed the sound of the cries and saw a small girl in pain with her mouth wide open and several concerned adults looking in. Remembering my training, I immediately recognized that it was some kind of dental problem. I went over, took a look, and to my horror saw that several teeth were abscessed and the infection had spread into the lymph system on her right side. She was swollen all the way from her temple down through her armpit. I learned that she had suffered this way for over a month with only occasional complaining, simply because no one knew what to do about it. Left untreated she would eventually die. I explained to the family that I was a "tooth doctor" and could take her to a nearby field hospital for treatment. I was planning to visit there that very day.

Her seven-year-old sister came along for moral support. Together we made the four-hour walk up to the hospital, climbing from 11,500 to 13,000 feet on the rugged and winding trail. During the tiring trek I secretly hoped that the physician who worked there would be the one to take care of the tiny five-year-old because of the seriousness of her condition.

When we got there I explained the grave situation to him. After he learned I was a dentist he said to me, "You know more, you better do it!" He called to the Sherpa assistant to bring out the "dental stuff" which consisted of a shoe box containing several pairs of pliers and a few other useless instruments all rusted together into one solid mass! There was no electricity. The room was dark except for some dim light coming through a dingy corrugated skylight. I was handed an unfamiliar-looking vial with mysterious foreign writing on it, supposedly filled with anesthetic and a needle that was four inches long. I had to bend it into a Z-shape in order to fit it into the little girl's mouth. When she caught sight of it, her eyes got very big, but she didn't cry. As I injected, I prayed that this really was anesthetic, and that she wouldn't die from some toxic overdose.

The only useful instrument I had for the surgery was my Swiss Army pocket knife, a treasured gift from my father. As I pried out the infected teeth with it, the little girl trembled a few times but still no tears. After draining as much purulence from the wound as possible, I realized there was no suture available to stitch it closed. So I used a wadded up strip of cloth for her to bite on to stop the bleeding. After getting some penicillin tablets from the physician, we left.

As we walked slowly back toward the side of the mountain, I became increasingly troubled by the burden of having to care for this child. I was worried about her survival from the infection, her weakened condition because of the crude surgery, and the prospect that I would probably have to carry her down the steep slope back to her village. I was mostly bothered because all of this extra time would cause me to miss photographing the sunset on Mt. Everest which was only viewable from the ridge top across the valley. I would never make it down and back up the other side by dark at this rate, and I had to leave the area tomorrow never to see Everest again.

When we finally arrived at the edge we could see her own village almost 2,000 feet straight down below us. She immediately started running down the steep rocky trail. As I watched her jubilant and nimble leaps toward home, I knew I could never catch her, much less keep up. Suddenly, the enormity of my selfishness hit me and through a flood of guilty tears I watched her deftly disappear around a corner on the endless switchbacks. I knew she had the surefootedness and commitment to make it home safely. In that moment I learned about true courage and selflessness. I vowed I would return someday and really help out, and I did. She lived, and for the first time so did I!

"NAMASTE"

ONE OF THE most valuable lessons I ever learned was in Nepal. It was the meaning of "namaste." Each person you meet or pass along the way salutes you with a formal greeting. They put their palms together, bow their head toward you reverently and say, "Namaste." It literally translates, "I honor the Divinity within you." They say it with absolute sincerity and respect. The meaning of their whole existence is built around following this ideal.

It's the same everywhere you go in the hill country. It's the ultimate culture of unconditional Love, an addictive atmosphere of approval and admiration. When they look at you, they see past your physical appearance and personality and focus on the Essence inside. In this way they are constantly acknowledging and drawing forth the greatness of God.

When I returned home from this trip I wasn't the same. I couldn't pass anyone in the grocery store aisle or on the street anymore without recognizing their presence by saying hello and honoring their greatness with a silent confirmation from my heart. It was a lesson of Truth I never would have learned here at home. It changed my life and those around me for the better.

I explained all this to Jerri and told her how children there were dying from infected teeth simply because they had no access to a toothbrush or knowledge of how to use one! How could I turn my back on this needless suffering when it was so easily eliminated? Besides, I wanted to return as a dentist, with Jerri, so together we could share their overwhelming environment of honor and respect and have a legitimate excuse to help and touch these people who had taught me so much.

In 1992, we gathered together some basic medical and dental supplies and a bunch of free toothbrushes. We tied our bulky bags on the hairy backs of two yaks and followed them and my trusty friend Pemba into the mountain villages of the Sherpas in the magical country of Nepal. I didn't believe it could be possible, but that experience was even more extraordinary than my first trip.

The majestic mountains had become a beautiful but secondary backdrop. The spirit of the people who lived there was the number one draw. The sense of fulfillment that came from helping and befriending them flooded our being. It added an exponential factor of thrill and satisfaction to an already sensational adventure in the exotic "Land of Namaste." We returned home filled with a new understanding of the world and what was possible for people to achieve. We had discovered a highly refined source of important knowledge that seemed to be largely missing in the lifestyles of the West. We resolved to share these uplifting virtues and values with all. Suddenly, it was obvious that the origin of true fulfillment comes from the experience of unconditional giving, caring, and sharing. It's what all of us are looking for and it comes from within!

HONORS AND REWARDS

JERRI AND I were completely exhilarated by what we had learned from one cultural connection and we were hungry for more wisdom and experience. We started getting calls from people in other countries who had heard about our humanitarian outreach via our eco-travel agent's company. Before long, we had been shaken off the side of an erupting volcano in Costa Rica, shown the hidden wonders of the Yucatan rain forest by a Mayan shaman, conferred with the High Medical Lama of Tibet beneath the towering steps of the Potala Palace in Lhasa. We had been chosen by a Maori witch doctor to be the first white people ever to see certain sacred historical relics in the South Pacific, felt the power of the Incas in Machu Picchu, sat with the last of the Kallahuaya healers on the shores of Lake Titicaca, and counciled with the elders of the Hopi, Crow, and Navajo.

In every case we gave what we could to honor them for their knowledge and to help them with their health problems and concerns. In every case, we made heart-to-heart friendships with amazing people from all over the world who bid us farewell with tearful eyes, and pleaded with us not to forget them. In every case, we came away with valuable, new understanding and helpful insights that we wanted to share with others to make a positive difference in the world.

Thanks to the encouragement of my best friend Dick, I took a 35mm camera with me and learned by doing how to use it. At first it was just an afterthought because I had never used a camera before, but over the years the resulting collection of slides has provided an invaluable resource for helping to share our experience with others. The thrill of capturing priceless moments for posterity has contributed to my own personal growth. The images have shown others the magic in the eyes of our neighbors that unites us all in the fellowship of Life.

BABIES IN BOLIVIA

WE GOT A flyer in the mail asking for volunteers to join a humanitarian health team going to Bolivia. Bolivia is one of the poorest countries in South America and has the world's highest infant mortality rate. The population has lived a meager but self-sustaining lifestyle in their rural colonial villages for generations. More recently, the promise of a "better life" in the big cities has produced a massive influx of families who have no resources or skills to compete for jobs. Many of them wind up living on the streets. We were told that the city of 750,000 we visited has 30,000 homeless children.

Because of this situation, there is a huge orphanage system in place. Out of love, desperate parents who can't afford another mouth to feed give their children over to an orphanage because they believe they will have a better life there than on the streets. This is especially true of any children who are born with developmental problems or chronic ailments. It happens every day in a flood of sobbing tears. The families bring their precious children in and drop them off. When they leave there is a certain finality to their last goodbye. Everyone is crying, everyone is devastated, but it happens. It is the way it is.

In many other cases, babies are found abandoned, or the parents have died from accidents, untreated diseases, or attrition from a relatively short life expectancy. The result is many buildings contain numerous rooms filled with children grouped together by age and gender from newborn to age 18, at which time they are dismissed back to the streets.

The first time I visited I was led down a long hallway. The piercing screams of a distraught child echoed through the corridors and a pungent smell of urine and disinfectant hung in the air. I came to a room with a shade drawn over the glass. I let myself in. It was the nursery. There in front of me were 20 to 25 infants all lying on a mat-covered floor. One caring staff person was all that was available to feed and change and watch over them. It was all she could do to keep up with the overwhelming task. There was no time left over for any other personal attention.

As I moved through the room, stepping over the babies, each and every one of them raised up their tiny little arms begging for me to pick them up and hold them, hug them. It was like a huge nest of baby birds eager to be fed. They were starved for affection. They were like little love sponges, able to soak up everything we could give them and more. When you looked into their deep, dark yearning eyes you could see forever far into the void.

As I looked around, I realized that every one of these little people had the potential for becoming one of the world's greatest leaders, or for making the biggest contribution of peace or knowledge ever given to mankind. It could be any one of them.

Studies have shown there is an area in the brain of every infant called the "bonding center" that needs to be activated before that person can manifest their full potential. The only way to energize and turn on this center is with tender touch and loving interaction. It requires nurturing, holding, hugging, and cuddling, something that these orphans weren't getting enough of and never would without parents.

Behind every door in the long hall was another room filled with kids a little older than the last group. I found myself feeling angry and upset about this reality. I didn't think it should be this way. The whole system seemed to perpetuate itself. Why did this have to exist? I kept looking for a positive and rational explanation. I didn't discover it until I started working with the children. We were there to fix their teeth, but I could see there was something more important that needed to be done.

We became their surrogate parents and held and nurtured every one of them. Some of them were stiff and unresponsive when we picked them up. We had to teach them how to hug by stroking and massaging their little bodies until they relaxed and softened up enough to snuggle. We gave the older kids big hugs and little gifts that were donated by schoolchildren from our home town. The orphans were ecstatic and held them up proudly. It was the first thing they had ever owned! For them it was proof that somebody, somewhere actually cared about them.

I went back every day and was greeted by a horde of lovable children who jumped on my back and hung off of every arm and leg, clamoring for my attention. They looked up at me longingly and yelled, "Me papa, me papa." I was the only adult male they knew they could depend on for comfort.

I found myself wanting to give more and more in order to satisfy their craving. I started to realize that I could touch them all, one at a time. Sometimes it was just with a big smile or an adoring glance. I was surprised to learn that my capacity for giving was greater than I thought. I could feel myself opening up wider and wider. They were drawing it out of me. I never knew I had this much in me.

Compared to this experience, my previous life had been stingy, pent up, and held back. I was afraid that if I allowed myself to be unrestrained I would be exposing myself to danger; that somehow I could be injured if I didn't protect myself by being guarded with my sincerity. I learned the opposite was true. Now I could feel the power of love flowing through me like a funnel from somewhere in the universe. The more I opened up and gave, the more the power came into my life. I was connected with it and it was exhilarating, fulfilling, empowering! I couldn't have been any safer.

It was such a simple yet awesome realization. Now I understood why these circumstances existed. These captivating children were here to help us, to give us the opportunity to grow, and to become aware of our own capacity for greatness and giving. How else could we have experienced it? They were here to teach us.

When we left for home we were closely bonded to hundreds of the orphans, and now, when I see their angelic faces in my mind's eye, I honor them. I thank them for teaching me this great lesson. That each of us has unlimited capacity for giving to others, for making a positive difference in the world. We each have the unique ability to become the best that there ever was of whatever we choose to be. It could be the person sitting right next to you. It could be you.

⌒   ⌒

ISLAND INFLUENCE

LAST YEAR I was on a remote tropical island in the middle of the South Pacific. I was clawing my way through the dense jungle, trying to keep up with the local witch doctor. With every step, a dense cloud of insects billowed up around me from the low-lying bushes. Sweating profusely, we stopped in a small clearing and I strained to understand what the witch doctor was trying to tell me. Suddenly, slap, slap, slap! His Amazon-like daughter was swatting the bugs on my back with the flat side of her extremely long, razor-sharp machete! It jolted me out of my intently focused state, making me more keenly aware of the expanse and uniqueness of my exotic green surroundings. The savvy old witch doctor laughed with abandon and pointed to the vine covered entrance of a giant hidden cave. He said, "You are the first white man in history to ever see this." It was a sacred place filled with ghostly geologic formations, sightless birds, and swarming bats. A place where his distant ancestors had huddled in safety to hide from the giant tsunamis and raging cyclones of the past.

I started to realize then what a significant experience this was. I had come to this island because it was a very special place. The people who lived here exuded a profound and intense joy that was indescribable. It was so pure and powerful that I knew it radiated outward from there and affected the whole planet. That island is such a profound center of joy that it influences all of us, even now in this moment.

I learned from the witch doctor that each one of us is an important island of influence. We all have an equally strong influence on the world. No one's influence is any more powerful that anybody else's. It's the quality, not the quantity of our influence that counts, and we control the quality. It's how we're being that generates our influence, not what we're doing.

So we have this powerful influence but how does it work? What is the mechanism? Twenty years ago I attended a party at a friend's house. There were lots of people there who I hadn't met before, all enjoying a friendly but subdued atmosphere. A stately old upright piano stood lonely in the corner.

Someone asked if anyone could play it. I volunteered and sat down on the rickety bench then started banging out a lively tune. I was just making it up, playing by sheer inspiration. My fingers were acting as a direct extension of my happy frame of mind. The song coming forth was completely original. It even surprised me and it created a stir. Before long, everyone was caught up in it. The whole crowd starting drumming on pots and pans, beating on the walls, stomping their feet, clapping hands and dancing around. It was a special, exhilarating moment in time when everyone was in sync. I could feel a tingle of excitement wash over me and the hair stood up on the back of my neck from the realization that we were all locked into a common bond. The experience of complete unity made it feel so powerful.

When the song finally ended and the spell was broken, I wished that we had recorded it on tape because it was a one-of-a-kind event that couldn't be duplicated. I fretted about this exceptional performance being lost forever. Then I realized that the unique energy of those remarkable vibes was still with us, emanating out across the space and time of the Universe like an echo. They would exist and continue on that way forever! I felt glad for what we had contributed.

This world is like a vast tranquil sea. When you drop a pebble in it, the ripples start radiating out from the center and travel on forever. Those ripples change the face and the character of the world and become part of the permanent history of existence. It's the quality of our voice, the words we choose, our posture, the way we drive, the expression on our face, and what we believe about ourselves and others that is the pebble! What we are choosing to be at every moment is that pebble. We are a living statement of what we are being, and what we are being is our influence on the world.

If you are being sad, irritable, negative, and unworthy then that is your contribution to the world. If you are being happy, healthy, wealthy, and wise then you are adding happiness, health, wealth, and wisdom to the world. Many people underestimate the power of their influence. Each of us has a unique and special talent or ability that only we possess. It's something that when given makes the whole world a better place. Are we holding it back for some reason? If it's out of fear of rejection, then that fear is what we are putting out into our surroundings, and it's what we receive in return.

Demonstrate what you know. Put your special skill and talent out there for all to share. When you do, we'll recognize the special and genuine quality of your passion and we'll embrace it. We all have the power of the Universe behind us, so let it flow. It won't hurt you. It can only uplift you.

Think about what kind of world you want and then be that. We all have an unlimited potential for unlimited influence. When you change, you change the world. No one is any more powerful than you. If you want something to be different, then be that difference. You are the only one who chooses the significance of your life. Why hold back? Go for the utmost limit of your imagination and beyond. Choose the ultimate for yourself. The only way to get there, is to do it! Your action initiates the creative process and the Universe comes rushing in to provide the necessary structure and physical framework for the life you are living. Make the commitment, take action, and go forward. The details will fall into place.

Whatever you decide to be will play a central role in the ongoing history of our planet! What you are "being" now is what the world is becoming!

PUTTING IT ALL TOGETHER

I LEARNED A lot from the witch doctor and the Bolivian orphans, and from my childhood peers, my water-skiing accident, dental school, patients, family and friends, music, restaurants, the great outdoors, my jobs, traveling to distant lands and everything in between. I learned that my response to every event directly influences and predicts the character of the next events to follow. I realized that I was directly responsible for "The Meaning of Life." All of the events that unfold to make up one's life have no meaning in and of themselves. There is no inherent quality to any event except that which we choose give to it. When I finally understood the unlimited power of this realization, it completely freed me up. To be in complete control of my destiny is an awesome feeling. To know that we are all united by the one Principle of Life that lives through each of us inspires me to share Love and forget about fear. It's the one and the same Life force that many call The Great Spirit.

> It lives through the rocks and the trees,
> The animals and their fleas.
> The water and the sky,
> The bold and the shy.
> It twinkles through the stars way up above,
> And speaks of everlasting, undying love.

So when we put it all together, Jerri and I decided that since we're going to have an impact on history no matter what, let's have a big one. A grand and glorious one. We've set up an organization called "The International Smile Power Foundation." Our intention is to: provide health care and disease prevention education and supplies to under-served populations in developing nations; to train their local people to take responsibility for the continuation of the preventive education; to share the virtues and values of foreign cultures with each other in order to enrich all of our lives; to develop understanding between all peoples so that we become a planet of friendly neighbors instead of unknown strangers; and to set up an organization that encourages and facilitates humanitarian outreach by other interested people.

We know that by reaching out and helping others, we gain understanding and appreciation for their unique contributions to the world. In doing so, we discover that we all share the same divine spark of life that unites us all as brothers and sisters. We learned that giving is truly the key to happiness and fulfillment. We have combined our acquired talents in dentistry, medicine, music, photography, and travel and put them together into one big package doing multimedia presentations to schools and other interested groups. We want to provide opportunities for children to participate in an outreach project and experience the deep sense of fulfillment that occurs for both the giver and the recipient. We want them to discover at an early age the benefits and internal rewards that always come from doing humanitarian work. Hopefully, these uplifting experiences will compel them to continue in similar endeavors as adults and will build bridges of love and understanding between their peers all around the planet. The next generation is quickly becoming the new leaders of the world. With a solid framework they can turn it into a safe and sustaining home for one big happy and healthy family.

We are also working to maintain and provide supplies and personnel to existing health care sites in Costa Rica, Nepal, Bolivia, and the remote Cook Islands. In addition, we are working with community leaders in Nepal, Tibet, Vietnam, Cambodia, Papua New Guinea, Zambia, and the Philippines to establish new programs in under-served areas.

. . . So that's why we are here, to accomplish our latest dream. This is the culmination of all our thoughts, beliefs and actions to this point. We are one day short of reaching the colorful tribes of Papua New Guinea. It is providing us with another fascinating experience in Life, being shipwrecked! Sitting here on this remote and lush tropical isle waiting to be rescued, has given me the opportunity to think it all through one step at a time, retracing our progress along our chosen path. The dreams we dreamed together are coming true! This time to reflect has reaffirmed that we are on the right track and have already accomplished more than we envisioned.

A PERFECT RESCUE

THE HOURS OF reminiscing in the darkness floated by effortlessly. An excited wave of buzzing anticipation suddenly swept through the crowd of castaways interrupting my reflections and contemplation. A tiny cluster of lights had appeared on the pitch-dark curtain at the horizon that hung between us and dawn. The rescue boat was here to save us! As we reassembled to leave an interesting discovery was made. During the night the natives (possibly seeking compensation for the damage to their natural environment) had secretly taken the life-jackets, gas tanks, and navigation gear out of the lifeboats rendering them useless. Another dilemma arose.

The heroic crew reboarded and braved the treacherously tilting decks of our beached ship. They successfully salvaged two inflatable landing craft with outboard motors and began ferrying ten people at a time toward the distant lights bobbing in the inky blackness. Simultaneously, a full blown storm that had been gathering off-shore blew in with full force to further heighten the suspense and enigma of the circumstances. Lightning flashes solarized the sky, illuminating the frightened flight of flying fishes darting across the wave crests. Resounding peals of thunder crackled in our ears, challenging our communication. Driving rain and stinging spray breaking over the bow soaked us to the skin and threatened to blind us as we bounced along, dearly hanging on to the safety lines. But it was all okay. Anything could have happened, but our confidence never faltered. The courageous crew had already proved their valor and earned our complete trust. They remained cool-headed, unruffled, helpful, and compassionate. They were complete professionals who were totally committed to zero tolerance for mistakes. There were no accidents, no injuries, no regrets. Eventually, all 200 people were safely evacuated in the midst of the storm. Forty-eight hours later we were back at home with a whole new set of unforgettable memories.

Mostly we were inspired by the unselfish service and dedication of that crew. It was the perfect display of how to be successful in the face of unforeseen obstacles, predicaments, and problems. When we hold to our vision and refuse to give up, these trials become opportunities to help raise us to new heights of awareness and accomplishment. Watching those people in action was proof that we all possess an important piece of a big puzzle. The only way to get it together and see the whole picture is to share what we have with others.

This grand adventure has spurred me on to learn and share even more about Life and living. So here we go, to see where Smile Power will take us next. We're off to make more great discoveries and a positive difference in the world. We are holding an image of the fullest expression of our potential in our minds and living it out now. We're not afraid to upgrade, improve, and expand it as we go along. There are many more exciting adventures, true stories, interesting people, terrific tales, and good books to come for all of us.

Order Information Page

To share this adventure with others, more copies of

Confessions of a Modern Dentist

can be ordered from:

Drill Press
c/o SMILE POWER
704-228th Avenue N.E., #204
Sammamish, WA 98074

or visit
www.SmilePower.org

Discounts are offered for quantity orders.

*Book proceeds provide health care to
children in developing countries.*